PLANNING
IN THE
UNIVERSITY LIBRARY

PLANNING
IN THE
UNIVERSITY LIBRARY

STANTON F. BIDDLE

New Directions in Information Management
MICHAEL BUCKLAND, Series Editor

GREENWOOD PRESS
Westport, Connecticut • London

Library of Congress Cataloging-in-Publication Data

Biddle, Stanton F.
    Planning in the university library / Stanton F. Biddle.
       p.   cm.— (New directions in information management, ISSN
  0887–3844)
    Includes bibliographical references and index.
    ISBN 0–313–27788–5 (alk. paper)
    1. Libraries, University and college—Administration. 2. Library
  planning. I. Title. II. Series.
  Z675.U5B54   1992
  027.7— dc20   92–8678

British Library Cataloguing in Publication Data is available.

Library of Congress Catalog Card Number: 92–8678
ISBN: 0–313–27788–5
ISSN: 0887–3844

First published in 1992

Greenwood Press, 88 Post Road West, Westport, CT 06881
An imprint of Greenwood Publishing Group, Inc.

Printed in the United States of America

The paper used in this book complies with the
Permanent Paper Standard issued by the National
Information Standards Organization (Z39.48–1984).

10 9 8 7 6 5 4 3 2 1

Contents

Preface and
Acknowledgments

Comprehensive planning has become an essential element in the management of the modern university library. Students, faculty, and the general public depend more heavily than ever before on university library resources and services to meet their information needs. Librarians and other information professionals cannot effectively develop resources or deliver services without adequate planning. They cannot be confident of responsible management unless there is evidence of planning. Over the years the practice of planning and the nature of plans have changed. The advent of computer technology, along with the rapidly changing capabilities of electronic information storage, processing, and retrieval, has revolutionized libraries and librarianship, necessitating more sophisticated planning in order to maximize the effective development of resources and delivery of services. The interconnectedness of the information community requires that each component relate to all others, and that libraries plan their resource and service programs carefully in order to participate in the interchanges. The purpose of this book is to help those now engaged in this important management function by summarizing the history of academic library planning, and analyzing its practice in a group of major libraries over the past several decades.

This book draws on my years of interest and involvement in university library planning. It is based on, but goes beyond, my doctoral dissertation, "The Planning Function in the Management of University Libraries: Survey, Analysis, Conclusions, and Recommendations," School of Library and Information Studies, University of California, Berkeley, 1988.

It would be impossible to recognize all those who helped and encouraged me in this effort. The grants and fellowships from the University of California at Berkeley and the Association of College and Research Libraries were appreciated, as were the released time from the State University of New York at Buffalo and administrative support from Baruch College, City University of New York.

I am thankful for the encouragement I received from my colleagues, especially Susan K. Martin, Charles Martell, Elfreda A. Chatman, and Rosario Gassol de Horowitz. However, the one person most responsible for my finishing the work is my dissertation committee chair at the School of Library and Information Studies, University of California, Berkeley, and editor of this series, Michael K. Buckland. I can never repay or thank him enough for his advice, encouragement, patience, and most of all persistence over the years and across the miles in pushing this effort to its completion.

One

Introduction

The university library has become a major organizational enterprise within the academic community. Many university libraries employ hundreds of individuals, spend millions of dollars, and are required to respond to an increasingly wide range of influences from both within the university and society at large. As such, the university library must articulate a mission, prioritize goals and objectives, allocate resources, evaluate performance, and develop strategies for addressing changing circumstances the same as any other entity in a large and complex network of organizations.

As library and university administrators have come to appreciate the maturation of academic libraries as complex organizations, pressure has increased for them to apply contemporary management theory in addressing problems. The use of strategic or long-range planning has been suggested as an effective way of helping libraries define themselves and develop strategies for surviving and succeeding in achieving their goals and objectives in an increasingly unstable and rapidly changing environment.

Strategic planning is a management tool that was developed in the private sector and widely advocated for government and nonprofit enterprises in the 1960s. It is based on the assumption that organizations can maximize their potential for success by developing strategies for accomplishing goals, by weighing options and selecting from sets of alternative approaches, and by preparing contingency plans where important factors are uncertain or subject to change.

Academic libraries have become more susceptible to outside influences as they have grown more complex, more sophisticated, more integrated into the total educational missions of their parent institutions, and more reliant on a network of information resources rather than being self-sufficient. Strategic planning has been offered as a tool for making these libraries more responsive to their environments and for helping them anticipate and prepare for change.

Change has always been an important factor in academic libraries. Chapters 3 and 4 describe their growth from the small collections of books donated to colonial colleges and universities and overseen part-time by interested or available faculty members, to the multimillion volume, multimillion-dollar-a-year colossuses employing hundreds, characteristic of major research university libraries today.

The most significant changes confronting academic libraries for the past several decades have been technological, social, and economic. All three forces continue to exert a tremendous influence on libraries and their changing role in society. The advent of the computer has totally revolutionized information, libraries, and the ways librarians provide access to information. New technologies are changing the ways information is generated, recorded, gathered, stored, preserved, transferred, analyzed, and used by the individual. Computer technology continues to change many of the ways in which librarians and other information professionals organize themselves, their work, and the services they offer their users.

Changes in technological capabilities have stimulated a restructuring of libraries and the ways they go about providing both traditional and new kinds of services. Electronic bibliographic data bases have replaced card catalogs; on-line computer search services and compact disks are replacing many of the traditional printed reference sources; microfilm and microfiche are replacing bound periodicals; microcomputers and terminals linked to minicomputers and mainframes are providing access to circulation, acquisitions, periodical, and financial records once maintained in voluminous paper files.

Changes in technological capabilities have also brought about changes in the expectations of library users and changes in the way librarians and other library workers see themselves. The social implications of the shift to computerization and electronic information systems have yet to be fully appreciated.

At the same time as the technological revolution has been occurring, libraries have been undergoing dramatic social change. The struggles of the late 1960s left their impressions on academic libraries just as they did on colleges and universities and on the other symbols of power and authority in society. Participatory management, faculty status for librarians, unionization of support staff, affirmative action and equal opportunity employment, staff development, continuing education, job security, and written job descriptions detailing duties and responsibilities are now all accepted personnel practices and procedures and are integral parts of the ongoing system in most institutions. Librarians and other library employees expect a certain quality of life and level of satisfaction from their work in addition to the salaries, vacations, and other fringe benefits they receive.

The economic status of academic libraries is also subject to sometimes sudden and dramatic change. Upswings and downswings in the nation's economy have a direct impact on support for higher education. Increases or decreases in enrollment or basic changes in institutional priorities can affect the amount and distribution of funding available to colleges and universities and their libraries. Inflation can undermine the buying power of the dollar, salary increases can change the ratio of funds left for nonpersonnel expenditures, and international exchange rates can disrupt foreign publication purchasing programs. Mandates to computerize library operations are not always accompanied with sufficient supplemental funding to cover total costs of the endeavor, or supplemental funding does not cover related expenses associated with the implementation of computer systems.

Although strategic planning cannot offer solutions to all of these problems, it is presented by advocates as a way of approaching them. The library administrator is thus in a position to view the situation from a broader perspective and to make intelligent decisions based on more accurate information than he or she would otherwise have.

Planning occurs everyday in an organization, whether it is formal or informal, and whether it is intentional or subliminal, because decisions have to be made and actions taken based on these decisions. Strategic planning provides a guide for continuity in decision making. A strategic plan is meant to be a framework or context for decision making, not a set of instructions to be followed relentlessly. A plan should be flexible enough to respond to changing circumstances, and to incorporate basic changes in goals, objectives, priorities, or directions as circumstances warrant. Strategic planning is a continuous effort. Written plans are merely benchmarks or snapshots of where the process stands at a particular point in time. A plan should not preclude pursuing any course of action based on new information, resources, technology, or personnel.

A 1982 survey of the 101 university library members of the Association of Research Libraries (ARL) conducted by the author showed that nearly 57 percent of the 83 respondents (47 libraries) had either developed a long-range plan or were in the process of doing so. A 1990–91 update of that survey revealed that the percentage of libraries actively involved in long-range planning efforts had increased to nearly 90 percent (58 of the 67 responding). The objectives of this study are (1) to examine the extent to which strategic planning is being employed in ARL libraries, (2) to analyze the planning documents they have developed to determine the extent to which they meet the criteria set forth in the literature, and (3) to develop guidelines for improving the quality of future planning efforts. The study also contrasts library planning documents produced during the 1970s with those available in 1991.

An analysis of academic library planning is important to the profession because of the amount of effort that goes into these projects and because of the long-term effects their success or failure can have on library growth and development. The study places current and recent planning efforts into a larger context and provides information that can be useful for improving future endeavors.

Chapter 2 begins this study with a discussion of definitions of strategic or long-range planning taken from the literatures of both management and organization theory. Chapter 3 reviews the historical development of large academic libraries in the United States and the history of the application of contemporary management theories and practices to their administration from the 1920s through the 1950s. Chapter 4 focuses on the widespread frustration and dissatisfaction with traditional approaches to library management that emerged in the late 1960s and on efforts to address these concerns in the early 1970s.

Chapter 5 summarizes and compares the principal library planning source documents identified in the earlier chapters and proposes a list of library planning program components based on these writings, the experience of the author, and a preliminary review of contemporary library plans, which should be incorporated into the programs of new library planning efforts. Chapter 6 is an analysis of the planning documents of thirty-four libraries that were received in response to the survey of ARL university libraries in 1982–83, a summary of the analysis's findings, and a set of conclusions drawn from a review of the findings. Chapter 6 also compares the results of the 1982–83 survey with an update conducted in the fall of 1990 and the spring of 1991.

Chapter 7 concludes the study with a discussion of the findings and with recommendations for further research that might be undertaken to foster a better understanding of strategic planning and its applications to academic libraries, and to validate assumptions about the effectiveness of academic library planning.

Two

Strategic Planning in the Literatures of Management and Organization Theory

OVERVIEW

The past several decades have seen an unprecedented growth in the size and complexity of human organizations, and an acceleration in the rates of change they experience. Contemporary society requires the combined and coordinated efforts of hundreds, and often thousands, of individuals in order to achieve its goals. Even the most basic human needs for food and shelter can no longer be met by the individual alone. Instead, they are satisfied by participation in worldwide networks of organizations, institutions, and individuals. The era in which an individual, a family, or even a community can live in isolation has passed. As human society has moved toward realizing dreams of conquering the earth and reaching for the stars, a growing concern has developed about the organizational structures and social mechanisms it has created to attain these ends.

Organization theory and management theory are attempts to understand and explain how human beings function in organizations, how organizations interact with each other and their environments, and how they can be made more efficient and effective in meeting their goals and objectives.

In view of the tremendous increases in the size and complexity of human organizations, the acceleration in the speed in which they must respond to changes in the environment, and their all encompassing role in modern society, it has become essential that leaders, managers, and administrators become as knowledgeable as possible about the character and nature of organizations and that they gain as thorough an understanding as possible about how organizations function and how their components interact.

Some scholars have identified strategic or long-range planning as a potentially important tool in organizational theory and management. It has become more obvious that organizational efficiency and effectiveness depend on how well administrators and managers coordinate an organization's efforts and allocate its resources.

Even in the United States there has come a realization that the nation does not have unlimited resources. With the rise of the systems approach to viewing the world has come a perception that all things are interrelated and that an action by one individual or one organization in one sector has repercussions affecting others throughout the larger system.

Large-scale planning in the public sector in the United States can be traced back to the 1930s when the nation struggled to overcome the adverse effects of the Great Depression. Later, in World War II, the nation was forced to reorder its priorities and to direct its energies toward overcoming an external enemy. Strategic planning was formally introduced into the federal government when President Lyndon Johnson acknowledged its apparently successful application in the Department of Defense under Robert S. McNamara and Charles J. Hitch. In August 1965 he directed all federal agencies to institute the Planning-Programming-Budgeting-System (PPBS) approach to management. Immediately after his presidential order the use of PPBS and other strategic planning tools received widespread attention at all levels of government and within other organizations seeking more effective ways of controlling, directing, and sustaining their operations (Mason, 1969, p. 10). The "War on Poverty" and other Great Society programs included a heavy reliance on the systems approach and the use of strategic planning tools for their development, implementation, and evaluation.

In the 1970s American society was confronted with other crises, again requiring careful analyses of goals, objectives, and priorities. Many had come to realize the limited nature of resources and to understand that in order to continue to function they would have to find less wasteful ways of meeting needs. Concern about the environment forced some segments of society to reappraise the effects industries have on the air, the land, and the water. Reliance on cheap sources of energy had been undermined by developments in oil producing countries. The message sent through oil pricing structures was that fossil fuel had become a limited source of energy to be bought, sold, and used more carefully if its long-term value to oil producers were to be fully realized. Events at several nuclear energy plant sites dramatized the fact that even the atomic alternative carried with it hazards that could poison the earth for thousands of years to come.

As organizations have struggled to survive in a rapidly changing environment, managers and administrators have become more aware of the need to be able to anticipate, or even to control change, and to develop plans and programs to minimize its negative effects. Viewing immediate profits, or specific accomplishments, as the criteria for success could no longer be used if, in the process, an organization destroyed its environment or threatened its prospects for long-term survival.

Strategic planning is a management tool that enables one to project possible long-term consequences of current events and to anticipate future effects of events and trends outside of the organization. It is useful to look into the meanings and definitions of strategic planning in order to develop an understanding of the tool and how it can best be employed in the management of libraries and other organizations.

DEFINITIONS

In his description of a 1973 library planning effort at Cornell University, William E. McGrath stated that "in modern management there is no universally accepted planning procedure, vocabulary, or model" (McGrath, 1973, p. 5). In his proposal for the same planning effort, Cornell Library Director David E. Kaser stated, "It is important to note that today's concept of planning came into the general arena of management only a scant decade ago. . . . Simple as it may sound, recognition of planning as 'an impersonal organizational structure for determining future action' was not postulated until 1961" (ibid., p. 78).

Kaser was referring to the publication of works such as *Planning Theory* by Preston P. LeBreton and Dale A. Henning. According to these two authors, "We were prompted to write this book because of a void in the literature on management theory: an absence of writing dealing with the planning function. As a result of this void we found it necessary to develop our own structural framework" (LeBreton and Henning, 1961, p. vii). LeBreton and Henning view planning as the process of determining a course of action. The process must include three essential characteristics: (1) it must involve the future, (2) it must involve action, and (3) it must be the result of personal or organizational causation.

In *A Concept of Corporate Planning* (1970), Russell L. Ackoff presents a related, though somewhat different, discussion of planning. According to Ackoff, there are two basic types of planning: strategic and tactical. Strategic planning deals with long-term goals and objectives. An organization decides where it ultimately wants to go over a period of time. Tactical planning deals with specific decisions in a given time frame. It is primarily concerned with day-to-day decisions that lead the organization toward its long-term goals. Tactical planning is therefore influenced by strategic planning decisions, just as strategic planning decisions are strongly influenced by the successes, failures, and feedback provided by tactical planning.

Ackoff's distinction between strategic and tactical planning refers to the concept of strategic management, which, despite its relatively recent emergence in management literature, has a long history in human endeavor. The word *strategy* comes from the Greek *strategos*, a general, which in turn is derived from roots meaning *army* and *lead*. The Greek verb *stratego* means "to plan the destruction of one's enemies through effective use of resources" (Bracker, 1980, p. 219).

The concept of strategy in military and political contexts was discussed by Homer, Euripides, and other early Greek writers and is evident in the works of such writers as Shakespeare, Montesquieu, Kant, Mill, Hegel, and Tolstoy. Early discussions of strategic planning focused on its application in military and diplomatic affairs, such as the strategy that enabled Philip II of Macedonia and his son Alexander the Great to overwhelm the Greek city-states and establish an empire which eventually stretched from the Mediterranean Sea to India, or the various strategies European countries used during and between the two world wars to further their interests or defend themselves.

According to James Brian Quinn, these military-diplomatic strategies provide some essential insights into the basic dimensions, nature, and design of formal strategies. They contained three essential elements: (1) the goals or objectives to be achieved, (2) the policies guiding or limiting actions, and (3) the action sequences or programs that were to accomplish the defined goals within the limits set (Quinn, 1988, p. 7).

The effective strategies were developed around a few key concepts and thrusts that gave them cohesion, balance, and focus. They dealt with not just the unpredictable, but also with the unknowable by building a posture that was strong enough to resist some changes yet flexible enough to take advantage of opportunities that might contribute to achieving goals. The military-diplomatic strategies were also subdivided into networks of strategies to achieve different goals, and assigned to different components of the organizations as their contributions to the overall effort (ibid, p. 8).

The application of strategic planning to business is mentioned by Socrates in comparing the duties of a general (Nichomachides) to those of a businessman (Antisthanes), but according to Bracker (1980, p. 219), does not appear again for several centuries.

In addition to differentiating between strategic and tactical planning, Ackoff has identified five elements in the planning process:

1. Ends—the specification of objectives and goals
2. Means—the selection of ways in which goals and objectives will be pursued
3. Resources—the determination of types and amounts of resources required, how they will be generated or acquired, and how they will be allocated to activities
4. Implementation—the design of decision-making procedures and ways of organizing them to carry out plans
5. Control—monitoring implementation and adjusting where necessary (Ackoff, 1970, p. 6)

Ackoff also describes three basic philosophies that should be considered in discussions of planning. These are identified as (1) the satisficing approach, (2) the optimizing approach, and (3) the adaptivising approach.

The goal of planning under the satisficing philosophy is to identify and attain minimally satisfactory levels of performance. In its practical application, this type of planning is seen in efforts to meet previously agreed upon standards, or in efforts to conform with established guidelines.

The goal of planning under the optimizing philosophy is to attain the highest possible yield, given the resources available. In its practical application, this type of planning can be seen in efforts to maximize productivity and efficiency. Because of its highly quantitative nature, optimizing planning tends to involve extensive use of statistics, mathematics, and simulated models.

The third philosophy, adaptivising, views planning as a tool for gaining a better understanding of the organization and how it functions. Under this philosophy, planners are just as concerned about the effects their efforts have on the organization as they are about how successfully, or unsuccessfully, an organization attains its goals. Theoretically, future plans based on either of the first two philosophies can be made, based on the knowledge gained from adaptivising efforts. The key concern of the adaptivising planner is involving people in the process. Participation in the planning process gives individuals a better understanding of the organization and how it functions, and enables them to make more effective contributions toward its successful operation (ibid., p. 30).

Peter F. Drucker defines strategic planning as

the continuous process of making present entrepreneurial (risktaking) decisions systematically and with the greatest knowledge of their futurity; organizing systematically the efforts needed to carry out these decisions; and measuring the results of these decisions against expectations through organized, systematic feedback. (Drucker, 1974, p. 125)

Robert D. Stueart and John Taylor Eastlick define planning as

the process of getting an organization from where it is to where it wants to be in a given period of time by setting it on a predetermined course of action. It is deciding what to do, how to do it, when to do it, and who is to do it. Planning consists of making decisions now regarding possible courses of action in light of established missions, goals, objectives, and other available information. (Stueart and Eastlick, 1977, p. 27)

George A. Steiner, another writer frequently cited in planning literature, describes planning from several points of view. First, planning deals with the futurity of current decisions. Planners look at the future consequences of an actual or intended decision. Strategic planning also looks at the alternative courses of action open now, and in the future, and considers the impact of current decisions on future options. Second, strategic planning is a process, a process that begins with the setting of organizational aims, the definition of strategies and policies to achieve them, and the development of detailed plans to make sure that strategies are implemented so as to achieve the ends sought. Third, strategic planning is an attitude. It is an approach to life in that it necessitates dedication to acting on the basis of a contemplation of the future, and a determination to plan constantly and systematically as an integral part of management. Fourth, strategic planning must have a structure. It involves a network of mutually dependent plans, both long-term and short-term, tactical and operational (Steiner, 1979, p. 13–15). The absence of consistent terminology in the field is illustrated by the fact that in Steiner's definition he uses long-term and short-term, tactical and operational, to express the same contrasts as Ackoff when he uses the phrases strategic and tactical planning.

There may be nearly as many definitions of planning as there are definers. However, several common themes consistently appear in the various definitions, which are elaborated upon in the various models. Planning, first of all, is concerned about achieving some objectives or goals in the future. It involves defining these goals, evaluating factors (economic, social, political, technological, etc.) that might influence achieving the goals, and taking the actions necessary for maximizing prospects for success. Possible alternative courses are considered, evaluated, and selected based on their overall effects on the organization, both in the present and in the future.

Planning may therefore be seen as a process which, if effectively employed, can provide substantial rewards to managers and administrators. Furthermore, in a rapidly changing environment, planning provides the organization with tools for anticipating change and developing alternative strategies for dealing with it.

WHAT PLANNING IS NOT

Several writers make a strong point of describing processes which, contrary to popular misconception, *are not* planning. George Keller presents an interesting summary of these efforts and contrasts them with what planning *is* in *Academic Strategy* (1983, pp. 140–141):

1. *It is not the production of a blueprint.* The idea is not to produce a fat, detailed document that everyone should follow but to get all the key people thinking innovatively and acting strategically, with the future in mind.

2. *It is not a set of platitudes.* Strategic planning means the formulation of succinctly stated operational aims. It is specific, not vague and vapid.

3. *It is not the personal vision of the president or board of trustees.* A strategy includes the hopes and aspirations of key leaders; however, these are balanced by constraints imposed by the environment and take into account opportunities that may lead in new directions.

4. *It is not a collection of departmental plans, compiled and edited.* While strategic planning must incorporate to some extent the goals and objectives of the individual components of an organization, its focus is on the long-term survival and growth of the whole organization rather than achieving the specific aims of its parts.

5. *Strategic decision making is not done by planners.* Planners provide the structure for planning. They provide the information about the organization, generate and analyze data on efficiency and effectiveness, project possible implications of different alternatives, and recommend courses of action. However, the strategic decision making, the selection of options to be followed, can only be done by the leadership of the organization. "Unless the chief operating officers subscribe—or at least feel they cannot ignore or torpedo the strategy—the plan will not sail."

6. *It is not a substitution of numbers for important intangibles.* Data are used, computers employed, financial forecasts made, and models tried, but these are introduced to sharpen judgments, analyses, and decisions, not to substitute for them. The computers do not make the decisions—people do.

7. *It is not a form of surrender to market conditions and trends.* Formulating a strategy does not mean going with whatever happens to be popular or appears to be temporarily successful. It requires an awareness of current trends and

maximizing their effective use in support of achieving predefined long-term goals and objectives.

8. *Strategic planning is not something done on an annual retreat.* Special sessions are necessary during the formulation or review stages, but planning itself is integral, not occasional.

9. *It is not a way of eliminating risks.* It enables one to calculate which risks to take, to capitalize on those with great potential for success, and to avoid those with either little possibility of success or benefits unequal to the investment of resources required.

10. *It is not an attempt to read tea leaves and outwit the future.* Strategic planning is an effort to make this year's decisions more intelligent by looking toward the probable future and coupling the decisions to an overall institutional strategy.

The mere application of standards or adherence to guidelines in evaluating an organization, or for comparing it to others, is not planning. Many librarians have come to rely heavily on suggested standards developed by national professional organizations and accreditation agencies. Although these standards may be useful as planning tools, their application to a library for evaluation is not, in itself, planning. Planning occurs when the library accepts the standards as goals and develops a comprehensive program for attaining them. Robert E. Kemper, one of the earlier writers on strategic planning in libraries, sees a danger in this course of action. Standards are meant to be used as guides that must be adapted to meet a given situation. Recommended standards may be inadequate for a specific library, or may not address the particular needs at a given point in time. On the other hand, national standards could be used to reduce support in cases where a library has managed to rise above the norm.

Forecasting is not planning. Forecasting also deals with the future. However, planning requires that a predetermined course of action be involved to affect the future. Forecasting is a tool of planning, but it must be combined with present decisions and the development of possible alternatives that can be taken in anticipation of future events in order to become a part of the planning process.

Making decisions for the future is not planning, although planning is concerned with the futurity of present decisions. "The question that faces the long-range planner is not what should we do tomorrow—it is what do we do today to be ready for an uncertain tomorrow" (Drucker, 1974, p. 125).

Planning is not a document. Planning is a dynamic, ongoing, ever-changing adapting process. It requires a constant evaluation of results of previous decisions in order to maintain a valid basis for present decisions. Planning documents, master plans, and other reports are "snapshots" of the planning process at given points in time. Ideally, the process continues after the report is completed. Subsequent updates or periodic reviews document the organization's continuing interaction with its environment and its adaptation to change.

RESEARCH FINDINGS ON EFFECTS OF FORMAL PLANNING

The question has been raised by some about whether there is documentary evidence that formal long-range planning improves an organization's efficiency and effectiveness. In his 1980 book *Management for Librarians: Fundamentals and Issues,* John R. Rizzo states that "research findings are strong and fairly consistent that organizations that plan are more effective than those that do not" (Rizzo, 1980, p. 39). He cites several studies to support this position.

In an article titled "Where Long-Range Planning Pays Off: Findings of a Survey of Formal, Informal Planners," Stanley S. Thune and Robert J. House (1970, pp. 81–87) describe a study they conducted on the effects of formal versus informal planning on thirty-six firms with sales of more than $75 million in six industrial groups (drugs, chemicals, machinery, oil, food, and steel). The study compared the performances of the companies over periods of seven to fifteen years ending in 1965, depending on the industry.

The study found that the formal planners significantly outperformed the informal planners in three of the five measures used (earnings per share, earnings on common equity, and earnings on total capital outlay). The study also found that the formal planners outperformed their own records based on an equal period of time before they began formal planning. Informal planners did not surpass formal planners in any of the measures of economic performance after long-range planning was introduced.

In a 1976 article surveying strategic planning research, Charles W. Hofer described the Thune and House study, as well as the work of D. M. Herold, which extended Thune and House's work by four years in the drug and chemical industries, and a third study by Ansoff, Brandenberg, Porter, and Radosevich, which reached similar conclusions.

Although subjective evaluation of results by management does not differ greatly between planners and nonplanners, objective financial measurements—sales growth rate, earning growth, eps growth, total assets growth, stock price growth, and so on—show a substantial difference . . . on virtually all relevant financial criteria, the planners of our sample significantly outperformed the non-planners . . . not only did the planners do better on the average but they also performed more predictably than did nonplanners. Planners seem to have narrowed the uncertainty in the outcomes of acquisition behavior. (Hofer, 1976, p. 263)

Hofer also cited other studies that found different correlations between performances of planners and nonplanners in different industries and which raised the question of whether formal planning might be more effective in some fields of endeavor than in others. In the end Hofer suggested that more cost-benefit studies were needed to resolve conflicting findings, and that new studies were needed on the value of strategic planning for nonbusiness organizations.

ADVANTAGES AND POTENTIAL DANGERS OF PLANNING

In a 1967 article titled "Long-Range Formal Planning in Perspective," Brian J. Loasby discussed the advantages and potential dangers of formal planning. He said that it helps the manager understand the future implications of present decisions, to understand the present implications of future events, and provides the motivation and mechanism for relating the implications of current decisions with long-range goals. What seems the right and rational decision in a given situation may be seen as a mistake when perceived in light of long-term ramifications (Quinn, 1988, p. 89).

Formal planning may reveal possible problems or opportunities, but over reliance on a formal system may miss or ignore signals it has not been designed to anticipate. Formal planning may secure a management commitment to a course of action; however, that commitment may inhibit spontaneity and preclude serious consideration of other courses of action. Planning provides a basis for evaluations of performance, but if the price of failure is greater than the rewards of success the system will not gain the support of the organization. An internal planning system is supposed to facilitate future decision making in other groups where external effects are important. Contingency plans are developed in anticipation of specific developments. However, if the approach becomes too mechanistic, communication and coordination between units within the organization become superseded by automatic programmed responses to change (ibid., p. 91).

Formal planning forces the organization to make its forecasts more explicit. Over reliance on the accuracy of information runs the risk of domination by sophisticated techniques. Effective monitoring is more useful than elaborate manipulation of data that is out-of-date before the manipulation is complete.

The great value of formal procedures . . . is in the raising and broadening of important issues that are liable otherwise to be inadequately considered. Much of this value can, however, be lost if these formal procedures are at all closely connected with the conflicting objective of controlling managerial performance. Planning procedures should be designed to illuminate, rather than obscure, the existence and implications of uncertainty. Finally, planning procedures should not concentrate on management action at the expense of the management system, and in particular should not be used to reconcile organization structure with the real structure: the design of a management system which facilitates quicker and more direct responses can be a better answer to some of the problems for which formal procedures offer only a second-best solution. (Ibid., p. 93–94)

Three

Planning in Academic Libraries: Historical Review—Through 1970

A study of the planning function in the management of university libraries should begin with a review of the historical development of the American academic library itself. Recent and current trends in academic library administration and management are as much a product of the growth and maturation of academic libraries as organizational entities as they are a response to the development and implementation of new theories for directing and coordinating group efforts within organizations. Until libraries were recognized as complex organizations exhibiting the same characteristics and phenomena as other organizations, theories of administration and management were not applied to them.

The problems and challenges confronting academic library administrators today are not unique to libraries. They are the same as those confronting other administrators in higher education, and, in fact, the same as those confronting administrators and managers throughout the public service sector of society. It is important that the university library of the 1990s be viewed in a historical context.

DEVELOPMENT OF THE UNIVERSITY LIBRARY

The contemporary American university library is a uniquely American phenomenon. It is a product of the development of the institutions and philosophies of higher education in the United States and of the development of libraries and philosophies of library service here. Both paths of development have bases in European models, but each has taken on new dimensions in its American adaptations and growth.

Academic librarians who have entered the profession in the last two decades frequently have not studied the history of libraries, or the history of American higher education. They therefore tend to accept what they find today at face value and to assume that what they see, except for some technological advances, is not radically different from what libraries have always been. They fail to appreciate the humble beginnings that preceded even the largest and greatest of today's academic and research libraries.

Higher education itself has taken on different meanings in twentieth-century American society than it had in the nineteenth century, and from what was originally brought to the Western Hemisphere from Europe.

The orientation of higher education has changed substantially over the past nearly three and one-half centuries. At first, it was toward preparation for the ministry, for teaching, and for community leadership in a frontier nation, with curricular emphasis on the Bible and the classics. Later it added preparation for the other ancient professions, specifically law and medicine. Then, after the American Civil War, attention was turned toward agricultural and industrial production, toward science, engineering, and later business administration. Increasingly in the past two decades, training has been added for policemen, firemen, nurses, and several of the skilled manual trades, among other additional occupations. More recently the mass market has become more important, particularly for the community colleges, but most colleges have placed additional emphasis upon it. Under the conditions of the next two decades, consumer sovereignty may well prevail largely undisputed in most institutions. (Three Thousand Futures, 1980, p. 29)

Academic libraries have shared in these shifts in emphasis in their parent institutions, and have participated in redefining the roles of higher education by redefining the roles of libraries and by developing new concepts of appropriate and adequate library service.

In *The University Library in the United States: Its Origins and Development*, Arthur T. Hamlin presents a comprehensive overview of the establishment, development, and growth of university libraries that helps correct the deficiency of historical knowledge from which many academic librarians suffer. Hamlin divides his overview into five periods of development, each with its own sets of problems, priorities, issues, accomplishments, and contributions to contemporary academic librarianship.

1. The Colonial Period (1636–1790): founding of the earliest universities
2. Growth and Development (1790–1876): a period of slow growth of the early libraries and of the founding of land grant colleges

3. Emergence of the Research Libraries (1876–1920): functional division between the colleges that stressed teaching, and the universities which emphasized research and the discovery of new knowledge
4. Between the Two World Wars (1920–46): a period characterized by the rising
   expectations of the 1920s and a pause in growth during the depression and
   World War II. The period also saw an increase in the amount of research and
   writing on library management.
5. Expansion in the Generation Since World War II (1946–Present): a period of
   explosive growth in higher education following World War II with a resur-
   gence in the 1960s. (Hamlin, 1981, p. vii)

Colonial Period, 1636–1790

The first American academic library is said to have been established at
a college in Massachusetts that later became Harvard University, shortly
after its founding in October of 1636. As reported by Edmund Browne,
"Wee have in Cambridge heere, a College erecting, youth lectured, a
library, and I suppose there will be a presse this winter." The "library"
referred to was probably a collection of donations made by "the Honoured
Magistrates and Reverend Elders" who gave "out of their libraryes' books
to the value of [£200 sterling]." This local effort was augmented by John
Harvard who bequeathed half of his estate and all of his personal library
to the newly established college when he died in 1638. That library
consisted of 329 titles in more than 400 volumes. By 1655 Harvard's
library collection had grown through other gifts and donations to 800 titles
in approximately 900 volumes.

It was not until nearly thirty years later that the first American "librarian"
appeared when Harvard adopted the "Library Laws of 1667" and chose
Mr. Solomon Stoddard, a recently appointed tutor at the college, as
"Library Keeper." The laws specified that only M.A. candidates could
borrow books (loan period—one month) and only fellows (tutors) could
study in the library. They also set forth rules regarding access to the library
key, records to be kept, sales of duplicates, and penalties for damaging
books. The hours set aside for borrowing and returning books were those
between 11:00 A.M. and 1:00 P.M.

Other academic libraries established during the colonial period include
those at the College of William and Mary (1699), Yale University (1701),
Princeton University (1757), the University of Pennsylvania (where an
appeal was made in 1749 in anticipation of the establishment of the
university), Kings College (Columbia University) (1754), College of
Rhode Island (Brown University) (1765), Rutgers University (1792), and
Dartmouth College (1792). Although each library has a separate history,

there are similarities in their beginnings. Each was started with gifts, donations, and bequests of books, money, or both from friends of the newly established or proposed institution.

Yale University's library is said to have been established in 1701 when ten clergymen met in the parlor of the Reverend Mr. Samuel Russell in Bradford, Connecticut. According to a later account by Thomas Clap, Yale's first president, each of the clergymen brought a number of books to the meeting, and before departing set them on a center table with the oath "I give these Books for the founding [of] a College in this Colony." The 40 folios thus donated form the nucleus of the Yale University Library. In 1714 Yale received a shipment of 800 more volumes collected from various donors by Jeremiah Drummer, an agent for the Massachusetts Bay Colony and supporter of the college. Another 1,000 volumes were donated in 1733 by George Berkeley, bishop of Coloyne. By 1791 Yale's printed catalog listed 2,700 volumes.

Princeton University's first reference to its library cites a bequest of Jeremy Belcher in 1757 that produced 474 volumes just in time to be housed in a special library room on the second floor the university's newest building, Nassau Hall. Princeton's catalog listed 1,281 volumes in 1760 and 2,000 by 1775.

The establishment of the library of the University of Pennsylvania predates the 1755 official founding of the college itself because of a 1749 appeal by supporters for books to serve the "publick academy." The appeal was followed by an authorization to spend up to £100 sterling for "Latin and Greek authors, maps, Drafts, and Instruments."

Kings College received a "fine library" from the bequest of the Honourable Joseph Murray in 1754, to which an additional 1,500 volumes were added shortly by another bequest from a friend in London. When the College of Rhode Island was founded in 1765, its supporters recognized the need for a library, and an appeal to English friends resulted in gifts of more than 500 books. Rutgers was chartered in 1766, but it was not until 1792 that any reference was made to a library, and then only to the fact that the only books available to students were those held individually by their tutors.

In addition to having similar histories, the colonial academic libraries had somewhat similar collections although no intentional "collection development" efforts were underway. Two-thirds of Harvard's 1638 collection was theological, primarily in Latin. It also included classical authors in the original and in translation, as well as Bacon, Descartes, Politian, and Erasmus. It contained a number of grammars and dictionaries, some English poetry, a very little classical drama, and a few medical books. Considering the time and location, it was an extensive collection.

Princeton's 1757 library was described as being heavy in the orthodox, moralistic writings of the period, and in classical literature. However, it also included modest holdings in history, biography, law, geography, navigation, and physics. Yale's 1791 collection is described as extensive and varied, containing the principle works on the natural sciences and representing all shades of theological doctrine.

A 1973 analysis by J. W. Kraus of the books listed in the available printed catalogs of the colonial colleges between 1723 and 1793 reveals that

about one-half of the titles were theological and . . . books on history, literature, and science comprised from 32 to 45 percent of the titles. With the exception of the 1793 Brown catalog, the distribution of subjects was remarkably similar despite the differences in size, and a time span of seventy years. A bibliographical review of the more important titles indicated that the range of subjects was impressive and that the significant authorities were available in many fields. (Kraus, 1973, p. 142)

It is noteworthy that in the 1790 Harvard catalog 73 percent of the titles were in English, 19 percent in Latin, with French and Italian ranking third and fourth in number.

The colonial academic programs did not require heavy reliance on library resources. Funding for the colonial academic libraries can be described as meager and sporadic at best. The College of William and Mary appears to be the first institution to use college funds specifically for its library. In February 1697 it authorized a "sizable expenditure" for that purpose. Supporters of the "publick academy" (University of Pennsylvania) in Philadelphia authorized the expenditure of up to £100 sterling for library materials several months after they issued their appeal in 1749 for gifts of books. Other important gifts of funds for libraries include the £1,170 given to Harvard by Thomas Hollis in 1726, £300 received by William and Mary from the Brafferton estate in 1732, £554 donated to Harvard by John Hancock in 1764, £700 raised for Brown University's library by John Brown, the university's treasurer, shortly after the Revolution, and £333 14s donated to Yale University by the Reverend Samuel Lockwood in 1789. The Columbia University trustees voted £750 for books for the library in 1792, and Rutgers received $1,800 from the New Jersey legislature in 1796 for repairing buildings and increasing its library.

In the colonial period no library received a regular appropriation for any purpose, or received funds on an ongoing basis except through student fees charged at several institutions. In its early days Dartmouth adopted the questionable practice of supporting the library by charging students according to their use of the facility. The income from circulation was largely applied to book purchases. Later this was changed to a flat fee of 2s per quarter. According to a 1793 document, one-quarter of the income from student fees went to the librarian and the other three-quarters to acquisitions. Princeton adopted a similar approach shortly after the Revolution when it instituted a library charge of 2s 6d per quarter for library support. In 1779 the faculty at William and Mary voted to require a contribution to the library from each student upon matriculation and annually thereafter. These contributions were to be recorded in a book kept by the bursar and would entitle the student to use the library. In 1782 the size of the contribution was set at 10s.

Other methods of obtaining funds for university libraries included the 1734 Virginia General Assembly vote directing the proceeds of a penny per gallon tax on imported liquor to William and Mary with the provision that some part be spent on books. At the University of Pennsylvania a 1752 rule levied a fine on behalf of the library of 1s on trustees who were absent from meetings, and a charge of 10s on students granted holidays. Graduation fees of 15s for a bachelor's degree and one pound for a master's degree also generated funds for the library.

The absence of sustained support for colonial academic libraries is not as detrimental as it might appear, since the only expenses were books and staff. As has been shown, gifts, donations, and bequests were the primary sources of library material. Louis Shores estimates that the proportion of acquisitions acquired by direct purchase was less than 10 percent of the total. The other 90 percent was obtained either through direct gifts or books purchased with money donated for that purpose (Shores, 1934, p. 109). The staffs of these libraries consisted of the part-time services of faculty members given responsibility for the library, usually without extra compensation.

Growth and Development, 1790–1876

Hamlin describes the period following the founding of the Republic as one of growth and development for American colleges and universities, but not for academic libraries. The period saw an increase in the number of institutions as the nation grew, but little change in enrollments (never more than a few hundred students each) or functions. In 1800 fewer than 30 colleges and universities were in operation. By 1850 there were 133, and by 1870 there were 369. A 1876 U.S. Bureau of Education report listed

305 college and university libraries with collections of 300 volumes or more. Many of the institutions established near the end of the period were products of the 1862 Morrill Land Grant Act, which provided public lands for the establishment and support of collegiate programs in agriculture and mechanic arts in developing regions of the country.

The academic programs of the new institutions were basically the same as those established during the previous period, with minimal reliance on library resources. There was a heavy emphasis on textbook study and class recitation. The curriculum tended to be classical, moralistic, and pedantic. With the notable exception of Harvard, colleges and universities demonstrated little appreciation of, or need for, library facilities beyond that which could be housed in a single room and would be occasionally opened for students for brief periods of time.

A 1907 *Library Journal* article on mid-nineteenth century college libraries by W.N.C. Carlton illustrates their status:

Eighteen college libraries in the states of North Carolina, Georgia, Alabama, Mississippi, Louisiana and Tennessee averaged 3,140 volumes. Five Kentucky institutions had an average of 5,100 volumes each; and seven in Ohio 2,957. Transylvania University had 12,000, Kenyon and Western Reserve 4,500, Indiana University 5,000, and the University of Missouri 675. . . . Excluding the University of Pennsylvania, seven Pennsylvania institutions averaged 2,839. . . . Georgetown College had 25,000 volumes and St. Mary's College, Baltimore 12,000; but these were exceptionally large collections; the 2,500 volumes at Delaware College, Newark, Del. and at St. James College, Hagerstown, Md. were more typical of this section of the country. (Carlton, 1907, p. 479)

Two movements developed in response to the absence of institutional support for library facilities. One was the "reading room," a student-run facility where newspapers, periodicals, and current books were collected and made available to students at their convenience. The other was the "society library" in which students pooled their resources through subscription memberships and established their own collections of books, newspapers, and journals. Some of the society libraries became quite large when compared with the college libraries. Prior to the Civil War many society libraries came to play a far more prominent role in the intellectual development and academic lives of their students than the institutional facility.

Just as the college library collections were small by today's standards, access to them was quite restricted. At the outbreak of the Civil War the Yale University Library was only open to juniors and seniors for a few hours in the mornings, and again in the afternoon "during a considerable portion of the year." Even those students who were allowed access to the library could borrow books only on Mondays and Thursdays. There was a charge of 6 to 12 cents on each volume, depending on its size, and a limit of three to a student. Before he could exercise even this limited privilege, a student would have to execute a bond or leave a deposit of $5. "Nearly all collegiate libraries were open for use only a very few hours a week until the 1850s, principally for the withdrawal of books. Consultation of materials within the library was virtually forbidden, if not by statute, by the lack of space, the lack of tables and chairs, and, in winter, the lack of heat" (Hamlin, 1981, p. 32).

The librarians at these institutions generally held dual appointments, with the emphasis on the other half of their responsibilities. At Amherst the librarian's position was held through fifty years by the following successors: the professor of Latin and Greek; the professor of rhetoric, oratory, and English literature; the professor of mathematics and natural philosophy; and the professor of Romance languages. These dual appointments were possible and functional because relatively little was required of the librarian. The collections were small and grew slowly. The hours of service were limited and levels of assistance given to students minimal.

Financial support for the collegiate libraries of the period continued to be irregular and weak, coming primarily as gifts of books, individual donations of money, occasional allotments from general funds, rare legislative appropriations as some public institutions, and in some cases library fees charged to students. In 1841, after two centuries of operation, Harvard had amassed a library endowment of $5,000 that generated an annual book fund of $250. By 1860 Yale had a total book endowment of approximately $26,000 that generated an annual book fund of $1,500. At the University of Missouri virtually no funds were assigned to the purchase of books for the first ten years of its existence. In 1849 the library was allotted $1,250, and in 1855 another $2,667 from the sale of public lands.

In summarizing the status of college and university libraries in the mid-nineteenth century in 1902, James Hulme Canfield, Columbia librarian and former president at the University of Nebraska and Ohio State University, wrote the following:

Fifty years ago the college library was almost an aside in education. Indeed, it was like the sentence which we enclose in brackets; to be read in a low tone, or to be slurred over hastily, or even to be entirely omitted without making any serious change in the sense. With rare exceptions, the position of the librarian was a haven for the incompetent or the decrepit. The appropriations for maintenance were pitifully meager. The expenditures for expansion were even less worthy. The efficiency, or the inefficiency, was, naturally, quite proportionate. (Brough, 1953, p. 2)

Emergence of the Research Library, 1876–1920

A number of events occurred in 1876 that Hamlin says marked the beginning of a new age for librarianship in the United States. These events included the establishment and first conference of the American Library Association, a national organization to articulate the needs of librarians and to serve as an advocate for the cause of libraries and literacy; the birth of *Library Journal* as a vehicle for the communication of library news, statistics, and articles of professional merit; the launching of the Library Bureau, a commercial enterprise to manufacture furniture and equipment for libraries; the Bureau of Education's publication of *Public Libraries in the United States of America: Their History, Condition, and Management*; Melvil Dewey's publication of the outline of the Dewey decimal system of classification; and Charles Cutter's publication of *Rules for a Printed Dictionary Catalogue*.

The period 1876–1920 saw the emergence of the research library, a part of a larger movement in the country to make higher education more relevant to the needs of society. The movement's beginnings can be traced to the Morrill Act of 1862, which provided for the sale of public lands to support "agriculture and the mechanic arts . . . and to promote the liberal and practical education of the industrial classes in the several pursuits and professions in life." Later the Hatch Act of 1887 created agricultural experiment stations, and the Second Morrill Act of 1890 provided direct appropriations to land grant institutions.

The movement was spurred on by the industrialization of the country during and after the Civil War, and by the interest many successful industrialists took in supporting research and higher education. Following the lead of Daniel Coit Gilman at Johns Hopkins University, many universities began adapting the German university model and emphasizing research. In addition, the shift from the classics and the textbook recitation to seminars and lectures had significant ramifications for the kinds of library resources and services that would be needed. Curricular offerings were expanded to new subject fields, and electives further expanded the scope of knowledge inquiring minds might seek to explore.

Hamlin lists seven areas in which the new emphasis on research altered the basic character of academic libraries and set them on the road to the developments we see today:

1. a shift in emphasis from conservation and protection of the book to one of putting material to effective use in the hands of the faculty and student body;

2. a recognition of responsibility to provide effective personal service in the use of the library and, more particularly, the efficient use of reference material;

3. recognition of the library's role as an educational force not only as a resource for the curriculum but also apart from it, to a very real degree independent of the curriculum;

4. the absolute necessity of classifying books according to subject and not to fixed shelf locations, which had to be changed as collections grew in size and movement became necessary;

5. the need to record each book with adequate bibliographic description and to make this information easily available to users by author, by subject, and, within limitation, by title, form, series, and other approaches appropriate to individual items;

6. acceptance of the role of departmental libraries within certain practical limits; and

7. the advantages of cooperation with other libraries principally in the loan of material. (Hamlin, 1980, pp. 48–49)

The recognition of these factors brought about many changes in the ways academic librarians saw themselves, the ways they interpreted their roles in their colleges and universities, and the ways in which university administrations began to view their libraries. Innovations of the period included longer hours, larger and more comfortable reading rooms and study areas, greater access to stacks, reserve reading rooms for high demand short-term circulation items, departmental libraries located near laboratories and faculty offices, library orientation sessions and courses in bibliographic instruction, public card catalogs, designated reference librarians to "counsel and direct readers," formalized interlibrary loan agreements, and even some cooperation between nearby libraries in collection development.

In 1876 only two institutions, Harvard and Yale, had collections of more than 50,000 volumes. By 1900 the number had increased to thirteen, with Harvard growing to nearly 1 million volumes. By 1920 Harvard had passed 2 million volumes, Yale had passed 1 million, and four others (Columbia, Cornell, Chicago, and Pennsylvania) had reached the half-million volume level. As the universities grew during this period in size and depth and range of studies, their libraries also grew, diversified, and began to develop the characteristics with which most librarians and library users are familiar today.

Between the Two World Wars

Hamlin describes the next period, 1920–46, as one of moderate growth and expansion for universities and their libraries overall, and divides it into three parts: the decade of the 1920s continued the expansion and redefining of roles begun during the preceding period, but ended with the stock market crash in 1929; the 1930s saw the Great Depression that stunted growth of collections and staff; and the 1940s saw the Second World War drain off energy and attention.

One example of the fluctuations of the period is illustrated in a 1944 study by Ralph Ellsworth of the library material expenditures of the fifty-three leading institutions. The average expenditure for books went from approximately $30,000 in 1920 to approximately $70,000 in 1931. Then it declined to less than $40,000 in 1934 and slowly grew to about $75,000 in 1941. Twenty of the largest universities spent well above $100,000 in 1929–32, then down to $80,000 in 1935, and up again to $100,000 in 1937–41 (Ellsworth, 1944, p. 1). Nevertheless, many significant achievements were made during the period, and several trends gained momentum in the years that followed. One of these trends was a publications program that saw the birth of *Library Quarterly* in 1931, the *Journal of Documentary Reproduction* in 1938, and *College and Research Libraries* in 1939. Until that time *Library Journal* and the *Bulletin of the American Library Association* had been the only major journals in the field. The 1930s also saw the establishment of the Association of Research Libraries in 1932, an association of the directors of the forty largest research libraries to discuss mutual concerns, and the Association of College and Reference (later Research) Libraries, which provided a forum within the American Library Association for all academic librarians in 1938.

Other accomplishments of the period included the construction of new central library buildings to house the enlarged collections at many universities, and the emergence of university librarians responsible for virtually all library services at an institution. Examples included those at Michigan (1920), Minnesota (1924), Washington (1926), Duke (1927), Illinois and North Carolina (1929), Cincinnati (1930), Yale and Rochester (1932), Columbia (1934), and Oregon (1937). These expanded facilities also saw the routine introduction of new services: browsing rooms for extracurricular reading, binderies, photostat services, incorporation of microforms in collections, and reserve reading rooms. In addition, "Friends of the Library" groups were formed at Harvard, Yale, and Columbia in the 1920s. Ten years later the number had increased from three to fifty, recognizing not only the contributions individuals made to the libraries, but also the more important and more visible role the library was beginning to play in the university. Interlibrary cooperation was another area in which significant advances were made during the period. One example was the establishment of the Joint Universities Library in Nashville to serve the needs of several local institutions. Others were the establishment of document centers; the development of union catalogs and cooperative cataloging programs; the publication of union lists of serials, newspapers, and archives; and the sharing of resources through microform reproduction of library materials.

Expansion in the Generation Since World War II, 1946–80

Hamlin ends his discussion of the development of the university library with the period that ran from the end of World War II through the 1970s.

Never had there been expansion of such magnitude, never had funds flowed so freely, never had technology had so much to offer the profession, never had the library had such opportunity to serve advanced study and research. Yet never had there been so much ground to cover, so many users, such criticism as demands were not fully met, such threats to the very security of collections, catalogs, and buildings, such widespread student rebellion, such general complexity of operations. (Hamlin, 1981, p. 68)

The key factor in describing the period was growth. Growth in the number of universities, growth in the numbers of students, growth in the sizes of collections, growth in the sizes of staffs, growth in the numbers of subjects included in the academic curricula, growth in faculty, and growth in the sizes of buildings to house everything. From the half-million students in colleges in 1939–40, enrollments went to nearly 10 million by 1975–76. In the 1970s both the University of Minnesota and Ohio State University each had more than 50,000 students.

In 1946, eleven of the twenty largest university libraries held 1 million volumes or more. Only three, Harvard, Yale, and the University of Illinois, held more than 2 million volumes. By 1978 all twenty had passed the 2 million mark, seventeen had passed 3 million, eleven had passed 4 million, five had passed 5 million, and Harvard was rapidly approaching 10 million volumes. From averaging 56,000 volumes per institution that were added in 1946–47, the fifteen largest university libraries went to an average of 144,000 volumes per institution in 1977–78.

With the growth in enrollments, diversification of academic programs, and development of other activities university administrations also expanded to manage these new institutions. New administrative units, often headed by vice presidents, were required for personnel, public relations, physical plants, computer services, research and development, security, extension programs, affirmative action, and for handling the special needs of the disabled and members of minority groups. These were in addition to the traditional roles of academic dean, financial or business vice president, and counseling or personnel dean. It is not unusual for a university to have eight or ten full vice presidents and thirty or forty associate or assistant vice presidents. This is a dramatic change from the era in which the university administration consisted of the president, a business-financial vice president, a librarian, a physical facilities manager, an athletic director, and two or three personnel deans who handled admissions, discipline, and student affairs.

Along with the increase in enrollment went an increase in the number of colleges that were upgraded to research institutions emphasizing graduate level work. The University of California (UC) at Santa Barbara, for example, went from a four-year college with a respectable library of 40,500 volumes in 1944, to a full-scale university with a library of 1,275,000 volumes by 1978. Similar developments occurred in other parts of the UC system, as well as in the state systems of New York, Texas, and Wisconsin. Federal funding for higher education fueled the growth. The Higher Education Facilities Act of 1963 aided in the construction of 605 separate library buildings in the six years before it was discontinued in 1969. Between 1967 and 1971 nearly $1 billion was spent on academic library buildings. Other movements in the period since World War II are the development of separate undergraduate libraries at many institutions, the development of large rare book libraries, and the clustering of departmental libraries combining related disciplines (health sciences, physical sciences, and biological sciences).

The growth and maturation of libraries also brought new problems, which will be addressed later in this study. These include overcrowding of facilities leading to the consideration of compact shelving and remote storage for little-used items; concerns about security, vandalism, and preservation of materials; inadequate supplies of professional librarians to staff the new facilities, followed by staff reductions as levels of funding either decreased or were eroded by inflation; the issue of faculty status for librarians; unionization of librarians and other university employees; greater emphasis on nonprint and audiovisual media; the role of specialists in libraries; and finally the advent of the computer.

The modern university library has come a long way from the collection of books donated to Harvard in 1636. It has grown large, dynamic, and complex. Its resources have changed, its philosophy and functions have changed, its scope has changed, and its problems have changed. As the university library has developed into a discrete organizational entity, it has become appropriate to approach its problems as organizational problems of efficiency and effectiveness and to apply the findings of management theory to the administration of the university library.

MANAGEMENT THEORY IN LIBRARIES

The application of theories and practices of management and organizational behavior to libraries has generally followed the same trends as found in other segments of society. However, a persistent time lag has been observed. In a study of the impact of management theories on public library administration after 1925, Arthur T. Kittle noted that concepts relating to library organization and management were emphasized somewhat in parallel with the development of organization theory generally, and that there had been a long-standing interest in management principles as they affect library personnel. However, he also noted that scientific management, for example, only gained serious attention in library management literature after World War II, "35 years after these concepts were stressed in the industrial world" (Kittle, 1961, p. 143).

In his 1976 text on library management, G. Edward Evans also referred to a time lag between the development of management theories in business, industry, and government and their application to library situations. Evans divided the development of management theory into four parts: (1) the prescientific period, before 1880 (emphasis based on power, fear, and ability to punish or reward), (2) the period of scientific management, 1880–1927 (emphasis on objective measurements of productivity and efficiency—Frederick W. Taylor), (3) the human-relations period, 1927–50, (emphasis on people as social entities participating in interpersonal and intergroup interactions—Elton Mayo and the Hawthorne Western Electric Company studies), and (4) the synthesis period, 1950–76 (a period characterized by an attempt to reconcile and broaden scientific management and human relations theories, and, to at the same time, incorporate a host of other schools, theories, and approaches to organizational analysis) (Evans, 1976, p. 29–32). One might view Evans's analysis as being overly simplistic. It did, however, set up a framework for contrasting the development of mainstream organization theories and their application to the administration of libraries. According to Evans, management theory in libraries followed the general pattern just outlined, with several differences. First, he saw three periods of library application, rather than the four periods for theory development. He described them as (1) before 1937 (based on the classic bureaucratic model), (2) the scientific management period, 1937–55, and (3) the human relations period, 1955–76.

Only relatively recently have many American libraries come to have the large budgets, collections, or staffs found today, or the managerial and administrative problems associated with organizational size and complexity. Prior to the twentieth century, American libraries were generally rather small endeavors, involving very few full-time employees. Little managerial expertise was required. In colleges and universities, the libraries were often built up and maintained by a single individual, or a small group of students or scholars. In those instances where library resources were combined, pooled, or centralized, one of these scholars, possibly with the aid of one or more assistants, would serve as the "librarian."

In the nonacademic sector, libraries, along with parks, zoos, and museums, were symbols of local culture and civic pride. The existence of the public library was fairly widespread, especially near the end of the nineteenth century. However, it remained a relatively minor aspect of municipal government. Typically it would be minimally staffed by a member of the community who happened to have a special interest in "books," "literature," or local history.

Whether public or academic, most nineteenth-century American libraries were simple, straight forward, uncomplicated operations requiring little special attention. The most important criterion for the "librarian" or the person responsible for the library's operation was that he, or she, be fairly knowledgeable about literature, scholarship, and academic pursuits. There was no apparent requirement for, or use of, administrative talents or training (Marchant, 1976, p. 29).

There were, of course, a number of exceptions to the situation just described. It is on the basis of these exceptions that Evans began his discussion of the application of management theories to libraries. During the first period, before 1937, the relatively few libraries of a size and scope to require the application of management techniques tended to imitate the administrative style found in business, government, and industry during that period, namely, the classic bureaucratic model. However, as one writer noted, the basically humanistic character of their activities "tended to soften libraries into benevolent structures rather than the exploitative ones that were stereotyped by the sweat shops of the time" (ibid., p. 29). Evans characterized the period 1937–55 as the scientific management period for libraries. It was ushered in by research activities and a number of doctoral dissertations produced in the late 1930s that advocated a more "scientific" approach to the study of libraries and library operations. It was a period in which the efficiency conscious measurement and analysis techniques of Taylor, Gantt, the Gilbreths, and others found wide applicability in libraries. It included research on cost analysis, technical services, cataloging, and the use of edge-notched cards for record control (Evans, 1976, pp. 29–32). In his 1932 introductory remarks to the *Proceedings of the Third Institute for Librarians*, sponsored by the Graduate Library School, University of Chicago, Carleton B. Joeckel referred to the change of emphasis in library circles about management theory and its applications to libraries:

The general subject . . . library administration . . . is at once old and new. It is old in the sense that questions of organization and management have long been discussed by librarians. It is new in the sense that the close and scientific study of library administration is a subject worthy of consideration in itself is only in its beginnings. (*Current Issues* . . ., 1939, p. v.)

Although these "discussions" of scientific management for libraries were occurring in the thirties, the widespread use of this approach did not come about until after World War II. This period was characterized by a dramatic increase in financial support for libraries. The small reading room-library was replaced by a multibranch municipal public library system. The "scholar-librarian" and his small staff of assistants were finding themselves increasingly involved with budgeting, accounting, acquisitions policies, building design, and complex matters of personnel administration. Discussion among librarians centered on the coordination of activities, division of services and processes, and the training of library administrators. The greatest emphasis was placed on the acquisition and processing of materials, activities that lent themselves to scientific analysis (Kittle, 1961, p. 88–102).

Evans characterized his third period of the application of management theory to libraries (1955–76) as the human relations period. He merged the third (human relations) and fourth (synthesis) periods he had defined for theory development into one period for theory application. He saw this third, and continuing, period as one in which a synthesis was occurring between the basically humanistic quality of library work and the scientific-technological advances being made on many fronts. The human relations school, defined and described by Mayo and the Hawthorne experiments, had little impact on library administrative practice. Evans felt that this may have stemmed from the fact that library administrators were already well aware of and concerned about interpersonal behavior. In fact, some used the findings of the Hawthorne studies to reinforce their opposition to the "depersonalization" and "dehumanizing influences" of scientific management. Evans's definition of the library human relations period referred to a period in which efforts were being made to integrate the worker into the organization's decision making structure on all levels. "Human relations in most libraries means democratic administrations, participative administration, great use of committees, and involvement, or apparent involvement, in the decision making process" (Evans, 1976, p. 32).

The current period of application of management theories to libraries (1991) appears to be one in which a large number of theories are being examined, evaluated, combined, and applied in a variety of library situations. A survey of library literature over the past twenty years reveals a number of writings on management, organizational and administrative theory, and strategic planning in libraries. The authors tend to take specific theories or groups of theories and interpret them as they may have relevance to the operation of libraries.

In his 1973 address to the Thirty-Sixth Annual Conference of the Graduate Library School, University of Chicago, Warren J. Haas, then vice president for Information Services and university librarian of Columbia University, commented on the increased amount of energy going into research and publishing on library management, and the applications of management theories to libraries. He saw this as a healthy sign that the time gap between the development of administrative theories and their application to libraries was rapidly closing.

EARLY PLANNING STUDIES IN ACADEMIC LIBRARIES

Despite David Kaser's 1971 comment that "planning, as now defined in management theory, was not postulated until a scant decade ago" (McGrath, 1973, p. 78), librarians have long been concerned about developing and improving their libraries' functions and services and have included comprehensive planning as one option for doing so. University and library administrators have also been interested in increasing the effectiveness and efficiency of their libraries. A review of these efforts presents a background upon which to base more recent evaluation and planning activities in libraries.

College and University Library Problems . . . , 1927

One of the earliest comprehensive analyses of American academic library operations surveyed the libraries of eighteen of the nation's leading colleges and universities in 1925. George A. Works was commissioned by the Association of American Universities to conduct a study of university libraries. The Advisory Committee for the study included such leaders in the profession as William W. Bishop of the University of Michigan, Andrew Keogh of Yale University, Sydney B. Mitchell of the University of California, Azariah S. Root of Oberlin College, and Frank K. Walter of the University of Minnesota. Initially the study was to have covered the period from 1875 to 1925. This was modified first to 1900 to 1925 and then later to 1910 to 1925 because of difficulties encountered in gathering and interpreting meaningful data, and because of concern about comparisons between institutions or between different periods in time when terms and definitions were not consistent (Works, 1927, p. vii).

Works's study is important because it is one of the earliest attempts to evaluate university libraries by making comparisons between institutions and drawing conclusions about them based on the study's findings. Today it is routine for a library administrator to examine his or her organization and make judgments based on information available about other libraries. Before George Works's study such an approach had not been attempted using such a large group of institutions. The fact that the lack of reliable and comparable data restricted the scope of his study is also important. Later library evaluation efforts were able to build upon this base and to encourage librarians to maintain more accurate records and to seek to standardize terminology for activities being documented. The study also made a number of significant observations about university libraries, library staffs, and specific problems and issues that are still of great concern to library planners, library administrators, and university administrators today.

College and University Library Problems . . . began with a statement of the functions of the academic library in 1925:

1. Facilitate and encourage research at least to the extent of securing the necessary printed resources when practicable . . . [assuming that] the lines of research for which materials are being gathered are in harmony with the objectives of the institution.

2. Facilitate the work of teacher and student in the processes of teaching and learning. This includes not only the instructional work for undergraduates but also special reading rooms and printed resources for such course work as graduate students may be doing in institutions having any considerable number of them.

3. Offer opportunities for the general or "cultural" reading of student body and faculty . . . making . . . an effort to have the library stimulate breadth of reading on the part of the student body. (Ibid., p. 5)

The report noted several situations that existed at the institutions studied that influenced the need for change in the ways many of the libraries were being administered. These included

1. the growth in the numbers of volumes available and in numbers of students to be served;
2. the growth in the number of graduate students and an increase in their ratio to undergraduate students along with an increase in the numbers of volumes required in order to meet their research needs; and
3. the effects of increased enrollments in summer sessions (eliminated catch-up time for behind the scenes work). (Ibid.)

The report found that the relationship between library and university expenditures was generally favorable, with the older collections stabilizing and the younger still catching up. It also found that expenditures for instruction and library salaries were generally favorable and showed an increased appreciation for the role of the library in the educational process.

Changes in methods of instruction during the period covered by the study were the same as those noted by Hamlin in *The University Library* . . . (1981, pp. 45–60), including increased reliance on outside readings, graduate study, and independent research requiring more and varied library resources. This increased use of assigned readings beyond standard texts stimulated the development of reserve collections and the purchase of duplicate copies for class assignments. Funds for the expanded service came from a variety of sources including student fees, general university funds, and departmental funds. Several formulas had been developed to determine how many copies might be needed, considering such factors as number of students in a course, and how many times a particular title was requested.

Works's report stressed the need for more accurate, thorough, and consistent documentation of activities undertaken in libraries. It found a general absence of such record keeping except at those institutions that also had library training programs (California, Chicago, Columbia, and Michigan). This absence of consistent documentation was the main reason the scope of the study had to be reduced first from fifty to twenty-five and finally to fifteen years. The report identified several trends, but called for more research, and more analysis of available data. It found a great variation in levels of service among the institutions studied, but found a general over reliance on student assistance. One interesting observation was the fact that many libraries seemed to have become "dumping grounds for elderly university employees who cannot afford to retire." The report found a steady ratio between expenditures for books and services during the period covered, but little documentation as to the extent to which the libraries were able to meet the demands of their users. General institutional funds had taken over the major responsibility for collection growth. Gifts and donations were no longer as significant a factor as they had been earlier. There had also been a steady increase in the use of interlibrary loan as a mechanism for expanding the scope of materials available to students and faculty.

Periodical literature stood out as a universal problem. There had been a dramatic increase in the number of titles published during the period studied (1910–25) and an increase in subscription rates. Works noted an increase of 162 percent in the domestic market and 205 percent in the non-English foreign market. There had also been a significant increase in the cost of binding titles once purchased. The 1927 initiation of a Union List of Serials project was cited as a possible way of alleviating this problem.

Extension services offered depended on the role of the institution in the region. Publicly supported institutions were by mandate more involved in this area than private ones. Across the board more money went into the sciences than into the humanities for library material, services, and capital expenditures. Even with the greater emphasis on graduate study, facilities (carrels or assigned desks) for graduate students were generally inadequate. Students in honors courses had special study areas and access to closed stacks. Hours of service in central libraries showed a general increase between 1875 and 1925 but this was not the case with departmental libraries.

The report expressed concern about the status of professional staff in libraries. Besides the issue of elderly university employees mentioned earlier, the report called for a clear distinction between clerical and professional work. It cited factors affecting the status of library staff that needed to be examined including salary, retirement provisions, vacations, tenure, relationships with classroom faculty, and conditions governing attendance at professional meetings. It contrasted the relative preparation requirements for library professional staff and teaching staff and called for changes in salaries to reduce the disparity.

The key recommendation of the Works study was to make a strong case for greater cooperation and resource sharing between libraries and between their parent institutions, a theme that is sounded repeatedly as subsequent reports and studies are examined. Works called upon *institutions* to determine specific areas of emphasis and to concentrate on them. "Competition drives up prices, scatters resources, condemns most efforts to mediocrity." University administrators—not librarians—must take the initiative in defining areas of emphasis through courses, research programs, and faculty appointments. The report quotes a 1913 presentation to underscore its point.

Is it wise or necessary or possible for all Universities to be all things to all advanced students? Are not the responsibility and the necessity upon most of us to be respectable in our library equipment in all the fields—where the personnel of the faculty justifies work for the Master's degree; to be good in what our location or traditions or special departmental strength justifies and to be best where all these three combine and make us the logical place where library excellence is to be expected? Should we not make our special treasures immediately available by special bibliographies, by generosity in inter-library loans, accepting commissions to photograph or copy whenever the demand is made and the expenses paid? Then in those fields where we are wisely and respectably mediocre let us depend upon loans ourselves and send our students on to the greater opportunities and that offer elsewhere in the fields where we have determined not to be a claimant for pre-eminence. ("The Library and the Graduate School," 1913, p. 44)

Existing cooperative arrangements between Stanford University and the University of California, between the University of Michigan and the Detroit Public Library, and between The New York Public Library and Columbia University were mentioned as illustrations of ways in which institutions could share resources and build upon strengths.

Although the Works study and report was not designed or executed as a planning effort, it holds a key place in the history of university library planning. It demonstrates that there were concerns about the adequacy of library resources and services among members of the Association of American Universities in 1925, and that there was an awareness that it would be beneficial to document library resources and services by collecting, comparing, and analyzing available data. The observations and recommendations included in Works's report were an attempt to draw conclusions about the status of the libraries studied based on the data collected and to give directions for future university library development based on some objective criteria. General goals and objectives were described, current and potential resources analyzed, problem areas discussed, and recommendations about priorities for action made. Perceptive library and university administrators should have found the report useful in addressing library planning in their own institutions.

Survey of Land Grant Colleges and Universities . . . , 1930

Another important early analysis of university libraries was that conducted by the U.S. Office of Education as a part of a larger study of land grant colleges and universities in the late 1920s (U.S. Office of Education, 1930, pp. 609–714). The overall survey was directed by Arthur J. Klein, chief of the Office of Education's Division of Collegiate and Professional Education, U.S. Department of the Interior. The library section of the survey was directed by Charles Harvey Brown, librarian at Iowa State College. Brown was an active leader in the profession who was later elected president of the Iowa Library Association, the American Library Association, and the Association of College and Reference Libraries. His most significant contributions, beyond the Office of Education survey, were in the area of collection development (Wilson and Tauber, 1956, p. 543).

The Advisory Committee on Library Facilities and Services, which assisted in designing and conducting the survey, consisted of Willard P. Lewis, librarian at the University of New Hampshire; Whitman Davis, librarian at Mississippi A & M College; Cora Miltimore, librarian at the University of Florida, Gainesville; L. L. Dickerson of the American Library Association; and Reba Davis, librarian at the University of Wyoming. The library section of the survey included sixty-three participants, forty-nine general and fourteen Negro land grant colleges.

The purpose of the survey was to determine the extent to which participating institutions met the five "requirements for good library service" set forth by the designers of the survey. Quoting a 1929 study of libraries of teacher-training institutions by G. W. Rosenlof, the report stated the following:

It has not been thought within the province of this study to challenge the place of the library in its relation to the newer theories and conceptions of educational philosophy or of the educative process. The newer methods of teaching and learning, the passing of the textbook as the only source of information, and the coming of new approaches to learning through the avenues of many supplementary reference materials have been accepted as prima facie evidences of a new day and a new responsibility in the field of library service. (Rosenlof, 1929, p. 150)

Referring to its specific charge the report continued:

There is general agreement as to the position of the library as the heart of the college. The object of this study, therefore, is not to justify this conception of the library but rather to ascertain the present status of libraries in land-grant institutions and the means and methods necessary to obtain and maintain efficient library service in these institutions. (U.S. Office of Education, 1930, p. 616)

The survey report began by outlining the "functions" of libraries in participating land grant institutions:

1. *The library in relation to effective teaching*: to aid directly in the instruction of students, both graduate and undergraduate, by supplying reading material, with suitable facilities for its use;
2. *The library in relation to research*: to provide for and aid research by making available the necessary source material;
3. *The library in relation to intellectual development of the individual instructors*: to aid faculty members to familiarize themselves with current developments in their respective fields;
4. *The library in relation to general reading of the students*: to make possible and to encourage general reading by faculty and students; and
5. *The library in relation to the state at large*: to aid in the extension of service of the institution by supplying printed material and information to persons beyond the campus. (Ibid., p. 613)

Having described these "functions," the report went on to set forth "requirements for good library service":

A library, to function effectively, requires an understanding by college administrators of the following necessary conditions:

1. adequate book collections;
2. suitable buildings and equipment;
3. satisfactory relationships of library to institutional administration and to faculty;
4. competent and sufficient library personnel; and
5. adequate financial support. (Ibid., p. 616)

The survey itself was an analysis of each of the sixty-three participating libraries, with a determination of the extent to which each, and the group as a whole, met the requirements for good service set forth. Six general categories were established for examining the libraries of land grant colleges and universities. Observations and recommendations were developed based on data and other information gathered about each.

1. Usability of Libraries and Methods of Facilitating Use
2. Books and Periodicals
3. Buildings
4. Administrative Control
5. Personnel
6. Financial Support and Library Budgets

Usability of libraries was determined by measurements of recorded use, and by the presence of tools, services, policies, and practices to facilitate use. Measurements of recorded use included the proportion of enrolled students using the library, number of books borrowed for home reading (not overnight use), amount of assigned reading, use shown of books borrowed from other libraries, and the ratio between the seating capacity of the library and the total number of students enrolled in the institution. The tools, services, policies, and practices to facilitate use included the presence of card catalogs and their efficiency, library instruction programs, delivery systems for books, telephone and messenger services, library hours, accessibility of books (closed versus open stacks), information services (to research workers, citizens of the state, and as perceived by faculty, librarians, and members of the survey teams), availability of titles beyond those directly related to instruction, the extent to which assigned readings were found to be available, and facilities for renting of books.

In evaluating the book and periodical collections the survey teams examined the quality and quantity of library materials provided. They looked at the roles faculty and librarians played in the selection of materials and the allocation of book funds. They noted the numbers of volumes added by purchase, holdings of typical titles, subscriptions to current periodicals, and holdings of scientific sets. They also looked into the handling of gifts, exchanges, books discarded or withdrawn from collections, duplicates, and availability of books through interlibrary loan.

Library buildings were examined for particular desirable and objectionable features. Ratio of seats to students was one of the most important, but the survey teams also considered the number of square feet per student, availability of special rooms for private or group study, and the adequacy of equipment provided.

Administrative control was considered important because it influenced the role the libraries played in the colleges' and universities' overall organization and administration. The survey teams looked at the relationships of head librarians to presidents, to faculty library committees, and to departmental and divisional libraries.

In the area of personnel the survey teams examined the duties and responsibilities of head librarians, professional library staff, and support staff. They compared the librarians with classroom faculty and made a number of observations and recommendations regarding faculty status, educational requirements for librarians, and the relationships between librarians and classroom faculty.

Financial support and library budgets constituted the final category of the study. The survey teams reviewed what was included in the various library budgets, by whom library budgets were prepared, factors that governed levels of library support, administration of library fees, and distributions of library expenditures. They also examined rates of growth for library expenditures, expenditures per student, and the relationship of the library budgets to the total budgets of the participating institutions.

The final report made specific recommendations in each of the categories examined and concluded with general recommendations. The following is a summary of the general recommendations:

Use of Libraries

- More attention should be given to the individual reader in order to see that he obtains needed material.

- Librarians should make additional studies, statistically and otherwise, of the use of their libraries, and especially of failures of students and faculty to obtain adequate service.

- Further studies by librarians are also needed to ascertain factors that affect present development and should direct future growth.

Books and Periodicals

- The selection of books should be organized; all instructors should see that the needed material in their field is available. The final responsibility should be placed upon the librarian.

- Inasmuch as it has been found that institutions with well-used libraries are expending not less than $10 per student for books, periodicals, and binding, this amount is suggested as a tentative standard. This need is shown by the pitiful condition of the book collections in more than one-half of the land grant institutions.

Buildings

- Institutions that have not erected library buildings within the past ten years should make a careful study to determine if their present buildings are fully conducive to the satisfactory use of books.

- In the erection of buildings in the future much more attention should be given to the use to be made of the building. Adequate provision should be made for future growth of the library and enlargement of the building.

Administrative Control

- The control of all libraries on the campus should be placed directly upon the librarian, who should be responsible only to the president for their administration. All purchases of library books and all appointments of library assistants should be made only upon his recommendation.

Personnel

- The library staffs of many land grant institutions should be enlarged. The number of persons found necessary by well-used libraries is 5 for the first 500 students, 10 for the first 1,000, and 4 additional for each additional 500 students. Part-time assistants are to be included and are to be figured on the basis given in this report.

- For all future appointments to positions on the professional staff of the library, a college degree and one year of library school should be required. In addition, adequate experience in scholarly, well-used libraries is recommended for all positions except those of junior assistants. More extensive educational and professional qualifications should be required for the higher positions.

- Salaries of librarians should correspond with the average salary paid academic deans or the salaries paid the most highly paid group of full professors. The salaries of library department heads should correspond with the salaries of assistant or associate professors.

- Many library staffs need reorganization. The present members of those staffs should be given positions for which they are qualified; new members should be appointed at salaries based upon the requirements of the positions and the qualifications of the appointee.

- There is need of a clear understanding of the duties of professional library assistants and a distinction between the duties of the professional and clerical staffs.

Financial Support

- In more than three-fourths of the land grant institutions much increased financial support is needed. In the group of libraries with the least use and smallest support the library budget should be increased to about four times the present amount. Institutions that are allotting less than 4 percent of their funds for library purposes or that are spending less than $20 per student should carefully examine the use made of their libraries, the adequacy of book collections, and the efficiency of the personnel as compared with libraries with larger ratios of expenditures.

The Survey of Land Grant Colleges and Universities . . . is important because it generated a large body of information on academic libraries, library resources, and library services at the time. It set forth "requirements for good library service" and, using the data collected in designated areas of study, sought to make objective evaluations of the extent to which land grant college and university libraries met these requirements in the late 1920s. It made observations and recommendations in each of the areas studied based on what was found among the sixty-three participating institutions and made general recommendations based on an overview of its findings.

Specific recommendations focused on how libraries could be made more effective. These included quantitative analyses of resources, services, and user satisfaction; identification of desirable and objectionable features in buildings; guidelines for administrative control of libraries; suggestions for relationships between library administrators and other campus officers; statements about the professional status of librarians and the education and training required in order for them to function effectively in academic environments; recommendations about financial support and library budgets; and the need for the development of specific plans for future growth.

The U.S. Office of Education survey gave guidance and direction to those seeking to improve conditions at individual institutions and gave them bases for comparing their libraries with those of other colleges and universities. The survey divided the participating institutions into roughly three groups: Those in the first group started their "modern" development early in the twentieth century or before, those in the second group began developing their libraries in the early 1920s, and those in the third group were only beginning the development of their libraries at the time of the survey. In an article published in the July 1932 issue of the American Library Association *Bulletin*, Charles H. Brown, director of the library section of the survey, described how a library director might make the best use of the study, its findings, and its recommendations (Brown, 1932. pp. 431–35).

The library director's first responsibility would be to read the report itself. Then the library staff should read it and determine how recommendations could be applied to the local situation. Next the library director would persuade the president of the university to establish a faculty committee to study the survey and its local applications. The committee would determine (1) into which group its institution fell, (2) where it did not meet the standards set forth, (3) whether these deficiencies should be remedied, and (4) if so, how. Once the self-study had been conducted,

Brown recommended bringing in an outside expert for an objective analysis and to give the self-study greater credibility. Finally, the library director would proceed to implement the recommendations received.

The Office of Education survey differed from the Works survey in several ways. It was a far more ambitious effort involving sixty-three institutions, and it was a part of an even larger survey of land grant colleges and universities. It benefited from having the sponsorship and support of the federal government and the full cooperation of the administrations of the participating colleges and universities. The initial purpose of the Works survey was to examine the development of a select group of academic libraries between 1875 and 1925. Problems cited earlier changed that purpose to an examination covering 1910–25. Works was responding to the desire of university presidents for guidance in evaluating and supporting library activities. The Office of Education survey was specifically designed to develop criteria for evaluating libraries and to provide recommendations on how library services could be improved. Works's recommendations tended to be general and were based on accepted assumptions about adequacy of resources and services. The Office of Education survey had the advantage of being able to build upon Works's study, but it also went a step farther by comparing "adequately" supported libraries with less well-funded facilities. Both studies are important efforts that warrant the attention of modern library planners. Many of the issues raised in these studies are as relevant today as they were a half century ago.

G. Edward Evans refers to the 1930s to 1950s as the scientific-management period of library management because of the increased interest on research in librarianship and an emphasis on applying scientific principles of management to libraries. The Works survey and the U.S. Office of Education survey were early products of this movement and both contributed to its further development. Both emphasized the importance of efficiency in library operations and established quantitative criteria for evaluating libraries. Both called for objective studies of library operations, more consistent record keeping, more data collection, and more data analysis, in order to determine how efficiently various services were being provided.

The interest of foundations in libraries, and the establishment of the Graduate School at the University of Chicago in 1928, resulted in the accumulation of a vast storehouse of data useful in the library survey, and created a climate in which the survey could thrive. The founding of the Association of Research Libraries in 1932 provided a formal structure for having directors of large academic and research libraries meet regularly and discuss mutual concerns. The founding of the Association of College and

Reference Libraries, a successor to the ALA College Advisory Board, in 1937 facilitated the dissemination of information resulting from the research and provided forums for the discussion of problems of library management among all academic library directors and among other library managers.

Library Surveys by Outside Experts

During the period following the publication of the Works and U.S. Office of Education studies a number of surveys of individual libraries were conducted in an effort to make local applications of research findings and to encourage the development of more effective and efficient ways of operating libraries. As suggested by Charles H. Brown, studies were undertaken by "experts" in the field in the belief that an objective outsider could conduct a thorough, unbiased evaluation of a library and its operations, and could provide valuable recommendations, guidance, and advice about addressing both special problems and general concerns. Although these experts were not management consultants per se, they were individuals who had gained a measure of recognition and respect in the field, and whose opinions were highly respected.

In an address to the third general session of the New Haven Conference in 1931, Louis R. Wilson spoke of the growth in research in librarianship and referred to the work of such scholar-librarians as George A. Works, G. W. Rosenlof, Charles H. Brown, Eugene Hilton, Edna A. Hester, Charles B. Shaw, Douglas Waples, and William M. Randall (Wilson, 1931).

Surveys of individual university libraries conducted during the scientific-management period hold an important place in the history of library management and library planning. The earliest of these is believed to be the one done of the University of Georgia in 1938 by Louis R. Wilson (Johnson and Mann, 1980, p. 24). Others surveys cited in the literature include those of the University of Florida, 1940; Indiana University, 1940; University of South Carolina, 1946; Stanford University, 1947; Cornell University, 1948; Virginia Polytechnic Institute, 1949; Alabama Polytechnic Institute, 1949; University of New Hampshire, 1949; Texas A & M University, 1950; Montana State University, 1951; and the University of Notre Dame, 1952.

According to Louis R. Wilson, author and coauthor of several of the surveys, there were two basic types conducted. There was the limited survey directed at a particular problem or issue of concern to a library or university administration, and there was the general survey with a wider scope.

In conducting the general surveys, several of the experts had an informal set of characteristics or "essentials" they sought in evaluating and comparing libraries. Louis R. Wilson (Wilson and Tauber, 1945, p. 12) outlined the "essentials that are fundamental to successful operation of the library and the coordination of its programs with the teaching and research programs of the university" in *The University Library* in 1945, as follows:

1. resources for instruction, research, and extension;
2. a competent library staff;
3. organization of materials for use;
4. adequate space and equipment;
5. integration of the library with administrative and educational policies;
6. integration of the library with community, state, regional, national, and international library resources;
7. adequate financial support; and
8. a workable policy of library government.

In response to criticisms that the positive results of these surveys were being exaggerated, Wilson admitted that they may not have been as extensive or as substantial as claimed by some supporters. However, they were still significant.

The criticism could be made that the surveys are very much alike in form and scope, that they are elementary, that when one is read there is little need to read the others. Such criticism is easy to make but is wide of the mark. They have been somewhat alike because they represent prescriptions for libraries, for different libraries, however, and they are directed at specific as well as general ends. They are elementary because they have been intended for administrative officers and faculty members who are not experts in library administration but whose sympathetic understanding and cooperation are essential to the carrying out of an effective, significant library program. (Wilson, 1947, p. 375)

Wilson identified seven specific results of the general surveys.

1. During the course of a survey the attention of the administrative officers and many members of the faculties is centered upon many aspects of library administration and service—it opens the channels of communication for the transmission of ideas about the library between administration, library, and faculty.
2. The education of the administration concerning the role of the library in the teaching and research programs of the university.

3. Codification of a library policy for the university.
4. A program of action for the library is developed.
5. Greater financial support has been obtained.
6. Solution of specific problems.
7. Stimulation of the library staff. (Ibid., pp. 368–75)

Wilson maintained that these general surveys were efforts to make libraries a more integral part of the college curriculum. They called for (1) more nearly adequate support, (2) more highly trained staff, and (3) a linking of collections to course offerings.

Maurice Tauber discussed surveys by librarians, their purposes, problem areas addressed, methodologies, and results in a 1953 presentation at the 39th Conference of Eastern College Librarians at Columbia University. "Very simply stated," he said "the major purposes of a library survey are to describe and evaluate. . . . The goal is to gather all the facts concerning [a situation] and to suggest steps for overcoming any shortcomings which are found" (Tauber, 1954, p. 189). He went on to describe the outline general surveys of libraries tended to follow:

- history and background
- governmental relationships
- financial administration
- organization and administration
- technical services
- readers' services
- personnel
- holdings
- use of libraries
- buildings and equipment
- cooperation

In 1958 E. Walfred Erickson completed a doctoral dissertation at the University of Illinois on surveys of college and university libraries between 1938 and 1952. His study dealt with the history of library surveys, their goals and objectives, and results. Erickson too responded to critics of the outside expert's library survey. In a 1950 article on library surveys, Herbert Goldhor had criticized them for being "unscientific" and questioned the technique of comparing libraries with past performance and with other libraries. He also questioned the use of outside experts: "While these individuals might have expertise in particular areas, the librarian and local staff were better equipped to handle a general library survey by themselves" (Goldhor, 1950, pp. 609–12).

Erickson examined the credentials of the experts who conducted twenty-five full-fledged general surveys between 1938 and 1959. All seventeen surveyors were men. Among them they held fifty degrees; eight held Ph.D.'s (four in library science and four in other subject areas); three did not have doctorates but had formal education beyond the master's degree; six had master's degrees in library science; and two held a total of six honorary doctorates. Together the surveyors had a total of 294 years of library experience (an average of 17.3 each) and 168 years of experience in library administration (an average of 9.9 years each) (Erickson, 1961, p. 14–15).

Whatever the validity of the criticisms, Erickson wrote, the general college and university library survey had reached a stage in its development when its results ought to be scrutinized and evaluated. The survey as a technique had achieved stature and was generally accepted as an instrument of evaluation. Erickson's basic thesis was that "the general library survey carried on by experts outside the institutional staff of the library being surveyed is an effective instrument in bringing about results conducive to the growth and development of college and university libraries" (ibid., p. 11).

Erickson's findings were published as ACRL Monograph No. 25 in 1961. For the purpose of his study Erickson defined a university library survey as "a scientific collection and analysis of data pertaining to the operation of a particular library, with a view toward the improvement of those operations and the establishment of a plan for growth within the limits of and the aims and objectives of the library and the university" (ibid., p. 1).

After reviewing library surveys conducted by outside experts between 1938 and 1952, he observed that they had eight major purposes in common:

1. to make a careful and comprehensive study of the entire library situation;
2. to submit recommendations for a long-range plan of development;
3. to set the library in the perspective of the history of the university, state, and region;
4. to discover ways and means of enabling the library to improve its organization and administration;
5. to indicate means by which the library resources of the university may be effectively related to and integrated with the libraries of the state, the region, the nation;
6. to discover the limitations that are at present retarding the effective operation of the library;

7. to contribute to an increased understanding of the library's needs, problems, and role both on the campus and throughout the state; and

8. to determine the present effectiveness of the library in playing its proper role in support of the stated objectives of the university. (Ibid., p. 5)

Erickson sought to support his thesis by analyzing the extent to which the recommendations of twelve of the surveys conducted between 1938 and 1952 had been implemented by the institutions studied. He was also interested in learning when the implementations occurred, what influence the survey might have had, and whether librarians involved agreed with the recommendations. Erickson first identified 775 specific recommendations made in the surveys and organized them into eight categories generally following the outline described by Tauber. He then sought to determine the extent to which each of them had been implemented as of 1958. Table 3.1 illustrates his findings.

Erickson found that more than two-thirds (531 or 68.5%) of the 775 recommendations identified in the survey reports had been implemented in whole or in part by the time of his study. Two hundred and sixty-nine (34.7%) had been completely implemented, 185 (23.9%) implemented to a large degree, and 77 (9.9%) to a small degree. Two hundred and fifteen (27.7%) had not been implemented at all, 19 (2.5%) were already in effect by the time the survey report was written, and there were 10 recommendations (1.3%) for which Erickson could find no information on status. In seven of the eight categories more than 50 percent of the recommendations were implemented either "completely" or in "large part" and in four categories the level was more than 60 percent. The highest level of implementation was in the area of Resources for Study and Research (78.7%), followed by Reader's Services (73.1%), Library Personnel (70.9%), and Technical Services (70.1%). The lowest level of implementation was in the area of Integration and Cooperation (52.8%).

From his study Erickson concluded that the college and university library survey conducted by outside experts was an effective instrument in bringing about results conducive to the growth and development of the libraries surveyed.

It has been shown . . . that something does happen after a survey. In most cases the survey report became a manual that the librarian followed assiduously, turning to it for guidance in the development of the library; pointing to it as a supporting document when trying to convince administration, staff, and faculty of needed improvements; and referring to it periodically to review progress. (Ibid., p. 104)

Table 3.1

Disposition of Library Survey Recommendations, 1938–52

Areas of Study	Number of Recommendations	Per Cent of Total	Recommendations Implemented
Government, Organization and Administration	146	18.8	95 65.1%
Technical Services	147	19.0	103 70.1%
Reader's Services	119	15.4	87 73.1%
Integration and Cooperation	53	6.8	28 52.8%
Buildings	76	9.8	50 65.8%
Resources for Study and Research	61	7.9	48 78.7%
Library Personnel	103	13.3	73 70.9%
Financial Administrartion	70	9.0	47 67.1%
TOTAL	775	100.0	531 68.5%

Summary of Dispositions

Recommendations Implemented Completely	269	34.7%
Recommendations Implemented in Large Degree	185	23.9%
Recommendations Implemented in Small Degree	77	9.9%
Recommendations Totally or Partially Implemented	531	68.5%
Recommendations not Implemented at All	215	27.7%
Changes Already in Effect at End of Survey	19	2.5%
No Information on Status	10	1.3%
Total Recommendations Made	775	100.0%

Source: E. Walfred Erickson (1961), p. 105.

He found that the impact of the survey was greatest during the first two years following the report. Two hundred and forty-two (45.6%) of the implementations occurred during that period. In the area of Government, Organization, and Administration the figure was 67.4 percent.

When one realizes that this figure represents such accomplishments . . . as the centralization of library resources and administration, the adoption of statutes or bylaws defining library resources and the duties of the librarian, the establishment or reactivation of library committees, the improved organization of libraries, and numerous other improvements, it must be agreed that considerable good came of the survey in a short space of time. (Ibid., p. 106–7)

The recommendations regarding library buildings took the longest to implement. The reasons given for nonimplementation included lack of funds, constitutional or institutional restrictions, personality problems, resistance to change, problems peculiar to particular institutions, and the opposition of librarians. It should be noted that although the opposition of librarians was listed as one of the reasons for nonimplementation, in the vast majority of instances the librarians agreed with the recommendations made by the surveyors. According to Erickson the percentages varied at different institutions from 86.9 to 92.2 percent. In response to the question of whether the changes that occurred were direct or indirect results of the survey, Erickson found it was hard to tell. He did state, however, that 67.9 percent were perceived as results of the surveys, and slightly more than half direct results.

Erickson's overall conclusion was that library surveys conducted by outside experts produced results. Nearly 60 percent of the 775 recommendations identified in the twelve surveys studied were implemented "completely" or "in large degree," and another 10 percent were implemented to a "small degree."

It has been shown that, in most cases following a survey, library organization has been improved, budgets have been increased, technical processes have been made more efficient, readers' services have been bettered, and corresponding improvements have been made with varying degrees of success regarding the other essentials of a good college or university library program. (Ibid., p. 109)

The role of outside experts was considered very important by the librarians involved. They felt that the surveyors impressed university administrators not only because they were outsiders, but also because they were unusually competent men who had established reputations for themselves and were known and respected by the administrators. The librarians felt that the very presence of the outside experts added emphasis to the needs of the libraries, and attracted the attention needed to correct them.

Erickson concluded his study with a list of the "by-products" of a library survey:

1. Professional stimulus for those staff who participated.

2. Attention of the academic community was focused upon the libraries.

3. The survey and its subsequent report proved an educational instrument for the administration and the faculty.

4. Publication of the report . . . provided a document useful to the librarian and staff in planning the development of the library and to students of library administration generally. (Ibid, p. 111)

Library Self-Studies as Planning Tools

Another approach to identifying and correcting library problems is the self-survey, self-evaluation or self-study. This approach gained wide acceptance in academic libraries because of its extensive use by accrediting agencies in evaluating colleges and universities. Under a self-study, the library staff itself undertakes an evaluation, usually with the participation of representatives from other segments of the university community. The earliest self-study of an academic library is said to be *The University Library* by M. Llewellyn Raney, director of the university library of the University of Chicago in 1933. Others include *A Faculty Survey of the University of Pennsylvania Libraries* (University of Pennsylvania Press, 1940), *Report of the Harvard University Library*, by Keyes D. Metcalf and his collaborators (1955), *The Columbia University Libraries*, by Maurice Tauber and his colleagues (Columbia University Press, 1958), and studies conducted by the staffs of the University of Michigan, 1961, and Florida State University, 1962 (Johnson and Mann, 1980, p. 24).

The intent of a self-study is to give the library staff and administration the opportunity to evaluate the library by allowing them (1) to articulate their own goals and objectives; (2) to review their progress toward meeting them in terms of the institution's own aspirations, taking into account prevailing professional standards and the performance levels of comparable institutions; and (3) to set forth recommendations for correcting deficiencies, strengthening weaknesses, or capitalizing upon assets.

In 1958 Morris A. Gelfand, then chief librarian at Queens College in New York City, conducted an analysis of library self-studies undertaken for the Middle States Association of Colleges and Secondary Schools between 1949 and 1958 (Gelfand, 1958, pp. 305–20). Although he was primarily interested in the techniques library evaluators used in determining the quality and effectiveness of library resources, facilities, and services, Gelfand also discussed the self-studies themselves and their role in the evaluation process as perceived by the Middle States Association.

The accreditation self-studies for the Middle States Association, and for the other regional accrediting agencies, were begun approximately a year in advance of the evaluation teams' formal visits, and were a part of the institutions' overall preparation for evaluation. These self-studies followed procedures outlined by the accrediting agencies in internal reports, guidelines, and other documents. One of the most comprehensive such documents for library self-studies was *Evaluating the Library: Suggestions for the Use of Faculties and Evaluating Teams* (Middle States Association . . ., 1957). The guide stated that

the primary characteristic of a good academic library is its complete identification with its own institution. The measurement of its excellence is the extent to which its resources and services support the institution's objectives. . . .

The emphasis in evaluating a library should be on the appropriateness of the collection for the instructional and research programs of the students and faculty, its adequacy in breadth, depth, and variety to stimulate both students and faculty, its accessibility, including cataloging, the competence and interest of the staff, and above all, what happens in the reading and reference rooms. (Gelfand, 1958, pp. 308–10)

Evaluating the Library went on to pose twenty-six specific questions a self-study team should ask about its library in order to gather the information upon which to base its evaluation. These questions dealt with such issues as the depth, variety, and currency of book and periodical collections in support of each undergraduate instructional program and the extent to which resources were able to support graduate programs in existing or proposed areas of study.

Once a survey team had completed a self-study, it had assembled a comprehensive body of information documenting the status of its resources and services. For the purpose of this study, however, we are interested in the self-survey as a planning tool, rather than an instrument of evaluation. There is very little in the literature about self-surveys as planning tools before the development of the Association of Research Libraries' Management Review and Analysis Program in 1970. The individual self-surveys at Chicago (1933), Pennsylvania (1940), Harvard (1955), Columbia (1958), Michigan (1961), and Florida State (1962) are cited as examples of self-surveys as evaluation tools. The library self-studies for regional accreditation agencies are described as excellent tools for evaluating library resources and services; however, very little is said about what should be done once a self-study has been completed and presented. In some cases recommendations contained in the library self-study were incorporated into the overall recommendations of the accreditation agency. In these cases their implementation may have become institutional priorities to be accomplished in anticipation of future accreditation reviews.

Accreditation self-studies are considered internal or limited distribution documents. They are not published per se and do not generally appear in the literature. It can be assumed that the library sections of these self-studies were not widely disseminated, read, critiqued, analyzed, or discussed among librarians outside the affected institutions. Their use as planning tools was limited to the home institution and depended upon the initiative of the library administration involved to take advantage of the availability of the information for planning or management purposes.

There appears to have been no voices in the forties or fifties urging librarians to capitalize upon the results of the accreditation surveys the way George Works and Charles H. Brown urged librarians to take advantage of the Works survey of 1927 or the U.S. Office of Education survey of 1930. There were no articles in the literature discussing accreditation self-studies as management or planning tools, or any analyses of the extent to which self-studies might have influenced changes in libraries comparable to Erickson's 1958 study of library surveys by outside experts. Morris Gelfand, widely recognized as one of the leading experts on library self-studies during the 1950s, ends his 1958 discussion of the self-study in an article in *College and Research Libraries* by stating that the questions raised in a self-study might best be addressed by having outside experts come in to analyze and interpret the data collected (Gelfand, 1958, p. 320). Library staffs were considered competent to answer questions about their resources and services and to identify areas of strength and weakness. However, it appears that an outside expert would be needed in order to validate their findings and to recommend solutions to problems that might be accepted and acted upon by library and university administrators.

The library self-survey appears to have been considered an effective tool for evaluating library resources and services into the early 1960s. However, it also appears that few librarians saw its potential as a management or planning tool or advocated that it be used as such. With the challenges of the mid-sixties, this attitude, along with many others about libraries and how they should be managed, was reexamined and new approaches•were considered.

STRATEGIC PLANNING IN ACADEMIC LIBRARIES

The preceding section dealt with early planning studies in academic libraries. Although all of these surveys and studies were useful mechanisms for evaluating libraries and for identifying weaknesses and strengths, it was not until the 1960s that a theoretical framework was developed for intentionally incorporating the information thus derived into an effort that would have a direct and ongoing relationship to library administration, management, or decision making.

The discussion of the application of strategic planning to libraries as it had emerged in management theory began in 1967 with Robert E. Kemper and the doctoral dissertation he completed at the University of Washington, *Strategic Planning for Library Systems* (Kemper, 1967). In that work, and in a major essay he contributed to the 1970 issue of *Advances in Librarianship* (Kemper, 1970), Kemper discussed the concept of strategic planning as described in management literature and addressed the need for library administrators to apply this management tool more widely to libraries.

Although there has been an increasing amount of information in the management literature on the strategic planning aspect of the administrator's job, there has been a dearth of comprehensive information available on the subject in library literature. The available information on actual library planning practice—strategic and otherwise—seems to be restricted to theoretical aspects adopted from other disciplines (operations research, behavioral science, and business administration), generalities, narrow phases of planning, and specific programs on the actual decision-making process.

Disciplines other than librarianship have made greater progress in the study of administrative practice and theory, in general, and strategic planning, in particular, because, until recently, even the largest libraries were small operations. Other reasons often cited in the literature are that library operations cannot be measured as readily as business operations for libraries do not use profit as a yardstick; libraries lack the money and manpower to spend in analysis and study of themselves; and libraries have few practicing managers and faculty members within the university environment who are interested in a theoretical exploration of administration. (Ibid., pp. 5–6)

Kemper set forth a theoretical approach to strategic planning to aid librarians, educators, and other institutional and organizational administrators responsible for library administrative decisions in their efforts to improve operations and services. The specific purposes of his study were to

- construct and test a usable model for strategic planning in library administration;
- determine the extent to which strategic planning is being used by a selected group of libraries and the relationships and differences between library

planning and that done by planning officers of the institutions to which the library is subordinate;

- determine the effects and amount of participation in the strategic planning process by library personnel, library boards, library committees, library trustees, institution administrators, and other legal bodies who have jurisdiction in regard to the development and approval of strategic policies, plans, objectives, forecasts, and practices;

- determine the sources utilized in recognizing the needs, in obtaining necessary data, in evaluating the data, in formulating conclusions, and in gaining approval of strategic plans;

- determine the length of time covered by and the types of specific strategic objectives, strategic plans, and forecasts being developed for achieving the objectives of the organization;

- determine the extent of use of procedures for periodic revision and comparing actual results of strategic plans; and

- discover the principal problems encountered in developing and the principal functions of strategic plans as viewed by top administrators. (Ibid., pp. 10–11)

In his study Kemper first developed a framework for strategic planning in libraries based on the works of such management theorists as Robert N. Anthony, Wendell French, Harold Koontz, William H. Newman, George A. Steiner, LeBreton and Henning, and William T. Newell, Jr. He then analyzed the current strategic planning policies and procedures in four case study library systems: the Bellevue Public School District libraries (Washington), the University of Colorado libraries, the Oregon State Library, and the Denver Public Library. After completing the case studies Kemper tested his findings and their applicability to other institutions with a questionnaire he sent to more than 300 libraries.

The theoretical approach to strategic planning or planning model Kemper developed began with a description of the "basic characteristics of a planning system" he derived from a variety of sources. The list of basic characteristics listed below is important because it was later used in other contexts for discussing and evaluating library plans and planning systems.

1. The planning system must be total and comprehensive, covering all aspects of the organization, including its environment.

2. Administrative plans and operational plans must be functionally related.

3. The planning system should designate responsibility, indicating exactly what would be expected of each subsystem of the organization.

4. The planning system should be dynamic and responsive to changes in the environment.

5. The plans should provide criteria to measure qualitative and quantitative outputs of the various systems. (Ibid., pp. 32–33)

Kemper's theoretical approach divided planning into three major categories: (1) strategic planning, (2) operational planning, and (3) task programming. Kemper adapted Robert N. Anthony's definitions of strategic planning and the strategic planning process. Anthony had described strategic planning as "the process of deciding on objectives of the organization, on changes in these objectives, on the resources used to attain these objectives, and on the policies that are to govern the acquisition, use, and disposition of these resources" (Anthony, 1965, p. 16).

Kemper's theoretical approach to *strategic planning* included the following:

- establishing general objectives
- identifying the environment (external, institutional, and internal)
- becoming aware of the need to change
- organizing for change
- forecasting the environment
- establishing specific objectives
- evaluating, selecting, and deciding on alternatives
- designing a plan of action
- gaining formal approval
- implementing change (Kemper, 1967, pp. 34–37)

Operational planning was seen as the process by which managers assure that resources are obtained and used effectively and efficiently in the accomplishment of the organization's objectives. Operational planning translates strategic planning into terms that can be applied to specific and short-term efforts. Specific goal projects are developed at this level based on guidelines established at the strategic level. Once the decision is made to implement a project, operational planners determine how resources are to be allocated within a prescribed hierarchy of priorities, and what specific tasks are to be accomplished in pursuit of the objectives. *Task programming* involved the basic day-to-day activities of the organization. It dealt with the actual implementation of plans according to specific instructions developed by operational planners and involved minimal decision making.

Ackoff and others had used the term *tactical planning* to describe the nonstrategic planning activities both Kemper and Anthony divided between operational planning and task programming.

After outlining his theoretical approach to strategic planning, analyzing the four case study library systems, and testing the general applicability of the results through a questionnaire submitted to other libraries, Kemper summarized his findings about the extent to which strategic planning was being used in the libraries studied and the libraries surveyed. He also described the major problem areas libraries encountered in developing and implementing strategic planning systems. The basic finding of Kemper's research was the fact that, although most of the libraries studied made use of some planning processes, procedures, and mechanisms, very few were engaged in formal strategic planning efforts. Sixty-eight percent of the libraries surveyed had no written plans.

Strategic planning has come to be recognized as an integral part of the function of managing an organization. Many organizations have developed strategies, established priorities, proposed a schedule of achievement development, and made a long-range commitment, but there appears to be a substantial number of organizations which do not engage formally in . . . strategic planning. (Ibid., p. 238)

Kemper developed a set of characteristics of a successful strategic planning framework based on his observations of the four case study libraries.

1. The library system must be concerned with differentiated and coordinated human activities, the impact of the system on people, and its effects on relationships among people.
2. Strategic planning should be a tool for decision makers.
3. There are three major levels of planning:
   a. Strategic—where services of the library are determined.
   b. Operational—where decisions in regard to the ongoing administration are made.
   c. Task—where specific tasks to be carried out are determined.
4. Strategic planning must be distinguished from, yet intimately related to, operational planning if it is to have any real effect.
5. The library system is immersed in a broader network of processes and systems from which it must receive informational inputs.
6. The strategic planning process in a library does not emerge as a highly developed process. It is created, frequently on an ad hoc basis, through

consideration of the future impact of institutional and external environmental factors.

7. Active participation in strategic planning by all levels of personnel is essential to effective strategic planning. (Ibid., pp. 239–42)

Although there were different approaches to strategic planning in the four case studies, and in the responses to the questionnaires, Kemper identified a common pattern that seemed to be related to the success of planning efforts. The common pattern included (1) the formal approval of objectives, (2) the establishment of target dates for achieving goals, and (3) an awareness of the need to plan (ibid., p. 242). Kemper also developed a list of activities he found were characteristic of successful planning efforts and therefore considered essential to a strategic planning model:

1. *Establishing specific objectives.* A critical element in developing an organizational image is the process of establishing major objectives and specific project objectives—with target dates.

2. *Identifying the Environment.* The terms of exchange between the library system and its environment, rather than the form of its structure, determined the policies and procedures the library followed.

3. *Becoming Aware of the Need to Plan.* Administrative groups usually decide that there is a need to plan based on their knowledge of operations and expectations.

4. *Organizing for Strategic Planning.* Successful strategic planning requires the active participation in the strategic planning process of all people involved.

5. *Forecasting the Environment.* Long-range forecasting does not seem highly developed; libraries tend to use figures provided by their institutions.

6. *Selecting, Evaluating, and Deciding on Alternatives.* The evaluation of alternatives requires expertise and access to a wide scope of information concerning the library, institutional, and external environmental systems.

7. *Development of Documented Strategic Plans.* Many strategic plans are informal and flexible and therefore not well documented. However, the successful strategic plan requires the circulation of written policies or guidelines to key library administrators so that operational plans can be developed.

8. *Review of Strategic Plan.* Strategic plans must be kept current and compared regularly with actual results if they are to serve as effective guides. When actual results deviate from planned results, a written explanation is recommended. The pattern for reviewing strategic plans should be based upon qualitative and quantitative criteria provided in the plans.

9. *Functions and Values of Strategic Planning.* The communication function that formal strategic planning serves between institution and library as disclosed

in the investigation implies more than the transmission of plans. It implies influence. (Ibid., pp. 243-49)

In summarizing Number 7, *Development of Documented Strategic Plans*, Kemper described the status of strategic planning he found in the libraries that responded to his questionnaire. The responses revealed that more libraries had developed plans for special projects than for general library operations. Sixty-six percent had developed plans for special projects, 61 percent for service activities, and 50 percent for financial activities. In general, libraries did not use target dates to indicate commitment to programs of action, but time periods covered by plans were usually three to six years.

A critical element in successful strategic planning is the circulation of key assumptions, forecasts, and objectives among decision makers, planners, and other organizations in the institution. Kemper's survey found that these assumptions were circulated in 57 percent of the libraries, but that the process of distribution was generally unstructured and informal.

Kemper concluded from his study that planning was vital to the success of the library programs in the institutions surveyed. However, the case studies and survey also identified a number of problem areas that affected whether a plan was successful or not, and which are worth noting in developing a model for a strategic planning system in libraries.

1. Strategic planning is not valuable unless reliable forecasts and other data are available to aid in surveying the competitive and environmental systems. As yet, librarians have neither tools nor research for accurate forecasts based upon reliable data.
2. Librarians spend too much time on operational aspects of the library and too little time on strategic planning.
3. Libraries must compete with other organizations within the institution for financial support and decision priorities.
4. There is the difficulty of defining institutional objectives and strategic plans and of reconciling institutional growth objectives with those of the library.
5. Where strategic planning is not done at the library level and various parts are handled by institutional administrators, the library may be forced to work at cross purposes with other agencies of the institution.
6. There is the tremendous problem of educating librarians in the administrative process. Librarians have not taken the opportunity to become knowledgeable in the planning process, and they do not realize the importance of strategic planning. The absence of an effective planning structure with adequate administrative information and controls has been due in part to the library administrator's lack of education in the management process. There is a

distinct difference between the job orientation of the bookman, the librarian, and the manager. Recent developments in analytical planning concepts and new library administrative training programs will reduce this facet of the problem. (Ibid., pp. 250–52)

Kemper also concluded that systematic strategic planning was growing among academic institutions, public schools, and local government. These institutions had come to realize that they had the same fundamental planning requirements as business corporations. As a result "librarians may be forced to develop formalized library planning information so that institution administrations can reflect library planning in the overall institutional planning programs" (Kemper, 1970, p. 224).

Kemper's recommendations for further research included the development of techniques for forecasting long-range social, economic, and technical library environments, and techniques for forecasting long-range institutional environments. He called for the formulation of analytical systems concepts and analytical operational planning concepts for libraries and for the development of sophisticated computer and mathematical models for use in forecasting environments. He saw a need for guidance in defining the roles of library strategic planning groups, in reconciling organizational uniqueness and specialization with national, regional, and institutional objectives, and in formulating strategic planning information and communications systems. Kemper also called for greater emphasis on developing planning concepts as a part of library education (ibid., pp. 252–53).

Kemper's study is important because it was the first significant effort to apply the strategic planning management tool to libraries. His list of the basic characteristics of a planning system identified the key elements essential to a comprehensive approach to library planning. After defining strategic planning as a process for decision making, Kemper outlined the components of a theoretical approach or model that could be used in developing, implementing, and evaluating planning systems.

Kemper's case studies and the results of his survey of other libraries revealed that, although there appeared to be a great deal of planning underway in libraries, it was rarely comprehensive or coordinated and lacked the conceptual framework likely to maximize changes for success. "For libraries, strategic planning has been largely the following of trends, of catching up" (ibid., p. 218). Kemper discussed activities that were characteristic of successful planning efforts and described the problem areas planners should try to avoid. His study and the essay he contributed to the 1970 issue of *Advances in Librarianship* provided a basis for later research on strategic planning in libraries and for the development of many of the planning efforts that followed. His 1967 findings, to a large extent, anticipated and supported those later confirmed by other research efforts. They all emphasized the importance of comprehensive, long-range planning as a basis for initiating all other efforts toward improving the management of libraries.

THE NEED FOR NEW MANAGEMENT TECHNIQUES, ARL 1968–69

The late 1960s was a critical period for academic libraries. They, along with the rest of American society, experienced major challenges to the basic assumptions under which they had operated for decades. Throughout the academic community students, and faculty, began to question the legitimacy of administrative authority and to demand greater participation in decision making at all levels, from dormitory councils to boards of trustees. These demands came in the form of petitions, class boycotts, student strikes, occupations of buildings, and in a few cases, full scale riots.

Academic administrators for the most part were unprepared to deal with these new demands and probably did not understand the widespread disaffection within the general society that had stimulated them. In an article titled "The Effect of the Revolution of 1969–1970," David Kaser, then director of libraries at Cornell University, described the situation confronting many library directors.

[There was a] frustration of unrealized expectations—expectations that had for the most part been unrealistic in the first place. It is difficult today to reconstruct the total sense of unbridled optimism that permeated the "Great Society" days of the early and mid-1960's. Somehow we had come to believe that we held all the aces, that we knew what society needed, that we knew how to deliver it, and that we had the resources to get the job done. As regards libraries, the press and public expected them to purvey extended services through instant computerization. University presidents expected them to cut costs. Faculty expected them to deliver everything they needed. Students expected them to stay open all night. Staff expected that work should never be dull and that salaries should rise 10 percent per year. (Kaser, 1977, pp. 64–65)

Academic libraries in the aggregate may have come closest to meeting the diverse and irreconcilable expectations in 1965. Soon thereafter, however, the directors began to realize that they were attempting to navigate troubled waters and that their budget increases were no longer adequate to meet the need. In 1966, 1967, and 1968 they were increasingly able to stave off disaster only by mortgaging their future. They found themselves in each successive fiscal year exhausting budget funds a month or two earlier.

In retrospect, it seems incredible that the profession did not get nature's message as the Association of Research Libraries watched its member directors fall one after another during those three years to coronaries and other stress-induced diseases. Individually, and in most cases also subconsciously, those directors recognized long before the rest of the library community that a day of reckoning was sure to come, that they were expected to do things for which the resources no longer existed, that there was no more straw for the making of bricks. (Ibid., p. 65)

The important issue for the purpose of this study is the fact that library administrators had come to the realization that existing ways of operating were no longer able to handle the new challenges. Hierarchical structures were not flexible enough or responsive enough to deal with the rapidly changing environment. Students, faculty, and library staff were demanding participation in decision making and were demanding a more active role in determining what libraries and library services should be and what they should become over time. At the same time funding sources (boards of trustees, foundations, state legislatures, and federal agencies) were requiring greater accountability for use of funds and more quantitative data in support of requests, not only for increases, but also for continuation of support at the existing levels. The advent of the computer to the university campus and other technological advances offered great opportunities for library applications. Few librarians were in a position to fully understand their potential or to project how they could be most effectively integrated into the ongoing operations of an academic library.

At the 72nd Meeting of the Association of Research Libraries (ARL) held in Kansas City, Missouri, in June 1968, Warren J. Haas, director of libraries at the University of Pennsylvania, chaired a session on research library management. The session was prompted by an intensification of interest in sophisticated approaches to the management problems of academic libraries and discussions that had been going on between ARL board members and Dr. Fred Cole, president of the Council on Library Resources. Haas raised a number of questions about how university librarians should go about meeting the new challenges. His first question was how to define good management:

We have good management when all parties involved (faculty, students, university administration, library staff, and even those "outsiders" we work with or assist) agree that stated library objectives are appropriate and that on-going operations designed to achieve those objectives are by and large effective. This definition suggests that the quality of management cannot really be judged until all parties involved know what library objectives are . . . and understand the operating methodology. The process of establishing objectives and then employing the right means to attain them is the essence of management. (Haas, 1968, p. 20)

Haas then reviewed the management tools that were becoming widely accepted in government, business, and industry as effective ways of helping managers adapt organizations to rapidly changing environments. He suggested that these tools might also be useful in addressing the management problems in libraries. The tools described included systems analysis (a process that involves the identification of principal operating functions and the explanations of their interrelationships); cost accounting and PPBS (Planning-Programming-Budgeting System) as developed and implemented at the Rand Corporation and in the U.S. Department of Defense; operations analysis (studies of time and motion, methods studies, standardizations, etc.); linear programming, simulation, and modeling—all acceptable ways of analyzing the efficiency and effectiveness of library operations and identifying ways of improving upon them. Haas commented that "enough of the techniques available to the management scientist have been identified to enable us to go on to the heart of the matter, which is to identify some of the parts of the library problem that need study and to suggest how a start might be made" (ibid., p. 22).

The question at hand, according to Haas, was "How do we work toward a solution?" A solution would mean (1) finding answers to many questions concerning library objectives and library operations; (2) gaining acceptance for the answers; and (3) applying the substance of the answers to library operations. He continued by posing groups of questions about validating existing assumptions, about relationships and alternatives, and about costs.

Validating existing assumptions:

1. What is the relationship between collection quality, collection size, and staff services on the one hand and the process of learning on the other?
2. What effect does each of the several elements that determine library quality have on research activity, subject by subject? For this, we have to determine first what elements of library quality are and establish their relative importance.

3. How important are speed of service and reliability of service?

4. What can (or should) librarians contribute to institutional administration and educational program formulation? What can faculty and students contribute to the formulation of library objectives?

5. How can cooperative ventures, such as coordinated collection and regional catalogs, be judged in terms of their utility and value to individuals who are members of the participating institutions?

Relationships and alternatives:

1. Are there any good alternatives to the fines system?

2. What is the relationship between loan periods and library performance?

3. What can reasonably be expected from computer applications to library operations in terms of more reliable and faster record maintenance, cost reduction, meaningful information services for library management, and so forth?

4. What is the effect on service and costs of storing collections in each one of the several possible ways?

Costs:

1. What are the costs of carrying out each of the many technical and service functions performed in libraries?

2. What are the costs of providing collections and services at several levels of comprehensiveness for various subject categories? In essence, how do costs for research support differ from costs for supporting programs of instruction?

3. What are the projections for worldwide publication and what are the implications for library operations?

4. What are the facts regarding staff utilization in the context of costs and individual capabilities?

5. What are the cost implications of some of the special library problems of great magnitude? For example, the paper deterioration problem is one that needs consideration in many quarters. Preserving or replacing existing collections implies real costs for each library.

Having posed the questions, Haas described three possible approaches to finding the answers. He suggested hiring a management consultant firm to investigate specific areas of concern to be identified by the directors. He advanced Dr. Russell Ackoff's idea of having three or four universities declare a "research year" during which the investigative and research efforts of students and faculty members in a number of academic departments and professional schools in each university would be mobilized and directed toward the library and the finding of solutions to its problems. He also referred to a proposal being considered by the Council on Library Resources that called for the use of an "idealization process" in which library experts would be invited to conceptualize the model academic library, completely in the abstract, and then find ways of incorporating its components into existing structures. Haas said that "while the management process is admittedly only a means to an end, there seems little doubt that some kind of carefully planned crash program to assess and develop research library management is necessary" (ibid., p. 27).

In January 1969 the ARL directors were still interested in learning more about new management techniques, about possible applications to academic libraries, and were still concerned about finding better ways to adapt their organizations to changes in the environment. Thomas R. Mason, director of institutional research at the University of Colorado, gave a presentation on "Program Planning for Research Libraries in a University Setting" at the 73rd Meeting of the ARL in Washington, D.C. In his presentation Mason described the Planning-Programming-Budgeting System and how it could be applied in an academic library setting. He concluded his discussion with the following observation:

We are now on the threshold of major advances in planning technique. Effective program planning is an essential to higher education. The old rules-of-thumb, the hallowed works of experienced authority, the casual, ad hoc response to short-range necessity, are no longer adequate to justify the resource needs and to order the management of our complex organizations.

In view of the identity of purpose between the university and the research library, the development of systematic, comprehensive program planning must proceed hand-in-hand. As a participant in the university planning process, I anticipate learning a great deal from the progress of the Association of Research Libraries in promoting the development of more effective library planning and management systems. (Mason, 1969, p. 20)

The directors were so impressed with the research potential of new management techniques and were so concerned that possible solutions to mounting problems be investigated that the ARL board established a Committee on University Library Management and charged it with looking into ways in which the new techniques might be utilized. The original committee was chaired by Warren J. Haas and included Douglas W. Bryant (Harvard University), Herman H. Fussler (University of Chicago), John McDonald (University of Connecticut), and Robert Vosper (University of California at Los Angeles). Subsequent discussions between the committee and Dr. Logan Wilson, president of the American Council on Education

(ACE), led to the establishment of a joint committee that included repre-
sentatives of the ACE and ACE cosponsorship of the effort. The ACE
representatives were Willard L. Boyd, president of the University of Iowa,
Allan M. Carter, chancellor and executive vice president of New York
University, Richard W. Lyman, vice president and provost of Stanford
University, and Howard W. Johnson, president of the Massachusetts
Institute of Technology. Stephen A. McCarthy, executive director, and
Louis E. Martin, associate executive director of the Association of Research Libraries, served as ex officio members of the joint committee. The
eventual goal of the ARL/ACE effort was to "develop management
techniques appropriate to academic research libraries and to promote their
use" (Booz, Allen and Hamilton, 1970, p. iv.).

One of the joint committee's initial actions was to commission a study
of academic library management by the consulting firm of Booz, Allen
and Hamilton, with the support of a grant from the Council on Library
Resources. The objective of the study was to "identify opportunities to
improve the ways in which university libraries plan and use their resources—collections, people, facilities and equipment, and finances"
(ibid., p. 1). The study focused on two aspects of university library
resource management: (1) an assessment of needs and opportunities to
strengthen the internal operations of the library, taking into account the
constraints and limitations of existing and anticipated budgets, staffing,
and program commitments; and (2) a review of long-range opportunities
to make more effective use of the collective resources of university
libraries through closer interinstitutional arrangements (ibid.).

Following an initial meeting with an advisory committee established
by the joint committee to oversee the management study, members of
the study team conducted field visits to six universities (Cornell, Duke,
UCLA, Connecticut, Iowa, and Pennsylvania) where 150 interviews
were held with presidents, chief academic officers, business officers,
physical facilities managers, planning officers, deans, faculty members,
students, members of library committees, university librarians, and
members of library staffs. In addition to the interviews, the operations
of libraries were observed, and available documents such as annual
reports and budgets were collected and reviewed. A literature survey was
conducted, a selected bibliography was developed, and extensive interaction took place between the study team and the members of the
advisory committee.

The end result of the study was the publication of *Problems in University
Library Management* (also known as the Booz, Allen and Hamilton report)
in 1970 by the Association of Research Libraries. The report marks a major

turning point in the history of academic library management because of the concerns and forces that brought the study about; the power, credibility, and influence of the organizations that sponsored it; and the actions that were subsequently taken based on its recommendations.

Just as the Works and U.S. Office of Education surveys had stimulated an interest in library management and research in librarianship in the 1930s, the Booz, Allen and Hamilton report, coupled with the increasingly overwhelming management problems discussed earlier, stimulated a revival of interest in management approaches to solving problems in the 1970s. The movement was strengthened by the support of the Association of Research Libraries, which established an Office of University Library Management Studies with a mandate to follow through on the report's recommendations, and of the American Council on Education, the Council on Library Resources, and other major funding sources in the fields of librarianship and higher education.

Four

Planning in Academic Libraries: The 1970s

PROBLEMS IN UNIVERSITY LIBRARY MANAGEMENT, THE BOOZ, ALLEN AND HAMILTON REPORT

The publication of *Problems in University Library Management* (Booz, Allen and Hamilton, Inc., 1970) was the culmination of a number of efforts to address library directors' and library administrations' apparent inability to successfully handle the demands being placed on them by their constituencies during the latter 1960s and early 1970s. The minutes of the meetings of the ARL and articles in library journals documented the growing sense of frustration and helplessness being felt by university library managers and administrators. According to a study by Arthur M. McAnally and Robert B. Downs, in 1971–72 the seriousness of the situation became dramatically evident when seven of the directors of the Big Ten university libraries (plus the University of Chicago) left their posts. Only one was a normal retirement because of age. These were major universities whose directorships had been stable in the past (McAnally and Downs, 1973, p. 103). An investigation of members of ARL found that "exactly one-half of the directors were found to have changed within the past three years, four of them twice. This is an extraordinarily high rate of change. If such a rate were to continue, the average span of service [for university library directors] would be five to six years" (ibid.).

When the ARL board of directors established the Committee on University Library Management in 1969 with the charge to investigate ways in which new management techniques might be used for finding solutions to library management problems, the effort was soon joined by the American Council on Education, an organization concerned with all dimensions of higher education. This action was reminiscent of the role the Association of American Universities had played in commissioning George A. Works's survey of "College and University Library Problems" in 1925, and the fact that the 1930 U.S. Office of Education survey of libraries had been a part of a larger survey of land grant colleges and universities. In all three instances the keen interest of university administrators in the state of university libraries was demonstrated by their support of research into addressing library management problems.

The Booz, Allen and Hamilton study was the most comprehensive investigation of university library management ever undertaken. The study team visited six universities selected on the basis of size, sponsorship, location, and interest and willingness of their staffs to participate in the study. The visits included 150 interviews with selected library staff, university administrators, faculty, and students—a wide variety of individuals with different involvements with academic librarianship. The interviews were supplemented by on-site observations, selected outside interviews, and a review of available operating documents, such as library and university budgets and annual reports. More significant than the number of institutions visited or the number of interviews conducted was the sweeping scope of the study.

Unlike previous library studies and surveys that tended to look at *what* libraries were doing, *how well* (efficiently and effectively) they were doing them, and to examine the *resources* being employed (staff, buildings and facilities, collections, acquisitions expenditures, etc.), the Booz, Allen and Hamilton study was a managerial study and as such was concerned with how decisions about what a library should attempt were made, and how decisions about the allocation of resources in pursuit of these objectives were being made. The study team was concerned about processes rather than products, and about the nature of administrative and managerial systems rather than the services they provided or the adequacy of the information resources they assembled. This was the totally different approach from library surveys and studies that had been called for by the ARL directors and which the American Council on Education and the Council on Library Resources sought to support.

The challenge of management in the university library is to make the most effective justification, allocation, and use of limited resources in relation to the needs and objectives of the university community. The task of management implies the use of the tools of organization and of systems in planning, budgeting, utilizing, and evaluating the resources and activities of libraries. (Booz, Allen and Hamilton, Inc., 1970, p. 5)

Before discussing its findings, conclusions and recommendations, the Booz, Allen and Hamilton study team identified key areas of concern in which it found serious impediments to efforts to develop and implement improved management systems in university libraries. These areas of concern provided the basis upon which the study team built its structure of observations and findings and provided a context for the series of recommendations resulting from the study. The eight key areas of concern identified were the following:

1. *Planning*—the need for more comprehensive library planning and budgeting systems, which, for the near and longer term, specify (a) the role and requirements of the library in relation to the academic program of the university; (b) the library's objectives and plans in support of academic programs; and (c) the library resources (financial, personnel, and physical materials, facilities, and equipment) needed to implement agreed upon plans.

2. *Objectives and Requirements*—the need for improved library statistics for use as tools to determine the cost and effectiveness of library programs and services in relation to academic program requirements.

3. *Operations*—the need for standards to measure and control the flow of work in the library; the need to explore feasible applications of automatic data processing that are transferable from one library to another; and the need for greater codification of operating policies, systems, and procedures for use in training library personnel, controlling operations, and delegating responsibility.

4. *Organization*—the need to strengthen the service delivery capacity of university libraries through formal organizational recognition of several management functions, such as planning and research, budgeting, and personnel development, which are vital to effective and efficient resource utilization, delivery of services, and communication flow in the library.

5. *Staffing*—the need for internal and external formalized programs for training library personnel in management techniques and skills.

6. *Facilities*—the need to undertake periodic analyses of space utilization in the library.

7. *Financing*—the need to explore more fully alternate sources of financing of university libraries, including increased federal support.

8. *Interinstitutional Arrangements*—the need for more effective linkages of library resources to realize improved bibliographical control of and access to

information and more effective use of national library resources. (Ibid., pp. 5–9)

The report itself was divided into four chapters. Chapter 1 discussed trends in higher education and their implications for university libraries and university library management. Chapter 2 described the major problems in university libraries outlined above. Chapter 3 contained recommended approaches to the solutions of the problems identified, along with general designs for subsequent research. Chapter 4 identified steps and discussed considerations related to implementing the recommended approaches. The overall goal was to strengthen the ability of university libraries to meet immediate and future management challenges, in cooperation with their parent institutions.

A basic theme of *Problems in University Library Management* was the fact that most university libraries had not adjusted to their new roles in higher education or society. Although all had experienced dramatic growth over the past several decades, they had not matured as organizations, and they had not developed the management systems required in order to cope with new demands.

The university library in the last century has evolved from a book, periodical, and manuscript repository for scholarly use—managed by scholars—to a large, intricate institution managed by professionals trained in library science and skilled in meeting the information needs of scholars. Because of the sheer size and complexity of contemporary university libraries, and the need to make effective use of scarce human, financial, and physical resources, the management dimension in library operations becomes a critical priority.

Increased reliance on industrial engineering approaches will be needed to assure that work of a routine nature is performed efficiently and that the best use is made of space. Operations research approaches to decision-making, involving systems and cost/benefit analysis will need to be used to assure that all feasible alternatives are explored before resources are committed to specific courses of action. In addition, librarians who now perform most management functions in the library will need to evaluate approaches used by analogous institutions and apply them in the management of university libraries. An example is the development of a distinctive career profession for the administration of hospitals, medical centers, and other health care institutions. (Ibid., p. 19–20)

The Booz, Allen and Hamilton study team found an absence of plans, an absence of planning systems, and an absence of the management and information systems from which plans might be produced. The study team found confusion about the goals and objectives of both the university libraries and the universities themselves. It found that operating policies and the organizational structures within the libraries were generally vague, ambiguous, and ill defined. It found an absence of standards for staffing and little emphasis on professional development to help staff adjust to the changes that were occurring all around them. The study team found that library facilities generally had not kept pace with the growth of collections, increases in enrollments, or expansions in academic programs, and that financial support had not been increased sufficiently to meet increased expectations of library users or university administrators. It found that interinstitutional cooperation, one way of sharing information and resources and of developing coordinated approaches to common problems, had been underutilized as a tool for responding to changes in the environment.

The Booz, Allen and Hamilton report recommended a number of approaches to correcting the deficiencies cited. A basic recommendation was that comprehensive long-range planning play a larger role in the management of university libraries. "Library planning as it exists today [1970] is not adequate to anticipate and reflect the changing educational environment" (ibid., p. 24). The study team found that although some universities evidenced a recognition of the systematic, cyclical, and continuous nature of planning and had undertaken some positive steps to strengthen the planning process, many essential elements for effective planning were not present. Therefore the resulting efforts did not meet criteria for good planning.

Compounding the problem of poor planning at the university level was the fact that even where adequate planning was done there were no effective systems for relating university planning to library planning.

Librarians are not initially a part of the planning process of the university. The libraries, as a consequence, utilized informal methods of obtaining information on university plans for changes in the educational program. These involved oral reports of library personnel assigned to work with academic departments, informal contacts with faculty and administration, and scanning of campus publications. This information, however, was not organized and maintained in a central location for planning purposes. (Ibid., p. 24)

In addition to calling for a larger role for planning in university library management, the study team recommended actions to clarify library goals and objectives, and research into improving operations and organizational structures. The report advocated a national approach to resolving personnel and staffing problems, and increased emphasis on management considerations in facility planning and space utilization. It supported efforts to identify additional sources of noninstitutional financial support for university libraries, and a more aggressive approach to exploiting the potential benefits of interinstitutional cooperation for solving problems and sharing information and resources.

The authors of the report realized that their recommendations were too general and sweeping to be responded to seriously by either library administrators or university administrators. Therefore, they recommended that a comprehensive library program planning system be developed that would incorporate the elements described. They recommended that the Association of Research Libraries assume a leadership role in this process by sponsoring a study to design such a system. The proposed library program planning system would specify objectives, program plans, and resource plans. It would provide for analytical narrative justifications, procedures for updating, and staffing requirements for its operation. Booz, Allen and Hamilton recommended that one university library be selected as a case study for the development of a program planning system. The study would include the following:

1. Design of a program planning system for that library which meets the needs of the librarian and university administrators.

2. Test and adaptation of the system at other universities, taking into account selection criteria based upon factors such as type of sponsorship, size, and nature of planning and budgetary requirements imposed by the university or state authorities.

3. Identification of personnel and organizational requirements for effective operation of the system.

4. Development of a report of the study including a manual for program planning in university libraries.

5. Provision of training programs to acquaint university librarians with the use of program planning techniques.

6. Review of the study effort by a selected panel of librarians and university planning officers.

Pending the implementation of such a study, Booz, Allen and Hamilton listed steps that could be taken by university presidents and university librarians to strengthen library planning efforts. A university president might involve the university librarian formally in the planning councils of the university. He or she might instruct a university planning officer to keep the librarian and library administration informed of plans for changes in programs that might have an impact on library service and resource needs. A university administrator might be made responsible for compiling information on faculty plans and decisions and for periodically informing the librarian. A president might establish a policy requiring that all new academic programs be reviewed by the librarian for library support needs. A president might provide university planning staff to assist the library in developing its plans and planning systems.

A university librarian might establish procedures within the library that provide for periodic collection, central compilation, analysis, and follow-up of information gained by library staff concerning anticipated changes in academic programs which might have library resource and service implications. The librarian might also assume the initiative in communicating information to university officials about the library implications of plans under discussion or decisions within the university community. He or she could establish a library plans and programs committee to assist in reviewing university plans, assessing priorities, and developing program plans in accordance with recommended elements of effective planning. The librarian might also seek staff or outside assistance in program planning, budgeting, and cost/benefit analysis.

Problems in University Library Management was a milestone in university library management. In recommending changes in the administration and management systems of university libraries, Booz, Allen and Hamilton called for a greater awareness of, and more responsiveness to, contemporary issues and trends in American society at large, especially in the area of higher education. They emphasized the fact that universities and their libraries would need to plan very effectively to ensure their ability to meet service requirements and make the best use of available resources. University libraries would be challenged to adapt their organizations to provide expanded and increasingly sophisticated services. Skilled staff would need to be trained or hired and used more effectively. Financial planning and control within the university library would become increasingly important and new approaches to financing their operations would need to be sought. Management approaches used in other fields would need to be explored and used when appropriate in the university library. In addition to recommending that the Association of Research Libraries sponsor a study to design a comprehensive program planning system for university libraries, Booz, Allen and Hamilton also proposed other actions the association could take to stimulate and facilitate the introduction of new management techniques to university library management.

As outlined in *Problems in University Library Management*, these actions included developing guides for defining the library's role in the university and guidelines for operating policy manuals. Booz, Allen and Hamilton encouraged the association to conduct research to develop library management information and reporting systems, work standards and model manual systems; to determine alternate feasible plans of library organization and staffing; and to assess existing and new opportunities for interinstitutional cooperation. The association should encourage research and exchange of information on library automation and the transfer of data processing systems. It should continue to encourage research to determine national human resource needs and training requirements and to act as a clearinghouse on human resource information. It should disseminate results of recommended studies impacting on facilities decisions and review space implications of the proposed study of manual systems. The association should also propose legislation for general support of research libraries.

The Booz, Allen and Hamilton report charged the Association of Research Libraries and the American Council on Education with assuming a leadership role in a concerted effort to bring about a change in the way in which university libraries were being managed, to encourage the utilization of new management techniques in their operations, and to make comprehensive long-range planning an integral part of university library operations.

RESPONSES TO THE BOOZ, ALLEN AND HAMILTON REPORT

ARL and the Columbia University Study

The association's response to the report and its recommendations was positive. In 1970 ARL established the Office of University Library Management Studies, with the support of a grant from the Council on Library Resources, and charged it with the overall implementation of the Booz, Allen and Hamilton recommendations. The office was given a permanent staff headed by Duane E. Webster, who was named director in October 1970. The specific objectives of the ARL Office of University Library Management Studies were

1. to identify areas of library management needing study and analysis;
2. to conduct and promote research on the fundamental issues relating to library management;
3. to develop effective approaches and systems that can be used by research libraries to improve management;
4. to operate an information clearinghouse in the area of library management;

5. to prepare and distribute materials that will provide information about desirable approaches and systems which can be used to improve management in research libraries;
6. to sponsor and participate in meetings that address areas of concern involving management of research libraries; and
7. to provide consultation and advice. (ARL/OMS/SPEC, n.d., p. 4)

In 1970 the association also commissioned Booz, Allen and Hamilton to conduct the comprehensive long-range planning design study the report recommended. Columbia University was selected as the site for the case study. One of the first activities of the Office of University Library Management Studies was to join with Booz, Allen and Hamilton in the study of the organization and staffing of the Columbia University Libraries. The widely publicized study was carried out in 1970–71 by a Booz, Allen and Hamilton consulting team with the advice and guidance of a joint committee including representatives from the Association of Research Libraries, American Council on Education, Council on Library Resources and a committee of Columbia University Libraries' senior staff. The specific purposes of the study were

1. to project the future requirements of the Columbia University Libraries;
2. to evaluate the existing organization and staffing of the Columbia University Libraries;
3. to suggest desirable principles of organization and executive staffing;
4. to recommend a plan of library organization; and
5. to prescribe a detailed staffing pattern for the Columbia University Libraries. (Booz, Allen and Hamilton, Inc., 1973, p. xvii)

In general the Columbia study recommendations stated that the libraries' administration should be based on modern management principles, should be geared to current trends in education, and should be prepared to meet the requirements of the future. The consultants called for the adoption of management principles being employed in government, business, and industry. They advocated placing a high priority on the development and utilization of human resources and greater utilization of group problem solving in order to draw on "appropriate" staff resources to formulate policies and programs that are relevant and based on accurate facts. The specific recommendations called for a reorganization of the libraries to better prepare them for planning and meeting the needs of the future. They supported the existing centralized system, but suggested that the executive officer should have the title and status of vice president. They also called for strengthening working relationships between the libraries and the university's top administration and faculties; for adopting a formal approach to library planning; and for having the new organizational structure reviewed and approved by various committees and advisory groups.

From a planning perspective, a number of other key recommendations included the establishment of a planning office for effective program planning and budgeting; the adoption of a new comprehensive plan of staffing, including executive, librarian, specialist, and clerical positions; utilization of group problem-solving methods to involve appropriate staff in library planning and development; adoption of multiple reporting relationships for staff with service and resources responsibilities; establishment of performance goals as a basis for effective planning and evaluation; the establishment and regular updating of clear policies; and the development of program budgeting approaches. The Booz, Allen and Hamilton report, in essence, called for the application of contemporary management theory to the operations of the Columbia University Libraries. It called for greater emphasis on staff participation in decision making and on coordinated planning as a way of giving focus and direction to all organizational efforts (ibid., pp. 8–12)

Responses at Other Institutions—Cornell, Chicago, Michigan, and Stanford

Another response to *Problems in University Library Management* came at Cornell University in late 1971 when Library Director David Kaser undertook a comprehensive study of that library system in cooperation with the American Management Association (AMA) under a grant from the Council on Library Resources. At Cornell a decision was made to employ AMA's Team Planning Program, an approach that had been developed for corporate management and which had been successfully used by several institutions of higher education. The Team Planning Program called for the establishment of a planning team consisting of the director of libraries, six members of his executive staff, five librarians elected by the Librarians' Assembly, and a team director—a member of AMA's permanent staff.

The team director was responsible for guiding the team through the entire procedure. After an organizational or "Likert Profile" questionnaire had been administered to the entire Cornell staff and the results analyzed by the AMA, the planning team met for a week at the AMA's Center for Planning and Implementation in rural Hamilton, New York. The team was charged with developing a group of statements about the Cornell University Libraries. These included mission, beliefs, basic policies, organizational personality, continuing objectives, specific objectives, strengths, weaknesses, internal analysis, action programs, and overall timetables (Johnson and Mann, 1980, p. 32).

During the following ten months, these statements were presented to the Cornell staff and were the subject of open hearings in which staff were encouraged to participate. The hearings served to validate objectives, identify strategies, provide data and documentation, and to generally assess and reassess what had been done by the planning team. The team held two interim meetings to evaluate the progress and direction of the process and held a final one-week meeting for a final review of the objectives, to establish priorities and strategies, and to develop procedures for the implementation and continuation of planning (ibid., p. 40).

In his report on the Cornell planning effort, William E. McGrath, an invited observer, noted that participative management became an important issue during the process and that the Likert Profile had shown that the staff saw the library as being in a state of transition from a "benevolent" to a "consultative" style of management. McGrath also wondered whether the shift from the traditional authoritarian administrative style characterized in most libraries to one based on McGregor's "Theory Y" in the space of a year or two, as envisioned in the emerging plan at Cornell, might be too much to expect of either management or the library rank and file (McGrath, 1973, p. 64).

In his evaluation of the process, David Kaser credited the effort with raising the staff's level of awareness about the library system and about its strengths and weaknesses. He felt that the process had been therapeutic for the entire organization and that it had provided the Cornell University Libraries with a continuing planning process which could be integrated into the regular management program and assure that the libraries would not again fall behind in their planning (Kaser, 1973, p. 17).

In 1972 Stanley McElderry was appointed director of the university library at the University of Chicago. He turned to the university's Industrial Relations Center for guidance in studying and resolving the library's management problems. The Industrial Relations Center recommended that the library initiate an organization improvement program using a Design Group which included representatives of all levels of library staff. The group was chaired by a Design Group coordinator and had a Steering Committee consisting of top library management. The Design Group received training in management theory, needs analysis, group discussion techniques, and leadership skills at the Industrial Relations Center.

During much of 1973 the Design Group developed and implemented a Needs Analysis Program. The program began with meetings with the entire library staff in small discussion groups over a two-week period. The 1,600 specific needs and problems identified in these meetings were condensed into a summary report by the Design Group and were presented to the staff at large for reactions, further discussion, and suggestions for solution. After the staff review the Design Group and the Steering Committee developed a general plan to pursue the staff suggestions.

The plan included recommendations for (1) a staff committee to develop an orientation program; (2) a personnel subcommittee to support the library's personnel function for librarians and support staff; (3) a training subcommittee to work on management and supervisory needs; (4) orientation training sessions for supervisory staff at the Industrial Relations Center; and (5) various subcommittees to work with library departments on specific problems that had been identified in these areas (Johnson and Mann, 1980, p. 35).

At the end of the first year the Design Group recommended that a standing group with rotating membership be appointed to identify organizational problems, to develop solutions to these problems, and to informally monitor the implementations of recommendations. In reviewing the whole effort afterward, Stanley McElderry noted that, although the analysis and review had been a slow process, the results were worthwhile because library staff had developed a greatly improved problem-solving capacity (ibid., p. 37).

At the University of Michigan a similar approach to analysis and planning was taken without the outside support other institutions had used. Aware of the *Problems of University Library Management* report and of the studies at Columbia and Cornell, the library administration decided to embark on its own self-assessment program using an internal University Library Planning Committee appointed by the director.

The nine-member committee appointed in 1973 was chaired by the associate director of libraries and included representatives of all levels of the professional staff. The committee identified the following reasons for undertaking the study:

1. Academic libraries are changing, but the rate of change is too slow to enable them to adapt successfully to the economic, technological, social, and educational developments that challenge them.

2. Many basic changes in academic librarianship have been introduced, but so rapidly that individual libraries and librarians need a crash program in order to assimilate them consistently throughout the profession, to explore fully

their implications for service, and for the organization and staffing of academic libraries.

3. Present forms of organization and staffing of academic libraries do not permit the fullest utilization of the human resources available to them and inhibit a flexible response to changing circumstances. (Michigan, University of, 1974, pp. 3–4)

The University Library Planning Committee was charged with reviewing the process of planning and decision making and for recommending changes to improve their effectiveness. The committee began its self-assessment by evaluating, discussing, and summarizing the internal and external problems facing the university libraries in the world of scholarship, the publishing field, declining funds in academia, and resulting pressures on libraries in institutional cooperation, the use of book funds, automation, services, and internal organization. In February 1973, a professional forum was held to discuss the statements of objectives prepared by the committee, to evaluate the performance of the library against these objectives, to recommend specific changes, and to recommend alternative forms of organization and staffing (Johnson and Mann, 1980, p. 39).

After the forum, the committee distributed a thirty-one page Library Staff Survey that eventually reached 186 library staff members. After the returns were received and processed, a series of small group meetings was held with librarians and committee members to discuss the results. These meetings resulted in the establishment of twenty-two task forces to deal with various aspects of the stated objectives. The planning committee's final report was a synthesis of the findings of the task forces with a set of general as well as specific recommendations. As with the Cornell and Columbia studies, the University of Michigan library study placed a great deal of emphasis on planning and on increasing staff participation in decision making. The committee recommended a network of standing advisory committees: planning council, executive council, technical services advisory committee, material selection policy committee, classification evaluation committee, personnel and staff development committee, and reader services advisory committee (ibid., p. 39).

Another internal self-study was undertaken at Stanford University where David C. Weber, director of libraries, created a Commission on Librarianship under the sponsorship of the Stanford University Librarians Association in May 1972. He charged it with examining the role and status of librarians at the university. The commission spent three years conducting its study and included investigations into the role of the library and the librarian; recognition of the library and the librarian; library instruction; peer review; library organization, definition, and classification; criteria for appointment and promotion; and salaries. These investigations were undertaken by subcommittees of the commission. They included wide participation from Stanford librarians and questionnaires administered locally and sent to librarians at twenty-six other institutions.

The commission's final report made twenty-three recommendations covering topics such as rank, appointments, benefits, peer review, professional development, work schedules, salaries, and other issues of concern to the librarians at Stanford. The commission's key recommendation was a call for the establishment of a librarians assembly to serve as a formal advisory body to the director of libraries.

ARL Office of Management Studies Publications Series

Beyond the studies at Columbia, Cornell, Stanford, and the Universities of Chicago and Michigan, and the national attention they were given, the *Problems in University Library Management* report had other important results. As a part of its mandate to assume a leadership role in the movement to improve the management of university libraries through the application of contemporary management theory, the ARL Office of University Library Management Studies (OMS) launched a sustained and coordinated effort to provide support to individual institutional efforts and to keep other library managers informed of trends and developments. One aspect of this role was the publication of *Occasional Papers* and *ARL Management Supplements*.

The *Occasional Papers* series was inaugurated in December 1971. It consisted of publications dealing with specific management problems facing research libraries. Each issue addressed itself to a single topic, which was presented as a paper, a summary, or a bibliographic review. The series was intended to serve as a guide to important research and publication in the management field, annual summaries of trends in various management areas, and information on current developments—including workability and success of innovations (Webster, 1971).

The *ARL Management Supplement* was another series of occasional publications, which was inaugurated in December of 1972. Each issue was a summary of the findings of an OMS survey of ARL membership on a particular topic. *ARL Management Supplements* not only summarized findings but discussed several specific institutional situations if there appeared to be significant developments or trends found. The *ARL Man-*

agement Supplements also included brief bibliographies (ARL/OMS, 1972).

For the purpose of this study it is important to note that the first issues of both the *Occasional Papers* and the *ARL Management Supplements* dealt with the issue of planning in university libraries. *Occasional Paper*, Number 1, prepared by OMS Director Duane Webster, was titled "Planning Aids for the University Library Director;" *ARL Management Supplement*, Number 1 was titled "Review of Planning Activities in Academic and Research Libraries."

In "Planning Aids . . ." Webster discussed the importance and benefits of planning and the problems library planners face. Drawing on the work of Kemper, the *Problems in University Library Management* report, the Booz, Allen and Hamilton work at Columbia, and the planning field in general, he set forth a model that was intended to assist library administrators who were interested in employing the techniques of planning or who might be interested in developing planning processes but who were unwilling, or unable, to undertake the full scale effort seen at Cornell, Columbia, Stanford, or the University of Michigan. Webster's model was based on seven elements:

1. formulation of objectives that can be used to guide future operations;
2. assessment of required changes within the library, such as a reduced budget or the need for improved services;
3. development of unit programs and alternate courses of action in a variety of circumstances;
4. determination of resources required for alternative action;
5. evaluation of proposed courses of action for both short- and long-term priorities;
6. installation and monitoring of programs; and
7. a review and updating of plans as part of the overall planning program. (Webster, 1971, p. 7)

"Planning Aids . . ." went on to describe the responsibilities of the planning-budget officer who was central to the planning process, as well as the director, senior planning board, and other library administrators and their staffs who all play a key role in the process, and who would ultimately determine its success or failure (ibid., p. 7).

ARL Management Supplement, Number 1, December 1972, featured an article reviewing planning activities in academic and research libraries. The summary of activities began with the observation that, since the publication of the Booz, Allen and Hamilton study of problems in the management of university libraries, developments in higher education had further emphasized the need for improving methodology involved in library planning.

Financial pressures particularly are forcing universities and their libraries to consider means of curtailing costs. University administrations are investigating new procedures and systems to improve resource allocation and utilization. Costs are being related to benefits. Responsibility for performance is being emphasized. These and other developments are creating operating conditions that need improved planning. (ARL/OMS, 1972, p. 1)

The review article listed some of the questions library administrators might consider in deciding how to approach the newly recognized problems of planning, and noted that emerging research library planning practices were still, to a large extent, in an experimental stage, involving efforts to apply proven management methods to academic situations. The article went on to highlight four major areas in which library planning efforts were being made and to summarize the status of those activities. The four areas featured were (1) The Library in University Planning, (2) New Organization and Staffing Patterns, (3) Procedures and Methods for Securing Planning Data, and (4) Experience with Long-range Planning Methodology. Under "The Library in University Planning" the article noted that three directors of libraries had recently had their areas of responsibility expanded to include coordination of services between major university units and involvement in university planning. At Columbia University the director of libraries had been elevated to vice president and at Indiana University he had been elevated to dean of libraries.

Under "New Organization and Staffing Patterns" it was noted that the application of scientific management techniques to the administration of libraries would require different skills from those traditionally needed by library managers. The role of the planning and budget officer described in *Planning Aids for the University Library Director* was used as an example. Also, several institutions had allocated staff and money to the operation of organizational units specifically responsible for planning and research. The Planning Office established at the Columbia University Libraries in 1972 and the Office of Research and Development established at the Joint Universities Libraries in 1970 were cited as examples. At Purdue University the Instructional Media Research Unit was moved out of the Audio-Visual Center, had its name changed to Library Research Unit, and had its responsibilities expanded to include research into library operational and managerial functions.

A September 1972 OMS survey of ARL member libraries revealed that seventeen of the eighty-nine contacted had established, or were in the process of establishing, a distinct administrative officer with major responsibilities for coordinating and promoting long-range planning. The most frequently cited responsibilities for this officer were (1) supplying data required in the planning and budgeting process, including statistical projections and data analyses, (2) supplying unit administrators with institutional guidelines for budget formulation and interpreting university guidelines in the context of library operations, (3) developing and applying management techniques to library planning and budgeting processes, and (4) preparing and monitoring the library budget.

Under "Procedures and Methods for Securing Planning Data" the article described several research projects examining the costs, benefits, and efficiency of library operations. There appeared to be increasing evidence that cost-reporting and accounting techniques were becoming more widely understood and employed in the management of university and research libraries. Information on cost and systems analysis of library operations was becoming more plentiful. Problems encountered in the collection and interpretation of cost information included incomplete data and standards of measurement and unclear statements of information systems objectives. However, several recent publications and research projects offered encouraging evidence of progress being made in the area of cost studies.

Under "Experience with Long-range Planning Methodology" the article described the American Management Association's planning program at Cornell University and the Booz, Allen and Hamilton study of organization and staffing at Columbia University. It also discussed ARL's own Management Review and Analysis Program.

ARL Management Review and Analysis Program (MRAP)

In addition to issuing the occasional publications that demonstrated the Association of Research Libraries' willingness to function as a clearinghouse for information on management theory and practice as it applied to libraries, in 1971–72 the OMS developed its own program for helping university libraries devise strategies for improving their management and planning systems. The Management Review and Analysis Program (MRAP) incorporated the experiences of the Columbia and Cornell studies and drew upon the findings of the American Management Association and Booz, Allen and Hamilton work in the corporate world. OMS personnel were actively involved in the Columbia study and OMS

Director Duane Webster was an invited observer at the Cornell Planning Team retreats.

The Management Review and Analysis Program was described as an "assisted self-study process" developed specifically for research libraries interested in reviewing and improving management activities in order to strengthen overall library performance. It is included in this study of planning because of the close relationship between the outcomes of self-study efforts and organizational planning efforts. As self-studies, MRAP studies were initiated, planned, carried out, and acted upon by persons directly associated with the libraries involved. Assistance from the ARL Office of Management Studies consisted of providing a framework or general set of procedures, study materials, training, resources, and consultation. The OMS also developed a comprehensive multivolume manual that outlined the entire process and guided each participating institution through each part. The manual was tested on the earlier participants and was revised based on the results of their experiences. The MRAP approach assumed an interested and able library staff, since staff involvement was necessary for producing practical recommendations and for assuring successful implementation of study results (Webster, 1980, p. 52).

The basic purpose of the Management Review and Analysis Program was to help libraries identify, describe, and propose needed changes in current organizational practices. The MRAP process was comprehensive and systematic. It examined the total library managerial system and its subsystems and the problems, goals, and outputs within these systems. Later, as more institutions went through the process, the MRAP manual continued to be refined, developed, and adapted for more effective use over the years the program was run.

The MRAP study was divided into seven components or phases. The first three were general and dealt with needs assessment and historical review, environmental analysis, and analysis of university and library goals and objectives. The other four were more detailed and concentrated on major library management functions such as library management systems, development and use of human resources, the personnel, communications and executive leadership for the future development of the organization, and implementation of change. MRAP studies emphasized the work of the central study team, which monitored and coordinated the overall effort, and task forces, which focused on specific issues for study, evaluation, and recommendation. The final product of the program was the MRAP report setting forth the recommendations with supporting documentation.

The MRAP approach drew heavily on contemporary behavioral sciences management theory as applied in industry and in the corporate world, and was modified based on the experiences of the Cornell and Columbia library studies. It also drew on the experience in self-analysis developed in higher education described in Chapter 3 under Library Self-studies as Planning Tools. It differed from the library accreditation self-surveys because it was a prepackaged program with specific rules, procedures, guidelines, and expected outputs.

The Management Review and Analysis Program was seen by the OMS as a strategy or a philosophy of organizational change.

While change is fast becoming an overworked and unclear term, it is apparent that academic libraries must deal with environments which will not remain the same. In the past managers have tried to cope with changing events; in the future emphasis must be on influencing the process of change. The challenge lies in determining how library managers can learn from past efforts and apply these lessons to managing libraries and, parenthetically, to developing new managers. Some lessons that have already emerged from [the MRAP studies] . . . include: By developing the management capability of the library staff there will be an improved environment for professional contributions. There is value in having different institutions address concerns in their own way assisted by current management techniques. There is a need for libraries to develop analytic and management skills within their own staffs rather than waiting for outside help. Libraries would profit most by developing their own teams of experts who can guide the library in assessing its strengths and building on them in a continuing fashion. There is a danger in resting on past accomplishments. Special efforts are needed to identify and develop new leaders. (Webster and Gardner, 1975b, p. 16)

The basic MRAP strategy was one of action-oriented research aimed toward producing effective, workable recommendations. The ultimate goal of an MRAP effort was to increase the effectiveness of the library by influencing the management decision-making processes and helping to develop a more open, candid, and constructive organization. Systematic fact-finding and extensive involvement of both professional and support staff were accomplished through the use of the two types of groups. The study team held the ultimate responsibility for each study. It conducted the general analyses and directed the more specific efforts of the second type of group—the task force. Task forces conducted analyses in nine management areas (Webster, 1980, p. 53): (1) planning, (2) policy-making, (3) budgeting, (4) management information systems, (5) organization, (6) supervision and leadership, (7) staff development, (8) personnel, and (9) general management. The MRAP approach had two types of goals:

process goals and issue or content goals. Process goals included (1) assessing present management practices; (2) securing a better understanding of the management concepts and principles by participating staff; (3) determining future actions for management improvement; (4) creating an open problem-solving climate; (5) developing group process skills; and (6) developing staff management and analytical ability.

Content goals were determined by each library at the outset of the process depending on its specific objectives, priorities, and areas of need. The issues most frequently addressed were (1) the need for clear library objectives that could be used for library planning and that were supported by key groups on the campuses; (2) low staff morale and how to improve it; (3) the need to develop a comprehensive library response to budget reductions; (4) identifying and training supervisory staff; and (5) development of more effective policy-making and communications systems.

One tangible product of an MRAP study was the final report. Each task force was required to produce a descriptive, analytical, and/or prescriptive report of its findings. The study teams were responsible for integrating the individual task force reports into an overall report including introductory, summary, and implementation sections. The introductions reflected on the background, the goals, and the general approaches of the study; the summary identified broad themes that cut across task force reports under which key recommendations were grouped; and the implementation sections provided study team perspectives of how to approach activities based on the recommendations. MRAP final reports were then reviewed by key groups within the libraries that considered the recommendations and developed programs for implementation in cooperation with directors, other library managers, and university administrators.

In August 1972 the first group of three ARL libraries (Iowa State University, Purdue University, and the University of Tennessee) began participating in a pilot operation of the Management Review and Analysis Program. After the pilot program had been reviewed and revised, a second group of six university libraries began MRAP studies in April 1973, a third group in October 1973, and a fourth group in 1974. By 1977 a total of twenty-four ARL libraries had participated in the Management Review and Analysis program.

In 1976 Edward Johnson, assistant dean of libraries, and Stuart H. Mann, professor of operations research, both of Pennsylvania State University, received a grant from the Council on Library Resources to evaluate the effectiveness of the program. Penn State had participated as one of the 1974 group of MRAP institutions and Johnson had served as chair of the study team there. At that time twenty-two institutions had participated, and it was felt that enough data had been generated to support a comprehensive evaluation and appraisal. One question to be answered was, "What has been the impact of the Management Review and Analysis Program on the libraries involved?" Another question was, "Is the MRAP an effective tool in improving the management of an academic or research library?" (Johnson, Mann, and Whiting 1979).

Unfortunately, from a planning perspective, the Johnson and Mann evaluation was highly process, rather than product, oriented. It approached the Management Review and Analysis Program as an organizational development effort rather than an application of a specific management tool. It emphasized behavioral, attitudinal, and organizational changes in the climates of the libraries that had participated in the program. It measured improvements in overall performance and effectiveness by the perceptions of MRAP participants rather than objective criteria. It did not attempt to ascertain the extent to which the findings and recommendations of the study teams and task forces had actually affected management systems or specific activities.

The evaluators described their approach to the program as one based on the organizational development goals outlined by the Office of Management Studies in its 1973 Annual Report. Specifically these goals were

1. to create an open problem-solving climate;
2. to develop group process skills;
3. to secure a better understanding of management concepts and principles;
4. to assess present management practices;
5. to determine future actions for management improvement;
6. to develop staff management and analytical capabilities; and
7. to improve the view of the university toward the library.

Since they were primarily interested in attitudinal changes, Johnson and Mann concentrated on the views of library administrators and library staff who had been involved in the program for their evaluation. They used questionnaires and key informant interviews to generate data for analysis. They also used a Delphi procedure to contrast the abilities of MRAP and non-MRAP institution personnel to articulate goals and objectives. Johnson and Mann concluded their evaluation with the following observation:

The study showed rather dramatically that, in the opinion of those who were involved, several improvements resulted in staff attitude and behavior and in the organization. These improvements were: creating an open problem-solving climate, developing group process skills, understanding management concepts and principles, assessing management practice, and determining future actions for management improvement. In summary, the results showed that overall, MRAP was viewed as worthwhile and successful by those who had participated in it . . .; although there were some variations between various levels of staff between institutions. (Johnson, 1981, p. 73)

Although the evaluation was comprehensive, structured, well-planned and implemented, since its emphasis was on attitude and behavior, it did not address questions of actual impact on decision making or on the accomplishment of specific objectives one might have expected.

When the 1930 U.S. Office of Education survey of land grant college and university libraries was conducted, the survey team was attempting to determine the extent to which the institutions examined met the requirements for "good library service" as defined at the outset of the study. Johnson and Mann made no judgments about the quality of resources or services found by the MRAP study teams, or whether these were considered adequate, inadequate, or unacceptable. When Erickson conducted his 1958 analysis of library surveys by outside experts, one of his criteria for determining whether the survey had been an effective management tool was the extent to which survey recommendations had been implemented by the libraries studied, and the extent to which these implementations could be attributed to the survey.

Since Johnson and Mann made no reference to implementations of recommendations their evaluation only documented participants impressions. Most felt that the process had improved attitude and behavior; it had created a better climate for problem solving; contributed to the development of group process skills; and heightened appreciation of good management concepts and principles. The evaluation did not document whether a single institution had demonstrably improved its services, increased its efficiency, or become more effective in meeting the needs of its clientele. The Johnson and Mann evaluation did not demonstrate whether a major effort involving literally thousands of individuals at the twenty-two institutions over a period of years had actually achieved its goal of strengthening overall library performance. The evaluation seemed to accept the Booz, Allen and Hamilton report's findings about the deficiencies in library management systems, and to conclude that the attitude and behavioral changes found in their study of participants would correct the deficiencies cited.

In response to the two questions raised—"What has been the impact of the Management Review and Analysis Program on the libraries involved?"

and "Is the MRAP an effective tool in improving management of an academic or research library?"—the evaluation addressed the first but not the second. What is still needed is an MRAP evaluation that would analyze the final recommendations of the study teams and determine the extent to which they were subsequently implemented. Such an evaluation would also have to determine, in quantitative terms, whether the implementations of the recommendations achieved the goal of improving library services.

Whether or not the MRAP experience was successful as an organization development effort, it did stimulate a great deal of activity in all the libraries involved. It focused attention on a wide range of problems and produced carefully considered and well thought out recommendations for dealing with them. Every MRAP participant came out of the process with a plan for correcting deficiencies and a plan for monitoring developments to assure that future efforts would be coordinated and directed toward specific agreed-upon ends.

Other ARL/OMS Programs

After its establishment in 1970, the ARL Office of Management Studies developed a comprehensive package of programs and services in support of efforts to improve library management. Its participation in the Columbia and Cornell University self-studies, its earliest publication series, and the Management Review and Analysis Program have already been described. The OMS continued to play a key role in stimulating, coordinating, and supporting individual library efforts to be more responsive to changes in their environments and to be more efficient and effective in meeting their goals and objectives.

During the 1970s and early 1980s the ARL Office of Management Studies operated four basic groups of programs and services (the following descriptions are based on OMS Annual Reports for 1979–84): (1) Academic Library Programs, (2) Information Exchange and Publications Programs, (3) Organizational Training and Staff Development Programs, and (4) Applied Research and Development Programs.

The *Academic Library Programs* (ALP) were an outgrowth of the Management Review and Analysis Program. The overall goal was to prepare the total library for the future by using the assisted self-study approach. They also provided a mechanism for training a large group of librarians in management and self-study techniques and for developing a resource pool for future library management improvement efforts. Staff members in each library planned and carried out selected programs with OMS staff and consultant assistance using manuals and other aids prepared by the Office. Thus ALP projects helped develop staff understanding and skills during the study process, as well as group cooperation and dedication to change. Academic Library Program projects were designed to help institutions make strategic assessments of their current positions and to determine alternative approaches to meeting external and internal challenges. Unlike the original Management Review and Analysis Program that attempted to be comprehensive in assessing needs, identifying problem areas, and making recommendations for improvement, the Academic Library Program consisted of seven different self-study procedures, each with a specific purpose.

General management review programs included the modified Management Review and Analysis Program (MRAP) for large academic and research libraries, the Academic Library Development Program (ALDP) for small and medium-sized libraries with staffs of twenty to one hundred, and the Planning Program for Small Academic Libraries (PPSAL) for libraries with staffs of fewer than twenty professionals. The Public Services in Research Libraries Program, the Preservation Planning Program, and the Collection Analysis Project studies permitted libraries to focus their efforts on particular functions, while the Organizational Screening Program was adaptable to a wide range of purposes and varying periods of time.

The *Information Exchange and Publications Programs* fulfilled the information clearinghouse function the Booz, Allen and Hamilton report recommended for the Association of Research Libraries. The Systems and Procedures Exchange Center (SPEC) was organized by the Office of Management Studies in 1973. Its initial impetus was a realization that while innovative library management techniques and procedures were being developed and utilized in libraries around the country, there were no formal, timely means of learning of their existence and acquiring descriptive material. The SPEC's objectives were

1. to collect information and documentation regarding current practices in specific areas of library management;

2. to make both the original documentation and the center's analyses available to the library community;

3. to publish analytical state-of-the-art reviews on management topics;

4. to identify library management expertise and facilitate its exchange; and

5. to promote experimentation and innovation on the basis of what has succeeded elsewhere.

The SPEC resources were developed by surveys of participating ARL institutions. The surveys were directed to each institution's SPEC liaison person who was responsible for responding to surveys and for forwarding relevant supporting documentation to ARL. The documentation included procedures manuals, policy statements, committee reports, brochures, and forms currently in use at the institution. While the SPEC files were a unique resource containing all documentation received by the center, representative coverage of management topics was presented in *SPEC Kits*, packages of illustrative material representing the range of approaches to management issues within ARL libraries. Each *SPEC Kit* was supported by a *SPEC Flyer* that defined the issue, described the various approaches being used, and indicated trends and problem areas.

OMS *Organizational Training and Staff Development Programs* focused on the development of staff skills and abilities critical to developing and implementing change strategies in libraries. A central concern was improving organizational performance through more effective library management and supervision. Individual programs included Basic Management Skills Institutes, Advanced Management Skills Institutes, Special Focus Workshops, Management Institutes for Library Directors, an Institute on Research Libraries for Library School Faculty, an Analytical Skills Institute, the Management Training Film Program, and a Consultant Training Program.

Basic Management Skills Institutes were generally held three times a year at different locations around the country. They were conducted by OMS staff and trained consultants to help administrators, supervisors, and those who wished to develop managerial skills to increase their knowledge and abilities. The Advanced Management Skills Institutes were held twice a year when demand warranted. They provided further training for those in senior management positions or for those who had attended other OMS training functions. Between 1978 and 1984 more than 2,500 librarians participated in the institutes. Special Focus Workshops were usually one- or two-day topically oriented training programs conducted by OMS staff for a specific library or group. During 1984 nearly 1,000 individuals participated in Special Focus workshops or OMS presentations.

The Consultant Training Program operated from 1979 to 1983 helping a selected group of seventy-seven librarians acquire the skills and knowledge needed to assist library self-study and training programs. Some Consultant Training Program participants later served as principle consultants for OMS self-study projects while others used the skills they acquired in the program primarily to benefit their home institutions in addition to accepting consulting work on an occasional basis.

OMS *Applied Research and Development Programs*, and consultation programs were practical developmental research projects that addressed issues of importance to research libraries. They were generally conducted in cooperation with ARL member institutions. Programs included the Collaborative Research/Writing Program, the Automation Inventory, Organizational Projections Project, and the North American Collections Inventory Project.

The Collaborative Research/Writing Program encouraged practicing librarians to prepare publications on library issues and problems. Participants worked in cooperation with OMS staff and with the support of OMS resources. Work under this program resulted in *SPEC Kits*, *SPEC Flyers*, and *Occasional Papers* on such topics as "Budget Allocation Systems for Research Libraries," "The Assistant/Associate Director Position," "Non-bibliographic Machine-Readable Data Bases," and "Staff Training for Automation." The Automation Inventory was a machine readable data base of information on the status of automation in ARL member libraries.

The Organizational Projections Project was a set of papers developed by the OMS staff and the ARL Task Force on Staffing. "Organizational Projections for Assessing Future Research Library Staffing Needs and Prospects" consisted of four different projections designed to assess options for change in library organization and staffing, particularly considering the potential impact of changes in technology. The alternatives were derived from varying speculations about how universities and their libraries would embrace and react to technological and other environmental developments over the next decade. In addition to a description of each situation, the papers included strategic concerns, staffing issues, and discussion questions. The projections were used with OMS self-study and training programs to help provide a framework for thinking about the future.

The North American Collections Inventory Project was a research effort supported by the Lilly Endowment. Its purpose was to expand the Research Libraries Group Conspectus Program into an inventory of North American research collections; to assist in participation by a broad representation of academic and research libraries; and to support collective action in the development, cataloging, and preservation of research collections.

STATUS OF LIBRARY PLANNING AT THE END OF THE 1970s

By the end of the 1970s most library managers had become far more aware of the advantages and importance of applying contemporary management techniques to libraries than they had been a decade earlier. As one of these management techniques, strategic planning had also become a generally acceptable tool for consideration. The library management deficiencies cited by the Booz, Allen and Hamilton report had been addressed locally by individual libraries and nationally under the leadership of the Association of Research Libraries, primarily through the Office of Management Studies.

The ARL/OMS efforts had the strong support of ARL member institutions and of such major funding sources in the field of higher education as the Council on Library Resources, the National Endowment for the Humanities, the Andrew W. Mellon Foundation, the General Electric Foundation, and the Lilly Endowment.

Between 1972 and 1979 twenty-five institutions had undertaken major comprehensive assisted self-studies under the Management Review and Analysis Program. In each case the library staff had reviewed its history and role in the university, conducted a needs assessment study and environmental analysis, and defined or redefined library and university goals and objectives. MRAP study teams and task forces had analyzed planning, policy, budgeting, and management information systems. They had addressed the issues of organization, leadership and supervision, and the need for staff development. They had studied their personnel and management systems, identified problem areas, made specific recommendations for improvements, and developed plans for implementing the recommendations.

Every MRAP library had completed a final report documenting its findings and setting forth its recommendations. On every campus, library staff, and the university community in general, had been given an opportunity to participate in the self-study process and to respond to the report and recommendations. The reports themselves were made available to other institutions and the library community at large, either directly from the MRAP participant or through the Office of Management Studies.

In 1978 the Council on Library Resources awarded the OMS a five-year grant of $870,000 to support the development and implementation of modified MRAP studies for medium-sized libraries under the Academic Library Program. The Lilly Endowment awarded a grant of $200,000 for a similar effort for independent college and university libraries with fewer than twenty professional staff. The Andrew W. Mellon Foundation awarded a $44,000 grant to facilitate the integration of the Collection Analysis Project into the Academic Library Program, further extending its support to individual library planning and analysis efforts. Other libraries had initiated their own self-studies and some had brought in outside management consultants to conduct studies and make recommendations on specific problems.

By 1980 the Systems Procedures and Exchange Center had assumed a major responsibility for functioning as an information clearinghouse for library planning and management. Between October 1973 and September 1980 the center issued nearly seventy *SPEC Kits* and *SPEC Flyers*, surveying and documenting the status of library activity in such areas as acquisitions budgets, systems functions, automated cataloging systems, planning systems, resource sharing, preparing for emergencies and disasters, on-line bibliographic search services, and remote storage.

The OMS had also encouraged the dissemination of information on library management issues through the *Occasional Papers*. Topics covered included "The Formulation and Use of Goals and Objectives Statements in Academic and Research Libraries" (No. 3, September 1974); "Changing Patterns in Internal Communications in Large Academic Libraries" (No. 6, July 1981); and "Salary Compensation Systems for Librarians" (No. 5, May 1981). *ARL Management Supplements* had been issued on such topics as "Performance Appraisal in Academic and Research Libraries" (Vol. 3, No. 1, May 1975); "Library Use Instruction in Academic and Research Libraries" (Vol. 5, No. 1, September 1977); and "Review of Management Training Activities in Academic and Research Libraries" (Vol. 1, No. 4, September 1973). A $30,000 grant from the H. W. Wilson Foundation supported the development of *Resource Notebooks* on staff development (January 1979), organization (January 1979), and planning (February 1979).

The ARL/OMS Management Skills Institutes had introduced hundreds of librarians to the basic concepts of organizational behavior and management theory. The Special Focus Workshops had helped many others develop management skills and participate in problem-solving exercises in a wide range of topics. The Consultant Training Program had been especially effective in helping to develop a corps of library consultants who could provide the expertise and technical skills to help individual libraries develop their own solutions to local problems.

The Office of Management Studies' Applied Research and Development Program further supported efforts of individual librarians to conduct research on selected topics, to get the results of their research published, and to get the information disseminated to the greater library community. The Applied Research and Development Program also provided a vehicle for focusing research on issues of concern to a number of institutions and to develop cooperative approaches to implementing solutions.

A decade after the Booz, Allen and Hamilton report on problems of university library management, academic library management had undergone a dramatic change. The mechanisms had been developed for addressing the problems identified by the Booz, Allen and Hamilton study. The personnel and information resources had been developed and, with the support of major grants from foundations, were now being made available to the general academic library community. The information necessary for successful strategic planning was finally available and the resources for developing and implementing effective plans accessible.

Five

Comparison of Survey/Planning Source Documents

REVIEW OF LIBRARY SURVEY/PLANNING SOURCE DOCUMENTS

Chapter 5 is a discussion of the key library survey and library planning documents presented thus far. Beginning with Works' study of a selected group of college and university libraries in 1927, there has been a continuing interest in studying academic libraries, identifying problem areas and deficiencies, and recommending ways in which they can be solved or corrected. The approaches have changed since Works' study, but some characteristics have remained constant.

There has been a basic assumption that there are more effective and more efficient ways of delivering library resources and services to the academic community than those being employed at any point in time. There has been a belief that by surveying and documenting libraries and their operations, library experts can define problems and recommend specific measures for improvements. Works' study was commissioned because a number of college and university presidents had become concerned that their libraries had not adjusted to the changes in emphasis in American higher education that had occurred between the 1880s and the 1920s.

With the establishment of the land grant colleges and universities and the emergence of the research universities (Hamlin, 1981, pp. 45–59), emphasis had shifted from the traditional education in the classics to scientific, technical, vocational, and research-oriented approaches. The requirements for library resources and services had changed more rapidly than existing facilities or management systems had been able to accommodate them. The university libraries needed to change from repositories for printed artifacts to working laboratories supporting student academic pursuits and faculty research. The librarians needed to change from custodians and guardians of books to active participants in the information transfer and learning processes.

The U.S. Office of Education survey of 1930 was undertaken in response to a similar concern on the part of the government about the extent to which land grant college and university libraries were meeting the requirements for "good" library service. The outside "library expert" surveys of individual institutions conducted during the 1930s, 1940s, and 1950s analyzed by Erickson (1961) responded to library administration, university administration, and funding source concerns about the adequacy of specific university libraries, and ways in which their resources and services could be improved. Again, the survey documenting existing resources and services and the development of a set of specific recommendations for action were seen as the appropriate approach to improving library management and library planning. The establishment of graduate library schools, the Association of Research Libraries, and the Association of College and Research Libraries provided staff to conduct these surveys, and audiences to receive, respond to, and disseminate information about the studies.

Robert Kemper's study of strategic planning in libraries brought a new dimension to the library survey and the study of library management by adding a theoretical basis. The "Essentials of a University Library Program" described by Wilson and Tauber (1945, p. 12) and the informal survey outline described by Tauber (1954, pp. 191–93), which had been followed by many of the outside experts, were now formalized in a theoretical approach that related the library survey and library planning to contemporary management theory.

The concerns of ARL library directors in the late 1960s echoed the concerns of university administrators and library directors in the 1920s about the extent to which libraries were responding to changes in higher education. Just as Works and the Office of Education survey teams had sought to define the problems and recommend solutions earlier, the Booz, Allen and Hamilton report identified major problems in university library management in 1969 and recommended solutions.

One basic difference between the traditional writings (Works, U.S. Office of Education, Wilson, Wilson and Tauber, and the surveys studied by Erickson) and the later management theory and systems writings

(Kemper, Booz, Allen and Hamilton, Inc., and Webster) was that the former tended to focus on the *specific* (number of titles, number of students, square feet of space, seating capacity, relative salaries of librarians, etc.) while the latter focused on the *general*—on organizational structure and the management process. Strategic planning was an undefined, unconscious goal of the traditional efforts; it was a clearly stated and intentional goal of the Kemper and the Booz, Allen and Hamilton recommendations.

Duane Webster's "Planning Aids for the University Library Director" (December 1971), the ARL Management Review and Analysis Program, and the activities of the ARL Office of Management Studies continued the Booz, Allen and Hamilton emphasis on management systems and the planning process as the most effective vehicles for carrying out the ARL directors' mandate to "identify opportunities to improve the ways in which university libraries plan and use their resources" (Booz, Allen and Hamilton, Inc., 1970, p. 1).

The following nine key library survey/library planning writings have been selected as source documents for the review of library planning theory, for the analysis of contemporary library plans, and for the development of an approach to examining future library planning efforts, which conclude this study. Each is a landmark document that contributed to the development of library management, library planning, and library planning theory. Each influenced those that followed and each helped shape the current body of library planning literature. It is useful to consider them here as a group in order to trace the development of trends and to identify constant themes in library management and library planning that persist and continue to need to be addressed. The outline used to analyze and compare these documents is contained in Appendix 1 of the author's doctoral dissertation (Biddle, 1988, pp. A-30–A-41).

KEY LIBRARY SURVEY/LIBRARY PLANNING SOURCE DOCUMENTS

Works, George A. 1927. *College and University Library Problems: A Study of a Selected Group of Institutions Prepared for the Association of American Universities*. Chicago: American Library Association, 142pp.

U.S. Office of Education. 1930. "Survey of Land Grant Colleges and Universities: The Library." Section of *Bulletin, 1930*. Vol. 1, no. 9, part 8. Washington, D.C.: Government Printing Office, pp. 609–714.

Wilson, Louis R. 1947. "The University Library Survey: Its Results." *College and Research Libraries* 8, no. 3, pt. 2 (July): 368–75.

Wilson, Louis R., and Maurice F. Tauber. 1956. "Essentials of a University Library Program." In *The University Library: The Organization, Administration, and Functions of Academic Libraries*. 2d ed. New York: Columbia University Press, pp. 19–25.

Tauber, Maurice F. 1954. [Survey Outline taken from] "Management Improvements in Libraries: Surveys by Librarians." *College and Research Libraries* 15, no. 2 (April): 191–93.

Erickson, E. Walfred. 1961. *College and University Library Surveys, 1938–1952*. ACRL Monograph No. 25. Chicago: American Library Association, 115pp.

Kemper, Robert E. 1967. "Strategic Planning for Library Systems." D.B.A. diss., University of Washington, 295pp.

Booz, Allen and Hamilton, Inc. 1970. *Problems in University Library Management, A Study Conducted by Booz, Allen and Hamilton, Inc., for the Association of Research Libraries and the American Council on Education*. Washington, D.C.: Association of Research Libraries, 63pp.

Webster, Duane E. 1971. "Planning Aids for the University Library Director." *Occasional Papers*, no. 1. Office of University Library Management Studies, Association of Research Libraries, Washington, D.C., December, 27pp.

LIBRARY PLANNING PROGRAM COMPONENTS

University libraries and their programs, resources, and services have many components that can be examined in conducting library surveys or in developing library strategic plans. The following group has been identified based on the contents of the source documents, a review of planning literature, the author's personal experience, and a preliminary survey of contemporary library planning documents.

1. Statements of goals and objectives
2. Responsive, functional, organizational structures
3. Evaluations of resources and services
   a. Collections
   b. Reader and technical services
   c. Personnel
   d. Physical facilities—buildings and equipment

e. General financial support

4. Use of contemporary technology and information management systems

5. Extent of interinstitutional cooperation

6. Examinations of the administrative relationships of the library to university administration

7. Library planning systems including

   a. Administrative support

   b. Provisions for assessing needs and weighing options—environmental analyses

   c. Mechanisms for establishing priorities and integrating them into ongoing operations

   d. Use of management information systems

   e. Formal planning documents—written plans

   f. Provisions for implementation and evaluation

Statements of Goals and Objectives: Defining the Purpose of the University Library

George Works opened his 1927 survey of selected college and university libraries with a description of the "primary functions of the university library." The U.S. Office of Education survey also began with a statement of the "functions of the library in land-grant institutions," and a statement of "requirements for good library service." The outside experts who conducted the individual library surveys covered by Erickson's study tended to accept the basic functions defined earlier and to measure the extent to which the libraries studied met the general requirements set forth. The functions of a university library as described by several writers included the following:

- facilitating and encouraging research by providing printed resources
- facilitating teaching and learning by providing adequate resources and facilities
- stimulating general, cultural, and recreational reading by the students
- providing for the intellectual development of the faculty
- providing information resource services to the general community
- integrating the local library with community, state, regional, national, and international library resources.

Kemper, Booz, Allen and Hamilton, and Webster used a different approach in relating the library survey, library evaluations, and library planning to management theory. Each suggests that a mission statement or definition of goals and objectives be developed early in the process— before a full-scale survey, evaluation, or planning effort is begun. One cannot assume that all parties have the same goals in mind. Until the goals and objectives are clearly stated, discussed, and agreed upon, it is not possible to determine the extent to which current activities or alternative courses of action are most likely to achieve success. In the end, the latter approach might produce the same set of primary functions as the former. However, the process of defining goals and objectives and of developing a mission statement focuses the participants' attention on a specific set of functions, and encourages them to think of quantitative and qualitative ways in which progress toward achieving various goals can be measured. The management theory or systems approach is primarily concerned with developing a process for planning rather than developing specific recommendations for correcting specific deficiencies.

Kemper, Booz, Allen and Hamilton, and Webster maintain that the mission of the university library, its goals and objectives, must not only be discussed, but must also be explicitly stated. Goals and objectives should be clearly defined, both officially and informally accepted, and measurable. "Facilitating and encouraging research by providing printed resources," is an inadequate statement of goal unless the writer includes ways of determining how research will be facilitated and encouraged, for whom, the scope of printed resources to be provided, and at what level research will be supported. With the variety of information media available today, such a goal would have to include nonpaper information resources such as microforms, machine readable data, and microcomputer software as well. The writer would also have to include means of measuring the extent to which a library would facilitate and encourage research.

"Facilitating teaching and learning by providing adequate resources and facilities" would also be an inadequate goal statement unless criteria were cited for determining adequacy of resources and adequacy of facilities in terms that could be objectively measured. Works tried to address the problem of defining adequacy by comparing the institutions surveyed and applying rules of thumb developed by respected members of the profession.

The U.S. Office of Education study defined adequacy basically the same way as Works, but in several areas it cited specific measurements.

Inasmuch as it has been found that institutions with well-used libraries are expending not less than $10 per student for books, periodicals, and binding, this amount is suggested as a tentative standard. . . .

Institutions which have not erected library buildings within the past ten years should make a careful study to determine if their present buildings are fully conducive to the satisfactory use of books. . . .

The library staffs of many land-grant institutions should be enlarged. The number of persons found necessary by well-used libraries is 5 for the first 500 students, 10 for the first 1,000, and 4 additional for each additional 500 students.

In more than three-fourths of the land-grant institutions much increased financial support is needed. In the group of libraries with the least use and smallest support the library budget should be increased to about four times the present amount. Institutions which are allotting less than 4 per cent of their funds for library purposes or which are spending less than $20 per student should carefully examine the use made of their libraries, the adequacy of the book collection, and the efficiency of the personnel as compared with libraries with larger ratios of expenditures. (U.S. Office of Education, 1930, pp. 713–14)

By the time of the studies analyzed by Erickson, professional standards had begun to be suggested by the Association of Research Libraries, the American Library Association, and the Association of College and Research Libraries. Objective criteria and standards for academic libraries were also being generated by the research being conducted at the graduate library schools and research sponsored by foundations and government agencies concerned about university libraries.

In addition to requiring that goals and objectives be stated, both officially and informally accepted, and measurable, Webster argued that those determining the goals and objectives should also examine the means required to achieve them. An unattainable objective might have to be restated in more realistic terms. For example, "Meeting all the students' information resource needs" might be changed to "Acquiring sufficient numbers of books, periodicals, and other information resources to fill at least 85 percent of the requests received from students with local sources, and obtaining the balance through interlibrary loan and resource sharing agreements." All of the management theory and systems writings agreed that it is important that the goals and objectives be integrated into the planning process, that they become an integral part of the day-to-day decision making and management process, and that they include staff participation, and to some extent library user participation, in their formulation.

Organizational Structure

All of the source documents refer to the need for an administrative structure capable of governing a large complex organization, what Wilson and Tauber referred to as "a workable policy of library governance." The earlier studies identified instances in which libraries had grown in size, but whose organizational structures had not matured in response to new environments. They also addressed a general need for universities to centralize the administration of all campus libraries and library programs under one office. This applied to centralized financial administration, the centralized acquisition, cataloging, and processing of materials, and the centralized administration of the main library as well as departmental libraries, departmental reading rooms, and special collections. The later studies included the application of contemporary data processing and automated library systems to routine, repetitive operations handled by centralized administrative facilities.

The Booz, Allen and Hamilton study discussed the need for the identification of the legal bases for policies, procedures, and relationships, for written policy statements, and for written procedures manuals to formalize and document ways in which specific functions are carried out. Kemper referred to the need to formally recognize the administrative, research, and educational responsibilities of university libraries mandated by the charters or legislation establishing them. Booz, Allen and Hamilton, and Erickson, described ways in which written policies and procedures could be communicated among library staff and users. These included organization manuals, library newsletters, and staff meetings.

The source documents describe the need for clear lines of authority within libraries, delegation of responsibilities among administrators and from the director through middle management to line operations. Booz, Allen and Hamilton discussed the need for written position descriptions documenting administrative relationships between individuals, the establishment of staffing patterns that respond to changing requirements, and the development of plans for coordinated organizational growth. Where libraries experience reductions in support, it is also important that the impact of reductions be minimized to the extent possible, by planned and controlled reduction rather than simple attrition.

The U.S. Office of Education study outlined appropriate duties of a "head librarian" and described the experience and the professional and educational qualifications directors of university libraries should have in order to effectively carry them out.

Booz, Allen and Hamilton, and Webster, emphasized the importance of examining the relationship among the budgeting system, the planning system, and the library's goals and objectives when analyzing a library organizational structure. All three components are important and there must be an integral relationship among them if an organization is to be effective in carrying out its mission. Perhaps in response to changes in management theory in general, the later writers also emphasized the importance of having an organizational structure that allowed for staff participation at all levels of decision making.

Resources and Services

Evaluating library resources and services can be divided into five basic areas: (1) collections, (2) services, (3) personnel, (4) facilities—buildings and equipment, and (5) general financial support. Although the source documents used different ways of dividing and integrating these, the same basic areas were addressed in each and recommendations were made about how they could or should be used for evaluating a library's overall adequacy and for planning improvements.

Collections

Although having a clearly stated mission and an organizational structure capable of carrying it out were described earlier as essential prerequisites to a successful, effective, and efficient program of library resources and services, the first things that one generally looks to when reviewing, evaluating, or analyzing a library are the size, adequacy, and accessibility of its collections.

Collection size and adequacy are measured in several ways: in absolute numbers (how many titles, how many volumes, how many current periodical subscriptions, how much is spent on new titles and subscriptions each year), in relative terms (how do the holdings of, and additions to, library A compare to those of libraries B, C, and D), and in terms of accepted standards (to what extent do the holdings and growth figures of library A meet the standards recommended by various entities). Collection accessibility is determined by bibliographical access through catalogs, indexes, and guides describing holdings, as well as physical access as measured by hours of service, use of open and closed stacks, and dispersion or centralization of library service facilities on the university's campus.

In evaluating a library's collection by size the absolute numbers are not significant in and of themselves. It is not until one begins comparing the sizes of holdings or additions between libraries, or between what is held and what is purchased by each to what is being published each year, that the numbers begin to take on meaning. Even then, one must be careful to take into consideration such factors as rates of publishing in different disciplines and during different periods of time, numbers of students and faculty being served, the scope and variety of academic programs being supported, and levels of research conducted at an institution.

Works looked at sizes of libraries and rates of growth and compared them among the institutions studied. His survey noted that the younger universities spent proportionately more of their total budgets on building their library collections than the older universities. The changes in emphasis from instruction to research that had occurred at many of the institutions included in the survey over the preceding decades had stimulated a demand for a greater variety of book titles, some duplication of heavily used titles, and a greater reliance on periodical literature. The number of periodicals being published had increased significantly at the same time as there were dramatic increases in the prices of individual subscriptions.

Works urged library administrators to maintain more accurate documentation of library resources and operations and to standardize terminology in describing what was being documented. Once resources and activities had been adequately documented, it would be possible to determine the relative extents to which libraries met the requirements of their users.

Works also observed that gifts no longer played the key role they once had in collection development. Unlike university libraries of earlier eras, the libraries of the 1920s did not rely heavily on gifts and donations for collection growth. At all of the institutions studied, general institutional or library funds had become the primary source for the acquisition of new library materials.

Although Works stressed that the university administrations should determine priorities and identify areas of concentration for research and instruction, he also maintained that the librarians, rather than the classroom faculty, should be ultimately responsible for the day-to-day selection of new material and for long-term collection development.

The U.S. Office of Education study encountered the same inadequacy of documentation in evaluating library collections, and expressed the same concern about the need for the development of standards for evaluating collections as Works. However, it placed greater emphasis on the quality of collections than on quantity, and it included in its measurement of quality the extent to which collections were used (accessibility). In discussing the "usability of libraries" it described use of books as "the sole purpose of libraries" (ibid., pp. 616–48). It went on to outline ways of measuring use of libraries and methods of facilitating use by increasing levels of bibliographic and physical accessibility. The measurements of use included the proportion of students using the library, the number of books borrowed for home reading as opposed to overnight (reserve) use, amount of assigned reading, use shown by books borrowed from other libraries, and the ratio between library seating capacity and numbers of students served.

The Office of Education survey advocated increasing bibliographic accessibility by use of standardized cataloging systems, instruction in use of catalogs and other bibliographic tools, and greater use of interlibrary lending and borrowing agreements. Collections were evaluated based on the number of volumes added per year by purchase (not including gifts), by holdings of "typical" volumes in various subject areas, by subscriptions to current periodicals, and by holdings of scientific sets. Other factors that might be included were loans from other libraries, gifts received, books withdrawn or discarded, exchange relationships with other institutions and organizations, and policies regarding handling of duplicates.

The Office of Education report also suggested that all instructors should see that needed material in their respective areas were available. However, the librarians rather than classroom instructors should be responsible for allocating acquisition funds and for overall material selection and collection development.

The survey's overall recommendations regarding collections were that librarians should (1) pay more attention to the individual reader in order to see that he or she obtains needed material, (2) make additional studies of the use of libraries—especially of failures to obtain adequate service—and (3) relate total library expenditures for material to the number of students served (a minimum of $10 per student was suggested as a beginning).

It is noteworthy that the founding of the Graduate Library School at the University of Chicago, the establishment of the Association of Research Libraries, and the Association of College and Reference Libraries in the American Library Association, along with the increased interest in academic library support by foundations, all occurred shortly after the release of the Works and later the U.S. Office of Education studies. Each was a factor in developing professional standards by which libraries, and library resources and services, could be analyzed and evaluated.

Erickson's study of library surveys by outside experts showed that only 7.9 percent of the recommendations dealt with collections or resources for study and research. The surveyors tended to agree that collections should be large enough to support the institutions' curricular and research needs, should be relevant to the specific areas of academic activity emphasized by the universities, and adequate according to the standards developed by scholars, library professional organizations, and the educational accrediting agencies. The recommendations addressed themselves to how these ends could be more effectively accomplished and how progress toward meeting them could be measured, rather than whether the goals were valid.

The self-studies that libraries conducted during the 1950s and 1960s also tended to accept the traditional positions on collection size, adequacy, and accessibility. They focused on how financial and other resources could be most effectively used to build collections, and on how collections could be evaluated to determine adequacy based on available standards. Because Kemper's study was a systems study rather than a library survey, and because he was interested in theoretical bases for management decisions employing strategic planning, he looked at how libraries planned collection development, and how they determined satisfactory levels of service rather than the actual size, adequacy, or accessibility of collections. The Booz, Allen and Hamilton study was a management study that also concentrated on how goals were determined, how decisions were made, and on how resources were dispersed, rather than on the extent to which specific objectives were accomplished.

However, both the Kemper study and the Booz, Allen and Hamilton study endorsed the earlier recommendations that collections be evaluated based on absolute and relative sizes, growth rates, expressed needs of users, and professionally determined minimal standards. Collection development policies should be formalized and should monitor changes in both the academic programs of an institution and in publishing trends in the various disciplines. Acquisitions funds should be allocated based on objective criteria derived from analyses of predetermined collection needs.

Services

A second area to be considered in an analysis or evaluation of a college or university library system, after its collections, is its services. The emphases have changed over the years, along with philosophies of service, perceptions of user needs, and the resources and technology available to meet them. Theories of organizational development and concepts of how organizations should mobilize their resources in pursuit of goals and objectives have also matured and become more responsive to the needs of both clientele and personnel.

The two primary service areas in a library are technical services and reader services. Technical services are those operations by which a library selects, orders, receives, pays for, catalogs, processes, stores, and repairs or preserves its information resource material. Reader services are those operations by which the staff of the library provide physical access to the resource material and assist library patrons in its use.

Approximately one-third of the 775 recommendations recorded in Erickson's study of library surveys dealt with technical and reader services; 71.4 percent of the recommendations were implemented in whole or in part by the time of the report. The library surveys recommended centralization of operations, standardization of procedures, formalization of policies for greater efficiency, and documentation of work performed—for later analysis and evaluation.

In technical services, libraries were encouraged to centralize the selection, ordering, and receiving of library materials, as well as the financial accounting associated with these operations. They were encouraged to apply uniform professionally determined criteria and standards for the cataloging and classification of material (including the purchase of Library of Congress catalog cards when possible) and to initiate and participate in cooperative cataloging programs. They were encouraged to formalize and document policies and procedures to assist in staff training and to assure consistency and continuity over time.

In reader services recommendations encouraged centralization of circulation records, standardization of loan policies, more comprehensive documentation of circulation activities, greater use of microform resources, and more active participation in interlibrary loan agreements. In reference work libraries were encouraged to provide professional help whenever public service desks were open, to push for longer hours of service, and to initiate or build upon library instruction programs to help library patrons make more effective use of the resources available.

In 1970 the Booz, Allen and Hamilton report emphasized the importance of applying appropriate electronic data processing and computer technology in all areas where routine repetitive tasks could be handled more efficiently by machines than human beings. It also stressed the importance of interinstitutional cooperation in all areas in which sharing skills, expertise, and resources could result in greater efficiency and less cost per institution through a pooling of efforts.

Personnel

Personnel was a third important *Resources and Services* area covered in the source documents. Studies of personnel generally dealt with the numbers of professional and support staff employed by the libraries relative to the number of students and faculty served, the ratio of professional to nonprofessional staff, the kinds and levels of training or experience required for each group, and the status of librarians relative to faculty and other professional employees of the universities. As illustrated in Chapter 3, the early librarians were usually members of the faculty who assumed responsibility for the libraries as an extra assignment. Librarianship as a distinct profession did not emerge until late in the nineteenth century when university libraries became large enough and comprehensive enough to warrant full-time, professionally trained staffing.

In 1927 George Works warned against over reliance on student assistance in the operation of university libraries and also warned against the libraries being used as a haven for the incompetent or "persons who have grown old in the service of the university" but cannot afford to retire (Works, 1927, p. 34). The need for a clear distinction between professional and support functions is emphasized in all of the source documents along with statements about the importance of establishing minimal educational requirements, staff development, continuing education, and formal criteria for appointment, tenure, and promotion of librarians. A delineation of the differences between the professional responsibilities of librarians and the functions of nonprofessional support staff was considered essential to protecting the status of librarians within the academic community. The earlier studies were concerned with having librarianship established and recognized as an accepted professional academic endeavor comparable to research and teaching, thus the emphasis on minimal educational requirements for librarians and appropriate training or experience. The Works survey, the U.S. Office of Education survey, and the individual surveys included in Erickson's study all showed great concern that librarians be perceived as professionals, receive salaries comparable with classroom faculty, and not suffer significant differences in fringe benefits (vacations, retirement provisions, eligibility for sabbatical leaves, access to research and travel funds, etc.).

The early surveys saw responsibility for collection development as a key issue between librarians and classroom faculty and an important factor in establishing the librarian's credibility as a scholar. They therefore recommended that librarians, the bibliographic experts, be recognized as such and be given the ultimate responsibility for material selection wherever they did not already have it. In view of the current volume of publishing in an era of the information explosion, it is hard to imagine nonlibrarians feeling competent to monitor the avalanche of new publications, or feeling current in mastering new information resources in electronic formats.

Kemper's work and the Booz, Allen and Hamilton report tended to be less defensive about the status of librarians and to focus on how staffing patterns and personnel policies and practices could be used to enhance professionalism and to simultaneously make the libraries more efficient, effective, and responsive organizations. Both advocated written position descriptions that clearly defined the duties and responsibilities of each individual, delineations between professional and nonprofessional support activities, and provisions for professional development and career advancement.

The Booz, Allen and Hamilton report specifically pointed to a need for more middle management positions to handle increasingly specialized areas of work. This could legitimately lead to an increased reliance on non-MLS professionals in finance and accounting, staff development and personnel administration, systems analysis and data processing, and fundraising. These are all areas in which the report identified a need to train or hire personnel to make better use of resources and technology. Both reports also called for job enhancement and greater responsibility for support staff in the rapidly changing technological environments.

Physical Facilities—Buildings and Equipment

The fourth *Resources and Services* area is facilities, specifically buildings and equipment. All of the source documents tended to be rather general in dealing with the issue. The primary concern was for the adequacy of facilities. While the Works study recommended "adequate" space and seating for students, the U.S. Office of Education survey defined adequacy by recommending that there be a ratio among the number of students to be served, the number of seats available, and the number of square feet per student a library contained. A standard of seating for 20 percent of the student enrollment and an overall ratio of 20 square feet per student was suggested.

The Office of Education survey also recommended that adequacy be determined by a library building's total storage capacity, its potential to accommodate future growth, and the extent to which it provided facilities or rooms for special purposes, such as individual and group study. Adequacy of library facilities also took into consideration the physical relationships between branch and department libraries and the central library building, and the extent to which the service patterns they fostered facilitated or frustrated students' use of libraries. The Office of Education survey concluded with a set of eleven recommendations regarding buildings, including one urging institutions that had not built buildings in the ten years preceding the study to examine their facilities in light of the standards cited in order to determine adequacy.

Erickson's study of surveys found that 76 or 9.8 percent of the 775 recommendations compiled dealt with buildings. These primarily addressed institution-specific building problems, but supported the overall position of the Office of Education survey in determining adequacy of library facilities and how it could be achieved. Comfort of facilities addresses the issues of physical accessibility, lighting, heating, ventilation, and so forth. Comfort had become an issue because the earliest university libraries included only the bare necessities and were not meant as places where students could study. Harvard University announced the introduction of artificial lighting in the Gore Hall library in 1895 (Hamlin, 1981, p. 50). This enabled the library to offer services beyond the daylight hours for the first time in its more than 250-year history.

The evolution of the university library from the small private collections reserved for faculty consultation to the multimillion volume research collections supporting the full academic spectrum necessitated a major change in attitude about the function of the library in the university, a change in attitude about what constituted "adequate" facilities, and a change in attitude about the role comfort of facilities should play in determining adequacy.

The physical facility requirements of the modern university library go far beyond those addressed by the early surveys. In addition to seating capacities, storage capacities, total space, and the provision of space for special functions, "adequacy" now includes comfort and safety of facilities, the extent to which buildings protect and preserve collections (temperature, humidity, and air pollution controls), the extent to which they provide access to materials by the handicapped, and the extent to which they house and provide access to such nonbook information resources as microforms, machine readable data, compact disk and video technology, electronic online data bases, and computer software.

Before the Kemper study and the Booz, Allen and Hamilton study, the source documents discussed here focused on the amounts and relationships of space. Although making no specific recommendations about buildings, space, or comfort of facilities, these two studies recommended treating facilities as any other management issue. Library administrators or planners should identify problems, determine alternative solutions, weigh relative costs of options, relate options to overall library and institutional priorities, and select courses of action to pursue.

The Booz, Allen and Hamilton report recommended space utilization analyses to maximize efficient use of existing space, to document the need for additional space where appropriate, and to provide guidance in determining how new space could be most effectively incorporated into a library's overall operational program. It also urged library administrators to be cognizant of emerging information technologies and to equip their facilities to make full use of them for both administrative and public service functions. The report suggests that library planners should view library facilities in the same light as other resources and services. Problems with buildings and equipment ought to be addressed in the same way as other problems. Thanks to the work of the ARL Office of Management Studies, and of professional organizations such as ACRL, a great deal of information is available about how different institutions have addressed these problems. A corps of library facilities planners has been developed that is adept at developing solutions to specific building problems based on the individual circumstances of almost any situation. The expertise has also been developed to plan and implement the integration of changing information technology into the operational program of any library.

General Financial Support

The fifth area under *Resources and Services* is general financial support. As seen in Chapter 2 in the discussion of the development of the university library, financial support for libraries and library services was generally not a high priority for university administrators until the mid-nineteenth century. The early university libraries were begun with donations of books or donations of funds to purchase books, and staffing was minimal and voluntary or lent by other offices or academic departments.

By 1925 Works observed that the libraries had assumed a more important role in the universities as evidenced by the amounts of money appropriated for library books and for librarians' salaries. By then gifts were no longer the major source of library material. Institutional funds had taken over the major responsibility for collection growth. In fact, it had been the concern that university libraries should play an even larger role, as expressed by the university presidents through the Association of American Universities, which led to the commissioning of Works' study. Individually and as a group the universities had dramatically increased the levels of funding for library materials and services; however, there appeared to be some question about how adequate the resources were, how efficiently the funds were being used, and whether the libraries were achieving the universities' information resource support goals.

Adequacy and efficient use of financial resources were also key issues in the U.S. Office of Education study in 1930. Again, the study was a part of a larger survey of land grant colleges and universities; however, the concern about the adequacy of financial support for libraries was a legitimate one, and the study group dealt with it appropriately.

The report listed "adequate financial support" as one of its necessary conditions for meeting the "Requirements for Good Library Service." It said adequacy could be determined by examining what the library budgets included, who prepared budgets, how growth in library expenditures correlated with institutional growth, expenditures per student, proportion of an institution's total budget allocated to the library, need for and use of library fees, and distribution of library expenditures among disciplines. It summarized its findings with a recommendation that universities should allocate a minimum of 4 percent of their total budgets to their libraries and that their expenditures for libraries should be an average of at least $20 per student (U.S. Office of Education, 1930, p. 714).

In a 1947 study of the results of library surveys Louis Wilson found that the libraries which had surveys done between 1939 and 1946 experienced increases in support immediately after the surveys. "It may not be correct to attribute the results entirely to the effect of the surveys since libraries, like other human institutions, are subject to many influences" (Wilson, 1947, p. 372).

Erickson noted a similar increase in financial support for libraries after the surveys by outside experts. However, he observed that a concern about adequacy of financial support, efficiency in the administration of funds, and a decision to increase funding may have been causes as often as results of surveys. The surveys reviewed tended to focus on how institutional funds for libraries were administered and by whom rather than where funds ought to come from. Seventy of the 775 recommendations recorded (9.0%) in Erickson's review dealt with financial administration. They fell into three groups: (1) those pertaining to actual budget needs; (2) those concerning budget procedures and the allocation of book funds; and (3) those recommending the central administration of all funds expended for library purposes (Erickson, 1961, p. 84).

By the time of Kemper's work on strategic planning in library systems in 1967, significant amounts of money had become available for academic library facilities, resources, and services from government agencies, foundations, and corporations, as well as the traditional private philanthropists. Therefore it had become important to incorporate accessibility to external funding into a library's planning priorities along with the continuing concern with the efficient administration of institutional funds.

Kemper maintained that the best way for a library to tap these newly available funds, or even to increase levels of ongoing institutional funding, was to present proposals that had been developed as a part of strategic planning efforts based on the model he described. The key elements in the model included the following:

* establishing general objectives
* identifying the environment (external, internal, and institutional)
* forecasting the environment
* establishing specific objectives
* evaluating, selecting, and deciding on alternatives
* designing a plan of action
* gaining formal approval (including funding)

Libraries that were able to articulate their objectives, to document their needs, to demonstrate that they had reviewed alternative approaches, and developed comprehensive plans of action as prescribed in the strategic planning model would be in a more competitive position to receive greater institutional support and external funding than those which could not.

The extreme frustrations of university librarians and university administrators in trying to meet the heightened expectations of academic libraries in the late 1960s were closely associated with the financial resources available to libraries, how effectively they were being utilized, and where they should come from. The concern had expanded beyond how best to administer institutional library funds seen in the surveys reviewed by Erickson, to how to identify significant amounts of external funding to provide resources and services beyond those the institution could or would support.

The Booz, Allen and Hamilton report identified financing as one of the eight major problem areas facing university libraries in 1970. It attributed this to "a disparity of expectations . . . between the university library and the university administration" and to the fact that "university libraries, to an increasing extent, are required to seek alternative sources of funding."

A lack of communications and understanding often exists between university presidents and librarians on the magnitude of the financial difficulties confronting higher education and their implications for future financial support of the library.

University presidents stress that libraries cannot expect financial support to continue at past levels which enabled some libraries to double in size over a decade. They believe that libraries can be more responsive to opportunities to effect cost savings through increased interlibrary cooperation, applications of new technology, and selectivity in acquisitions.

In contrast, many librarians indicate that university presidents do not appreciate fully the cost and operational difficulties inherent in moving more quickly in such fields. Also, librarians believe that the presidents are not fully cognizant of the dimensions of the operating realities of the library, including the problems involved in meeting faculty and student expectations for services within existing resources. (Booz, Allen and Hamilton, Inc., 1970, p. 35–36)

The report's major recommendation on financing was that increased emphasis be given to the pursuit of additional sources of financial support for university libraries. In addition to the federal government, which had become increasingly involved in developing bibliographic resources and supporting cooperative resource sharing arrangements, the report suggested private philanthropy, foundations, state governments, and the imposition of fees and royalties for special services.

Another approach called for the maintenance of cost data documenting the efficiency of operations and attributing extra costs to specific services (advanced programs in specific disciplines, special projects, support for institutional noninstructional research—costs of supporting grant-funded research projects). This approach, along with the use of objective criteria (numbers of students, programs, levels of research conducted at the university) for determining appropriate levels of support, would strengthen the librarian's position in seeking institutional funds through annual budget requests and support efforts to obtain external funds through fees, contracts, grants, or endowments.

The planning studies and management studies that have followed the Booz, Allen and Hamilton report have all taken into consideration the efficient utilization of institutional funds, the documentation of costs of providing resources and services, and the potential for finding new funds based on the needs and priorities of the institutions and the availability of alternative sources. The basic elements of good planning are integral parts of finding workable solutions and considering viable alternatives to the existing financial circumstances in which university libraries find themselves. The funding criteria introduced in the earliest studies, and refined in later works, are still useful tools for developing and implementing comprehensive fiscal plans.

Use of Contemporary Technology and Management Systems

Recommendations that contemporary technology and new management systems be applied in the operation of libraries are almost universal in library management studies, evaluations by library experts, self-studies, and master plans. Chapter 3 in this book, Planning in Academic Libraries–Historical Review, describes G. Edward Evans's portrayal of the history of the application of management theory to libraries and the three periods into which he divides the movement: (1) before 1937 (based on the classic bureaucratic model), (2) the scientific management period, 1937–1955, and (3) the human relations period, 1955–1976. The recommendations of the earlier studies appear to follow this pattern. The classic bureaucratic model seemed to be the base for many of the recommendations included in the Works report (1927) and the U.S. Office of Education report (1930).

Works suggested that the libraries he studied standardize methods of record keeping and develop common terminology to describe the transactions documented by these records. He found it impossible to compare resources, services, or the efficiency of library operations among the institutions studied when different terms were used to describe the same resource or transaction, or the same terms meant different things at different institutions and at different points in time.

Works's initial commission from the Association of American Universities was to conduct a study of college and university library problems from 1875–1925. The problem of gathering and analyzing comparable data for the institutions was so great that the scope of the study was reduced—first to 1900–1925 and finally to 1910–1925—in order to make observations more meaningful to those receiving the report. Works said that the establishment of common terminology would be essential for the study, evaluation, and comparison of library resources and services among institutions. The Office of Education survey came to the same conclusions in 1930 and suggested definitions for some of the more widely used terms, based on existing practices. Both surveys discussed the need for applying the principles of good personnel administration to libraries. These included the development of specific job descriptions, classification of positions, defining of levels of responsibility, distinguishing between professional and support activities, recommending planned staffing patterns, and imposing a requirement that librarians have the experience and meet the educational qualifications appropriate to the responsibilities they were to assume within the universities.

The Office of Education survey went even further than Works's survey by recommending that librarians conduct formal studies of library use, "especially failures of students and faculty to obtain adequate services." It recommended statistical studies of the efficiency of library operations and studies of the factors that "affect present development" and influence future growth (U.S. Office of Education, 1930, p. 712).

The report singled out library education as both a major area in need of attention and an area that could help librarians develop the management skills needed to maximize the effective utilization of personnel and other resources. It recommended a different type of library school program emphasizing

business methods, literature of subject areas, objective methods in determination of library needs and future library development, including tests on use of books, methods for determination of most valuable periodical publications, and place of reading in instructional work in various departments. (Ibid., p. 692)

Evans characterized the period from 1937 to 1955 as the scientific management period of library administration. The library surveys by outside experts studied by Wilson (1940–46) and Erickson (1938–52) picked up on the theme of applying research tools and scientific management to the operation of libraries suggested by the Office of Education report and expanded upon it.

The surveys Wilson and Erickson studied called for the application of the principles of personnel administration current in the 1930s and 1940s. They called for more specific classification of personnel, development of hierarchies of positions with associates and assistants with prescribed responsibilities and spans of control. They called for the standardization of cataloging and classification work in technical services. Ordering, receiving, cataloging, and processing of library materials within the universities were to be centralized in the libraries for greater efficiency. Libraries were encouraged to use Library of Congress cataloging copy whenever it was available and to reclassify according to the LC system in order to make greater use of shared resources. All record-keeping files were to be reviewed, and duplicate or unnecessary files eliminated. Where decentralized libraries with branches or departmental libraries existed, they were urged to develop union catalogs of university holdings and to develop central serial record files to maximize centralization of operations and minimize duplication of effort.

Although the outside experts did not go so far as to develop one best way of performing library operations as would have been the case under strict scientific management as advocated by Frederick W. Taylor, they did recommend that operations be studied and that more efficient processes and procedures be identified and implemented. The experts also recommended the development of objective criteria for the allocation of book funds that would take into account such factors as relative costs of publications in different subject areas, levels of research supported by an institution, sizes of enrollment in various disciplines, and the availability of resources through interinstitutional agreements within a state or region.

With Kemper's work, the approach to addressing library management problems shifted from specific recommendations on specific issues of concern to the development of processes to handle library management in general. In advocating the application of new technology and new management systems, Kemper, Booz, Allen and Hamilton, and Webster were not recommending specific solutions to specific problems, but rather the development of comprehensive new approaches to library management that would take into account developments in organization theory, management theory, and planning theory.

Kemper's strategic planning model required that library planners, managers, and administrators establish general objectives for their organizations based on an awareness of the environment, which included knowledge of the library's assets, liabilities, and areas of strength; the institution's priorities for library development; and the potential for support and development from the larger society in which both the institution and the library must function.

Booz, Allen and Hamilton expanded upon Kemper's strategic planning model by identifying eight "problem" areas in the management of university libraries in the 1960s and recommending how new management systems and computer technology could be used to accomplish goals and bring about desired change. Although the report emphasized new management systems, it also relied heavily on the ability of computer technology to assume a larger role in the operations of libraries. It recommended the use of online bibliographic utilities for shared cataloging and later shared acquisitions, serials, and periodicals records control; local computers for online catalogs, circulation systems, and internal administrative operations; and greater use of online electronic data bases for remote access and use of both numerical and bibliographic data.

Webster's writings followed up on the Booz, Allen and Hamilton recommendations regarding management systems and provided the apparatus, through the Association of Research Libraries' Office of Management Studies, for university librarians to operationalize the recommendations. The studies of university libraries in the early 1970s at Cornell, Columbia, Stanford, and the Universities of Michigan and Chicago, described in Chapter 4 of this book, were individual attempts to document the current status of library management and to determine the best ways to change the systems to more effectively address problems, taking advantage of new management systems and new technologies. The Management Review and Analysis Program (MRAP) and subsequent

Academic Library Programs (ALP), Systems and Procedures Exchange Center program, organizational training and staff development programs, and Applied Research and Development Programs were all efforts to build upon the experiences of individual libraries; to disseminate information on the application of management systems and technologies to academic library operations; and to develop a corps of library management experts capable of sustaining the effort in the future.

Interinstitutional Cooperation

Another approach to individual library problems is Interlibrary cooperation, which is almost universally recommended in library evaluations and in management and planning studies. Interlibrary cooperation is a way of reinforcing and sharing the strengths of superior libraries and a way of complementing and supplementing the resources and services available through less well-endowed libraries.

George Works discussed the benefits of interlibrary cooperation, especially at the more advanced levels of research, at length in his 1927 study. Although it is understood that every university library is responsible for meeting the basic instructional and curricular needs of its parent institution, and for supporting some faculty research, Works asked whether it was "necessary or possible for all universities to be all things to all advanced students?" He said it would be better for libraries to concentrate on building in their areas of strength, those areas in which they could make the best use of their personnel and material resources, and to refer advanced students and faculty to other libraries for research material in those areas in which their holdings were, by intent, only adequate for basic needs.

Works went on to describe specific ways in which cooperation between libraries could be beneficial to all participants. Examples included the preparation of union lists of serials, participation in interlibrary lending agreements, publication of bibliographies of holdings, exchange of photocopies of material upon request, and participation in coordinated collection development agreements. He cited existing relationships between Stanford University and the University of California, the University of Michigan and the Detroit Public Library, and Columbia University and the New York Public Library as models for examination.

The U.S. Office of Education study also advocated greater cooperation among libraries but with a more specific objective. A part of the mandate to the land grant colleges was to provide educational facilities and research support to the public at large. Therefore the land grant colleges and universities were responsible not only for satisfying the needs of their students and faculty, but also for addressing the educational and research needs of the cities, towns, and regions in which they were located. Thus cooperation with other college and university libraries, as well as with public libraries and local and regional government agencies, should already have been an integral part of each library's public service program. The Office of Education report underscored the obligation of each land grant college or university to participate in providing library resources and services to the local community, the state, and the region.

The library expert surveys of 1938–52 usually contained a separate chapter on integration and cooperation, which discussed problems involved in the "integration of the library into the academic community and in making the influence of the library felt at the state, regional, and national levels through co-operative ventures" (Erickson, 1961, p. 59).

Erickson found that the recommendations were divided into two groups: those dealing with integration and cooperation on the local level, and those dealing with cooperation on a state, regional, and national level. Integration at the local level usually consisted of recommendations for instructing potential patrons (whether students or others) on use of the library, and of publishing handbooks describing library facilities, resources, and services. Recommendations on the integration of libraries into the local community also dealt with the coordination of member libraries within a college or university library system. Recommendations on cooperation on a state, regional, or national level were confined to programs of cooperative acquisitions and exchanges of published bibliographies and participation in state extension services through interlibrary loans or the granting of special borrowing privileges.

The library expert surveys did not press for interinstitutional cooperation as strongly as either the Works or the Office of Education report had, but Erickson reports that even these relatively mild recommendations met with little success. Of the fifty-three recommendations made on integration and cooperation (6.8% of the total), only twenty-eight were achieved in any degree. "It has been clearly evident in this chapter that the libraries enjoyed small success in carrying out the recommendations made by surveyors concerning matters of integration and cooperation, particularly at the state, regional, and national levels" (ibid., p. 63).

By the end of the sixties the environment for interlibrary cooperation had changed considerably, reverting back to the position advocated by George Works in 1927. The social changes of the preceding decade, and the escalation of demands for a greater number and greater variety of library resources and services, coupled with unprecedented infusions of funds from private, institutional, and government sources, forced library administrators to consider all ways of maximizing the effective utilization of resources to satisfy needs. The answer to Works's question of whether it was necessary or possible for all university libraries to be all things to all advanced students had become a definite "no."

Kemper described the development of interlibrary cooperation as

one of the most powerful forces operating in the library environment today. This development is particularly strong in the complex urban areas. The number and size of cooperative library systems has shown a substantial increase. It is certain that these trends will continue. Library cooperation adds a degree of complexity to planning at the local level. (Kemper, 1970, p. 230)

He referred to the development of more rigorous accreditation standards, the influx of federal funds, recognition of the need for and support of developing library systems, library surveys, and programs of statewide library planning as factors that contributed to the heightened awareness of the need for more interlibrary cooperation. Kemper's strategic planning model incorporates interlibrary cooperation as an integral factor in all aspects of library planning: in establishing goals, in identifying environmental forces that define and limit library activities, in evaluating and selecting alternatives, in selecting specific objectives, in designing strategic plans of action, in gaining formal approval, and in implementing change.

The Booz, Allen and Hamilton report expanded on the theme of interlibrary cooperation as an integral part of addressing the problems of university library management. Problems related to interinstitutional arrangements were cited as one of the eight major categories identified. The report stated that inadequate priority was being accorded the strengthening of interinstitutional linkages among libraries, and that university libraries and university officials lacked adequate information on the impact of interinstitutional library arrangements on university costs and the work of individual scholars (Booz, Allen and Hamilton, Inc., 1970, p. 37–38).

The report recognized existing interlibrary arrangements such as interlibrary loan agreements, use of Library of Congress cataloging data, reciprocal borrowing privileges for faculty and graduate students, the Center for Research Libraries' program of joint acquisitions and common storage of little-used and expensive materials, participation in regional bibliographic centers, resource sharing between units of multicampus state university systems, and participation in electronically linked regional networks. However, it characterized these as inadequate in the face of existing demands. "Rising library costs, continuing expansion and duplication of collections at increasing rates, and the growing sophistication and specialization of the information needs of scholars combine to create a greater need for interinstitutional cooperation and planning among libraries" (ibid., p. 37). While not recommending any specific action to library administrators, the report did urge the Association of Research Libraries and the American Council on Education to sponsor research designed to define new approaches to and requirements for interinstitutional cooperation.

Although there have been periodic changes in emphasis, interlibrary cooperation has been a consistent theme in all of the source documents. Many of the earlier proposals may have been overly optimistic about institutions' willingness to share resources or provide access to their services. The current awareness of libraries' mutual interdependence has brought about a recognition that no institution can satisfy all of its users' needs. Well thought out, properly structured cooperative arrangements can complement the resources of strong libraries and provide access to resources and services otherwise unavailable to patrons of less comprehensive ones. Smaller libraries on the other hand can supplement the resources of larger ones by contributing to the regional availability of resources and by providing access to specialized materials that are too expensive or too infrequently used to warrant duplication of purchase by several institutions.

Present computer technology provides the capability to develop and implement comprehensive interlibrary cooperative arrangements unimaginable in the past. Any library plan must take into consideration the present and future potential advantages of interlibrary cooperation and make them an integral part of all decisions.

Administrative Relationship of the Library to University Administration

The administrative relationship of the university library to the rest of the university is another important factor in analyzing university library management. That relationship helps define the library's relative importance to the university and influences perceptions of its role in the overall educational process. Library planners, surveyors, and evaluators from the Works study on have discussed the importance of the administrative relationship between the library and the university administration and between the university librarian and the university president.

In the early universities where the president was, in effect, THE administration, there was frequently a direct personal relationship between the librarian and the president. As the universities became larger, and administrative staffs developed, the relationship became more and more distant. By the time of the Works study, although presidents still maintained a strong interest in their libraries, there was little active, daily involvement in the libraries' administration.

Library planners, surveyors, and evaluators have sought to define the proper relationship between the university librarian, the university president, and other officers of university administration. Every study included in this review recommended centralization of the responsibility for library resources and services in the university librarian who would be responsible to the president, or the chief academic officer of the university. Notable exceptions to this overall policy were the fields of medicine and law, where the need for a certain degree of autonomy was recognized. All other orders for books and journals were to be channeled through the librarian, and he or she would be responsible for fiscal accounting and personnel administration related to providing university-wide library services. Funds for university-wide library support services were to be the province of the university librarian who would also be responsible for the allocation of these funds within the library.

Although departmental libraries and reading rooms or faculty personal collections and student libraries might be retained, they were either to be linked administratively into a university library system, or be denied institutional funds for their support and operation.

In discussing areas of responsibility, George Works emphasized the point that the university must define its areas of interest through the courses offered, research programs supported, and faculty appointments. However, the librarians should then determine how best to provide the necessary support, given the resources the university makes available. The U.S. Office of Education took the same position as Works with respect to the centralization of operations and responsibilities under one administrator. It also discussed the role the faculty library committee ought to play in advising the librarian.

With the publication of *The University Library: Its Organization, Administration, and Functions* by Louis R. Wilson and Maurice F. Tauber in 1945, the profession had a very specific statement of appropriate duties and responsibilities of the university librarian and of his or her relationships to university administrators, library administrators, teaching faculty, and library staff (Wilson and Tauber, 1945, pp. 105–41).

Many of the surveys studied by Erickson seem to have applied these statements on duties and responsibilities to the institutions studied, and to have made recommendations based on the extent to which they found the intent of the statements being met in the organization and operation of the libraries. Where it had not already been done, the surveys called for the formalization of the university librarians' status and their relationships to other university administrators, for the integration of librarians into the academic governance structures of the universities (faculty status), and outlined appropriate roles for faculty library committees and other advisory councils, and friends of the library groups.

Before Kemper introduced the theoretical approach to library planning, the conventional wisdom advocated autonomy for the university librarian in determining mission, goals, objectives, and priorities for the library. The strategic planning model brought a new dimension to the relationship between the library and its parent institution by urging that the parent institution be more specific in articulating its expectations of the library, that the library administrator be more involved in the development of institutional priorities which would determine library resource and service requirements, and that strategic plans incorporate these institutional priorities into the libraries' own goals, objectives, and considerations of environmental conditions.

Kemper identified inadequate knowledge of the university's goals and objectives, inadequate knowledge of changes in the university's priorities, an inability to communicate library objectives in terms that are meaningful and understandable to university administrators, and a lack of consensus on library objectives between university administrators and librarians as major obstacles to successful long-range library planning. His planning model attempted to overcome these obstacles by incorporating communication between university administration and library administration into a formal structure and by requiring institutional approval of library plans before implementation.

The Booz, Allen and Hamilton report identified the same deficiencies in many components needed for effective planning, an absence of clarity in defining university goals and objectives, and inadequate communications between university administrators and library administrators. In describing problems related to organization it found that "the top management group in the library often does not have clear or appropriate standing within the university's organizational structure (Booz, Allen and Hamilton, Inc., 1970, p. 31). The report recommended that the university president "involve the university librarian formally in the planning councils of the university" and that he or she "instruct the university officer responsible for planning to develop arrangements between the librarian and the university administration on policies and procedures to keep the librarian periodically informed of plans or changes in programs having a potential impact on the library" (ibid., p. 43–44).

The formal involvement of the university librarian in university planning would facilitate the reconciliation of library and university expectations about the scope of library resources, programs, and services required and lead to a greater degree of success in meeting expectations.

Webster's "Planning Aids for the University Library Director" (Webster, 1971) discussed the problems library directors confront in trying to plan, and outlined a planning process that might be used to address them. "Review of Planning Activities in Academic and Research Libraries" (ARL/OMS, 1972), reported on planning activities underway in academic libraries at the time and included a discussion of variations on the status of university librarians in the administrative structures of the institutions involved.

Both documents addressed the need for a thorough understanding of university goals, objectives, and priorities on the part of library planners, involvement of library administrators in determining them, and close coordination between university and library administrators in developing and implementing appropriate programs for providing library resources, services, and general support. The relationship between the library administration and the university administration, and the status of the university librarian within the university administration, are important factors that influence the amount of communication which goes on and the extent to which librarians are able to plan and implement appropriate programs of service.

Library Planning Systems

The source documents reviewed and discussed here present a wide range of recommendations on how college and university libraries could improve their facilities and services and make more effective use of resources. The earlier documents, from the Works report through Erickson's analysis of surveys, focused on specific problems and made specific recommendations on how they should be addressed. With Kemper's introduction of a theoretical framework and a strategic planning model, the emphasis shifted to the application of management theory to libraries and the development of management systems and processes for identifying problems and finding solutions. The development and implementation of comprehensive long-term plans is an integral part of the systems approach to library management advocated by the Kemper model, the Booz, Allen and Hamilton report, and the various programs developed by Webster and the ARL Office of Management Studies. Strategic library management planning is a key factor in developing and implementing the changes in organizational structure, management systems, and coordination of resources necessary to enable libraries to adapt to changing environments and continue to meet the needs of their constituencies.

This next section combines the philosophies of "good library service" and the attitudes about meeting the needs of library users advocated in the specific recommendations of the earlier documents with the theories and management concepts espoused in the later systems recommendations, to produce a set of criteria for evaluating library management plans and planning systems.

The section also describes basic requirements of library plans and planning systems, incorporating the library survey and library evaluation program elements described earlier in the chapter. The set of requirements can then be used in evaluating specific library plans and library planning systems. The underlying assumption is that plans which meet the basic requirements present a stronger case for support and have a greater chance of being successfully implemented and of solving the problems addressed. Basic requirements for college and university library plans and planning systems include the following:

- administrative support
- apparatus for assessing needs and weighing options
- mechanisms for establishing priorities and relating them to day-to-day activities
- management information systems
- formal planning documents—written plans
- programs of implementation and evaluation

Administrative Support

Perhaps the most basic prerequisite for a successful library planning effort is the support of the endeavor and involvement by the library director and top library administrative officers. Webster's "Planning Aids for the University Library Director" (Webster, 1971) describes measures library directors can take to encourage and support planning efforts.

Administrative support can be determined by an examination of the ways in which the planning effort is introduced to the library staff and to the university administration. A plan or a planning effort is not a solution to problems but a tool to be used to define specific problems and establish structures to help find solutions. Planning is also not a "one shot deal." Planning ought to be a continuous process that does not end with the development of a final document or written plan. It is a process that becomes an integral part of ongoing library administration.

Another way of measuring administrative support for planning is looking at the structure that is established to conduct the initial effort. The structure should include a formal planning committee including both top library administrators and representatives of the rank and file, with a specific charge and timetable. The planning committee should have adequate staff support and should include administrators who have library program development, implementation, and evaluation as a part of their ongoing responsibilities. It should also have the involvement of those responsible for budgeting and other resource allocation, and those familiar with the university's governance structure and its mission, goals, objectives, and priorities.

While the library director must lend his or her full support to the planning effort, it should be headed by some other member of the staff. Frequently an associate or assistant director, or the library's budget officer, can best serve in this capacity. It is important that the individual charged with coordinating planning activities have the quantitative skills required to identify, gather, maintain, analyze, and interpret the information required by the process. It would also be useful if the planning officer were also designated the library's representative in university planning activities. Where this is not practical, the library director must make sure the planning officer has adequate access to university planning information.

A third way of demonstrating administrative support for planning is the extent to which the planning officer and/or the planning committee is involved in the preparation of library budget requests. The budget system and the planning process should be integrated so that once goals and objectives have been determined, and priorities have been established, budget requests can be reviewed and evaluated based on the extent to which they reconcile the elements of the plan with the daily operations of the library. The integration of planning elements must occur in the budget requests of individual units, departments, and divisions, as well as on a library-wide basis.

Apparatus for Assessing Needs and Weighing Options

A second requirement of a good library planning system is the presence of an apparatus for assessing needs and weighing options. Before a planning effort is initiated there should be a realization or agreement that something has to be done, that there are goals and objectives not being met, or there are more efficient or effective ways of achieving ends. Kemper refers to this requirement as "a recognition of the need for change" (Kemper, 1970, p. 217).

The realization can be a spontaneous response to accumulated frustrations on the part of library staff or dissatisfaction on the part of library patrons or university administrators. It can be a reaction to either reductions or increases in resources available to support library operations. It can be the result of a deteriorating physical plant or overburdened service facilities, or a recognition of the obsolescence of the technologies being employed in providing services.

Once there is general recognition of the basic need for change, the need can be more clearly defined and addressed. The planning committee can coordinate the identification of specific deficiencies in operations or services based on the professional judgment of the librarians or the expectations of students, faculty, staff, or university administrators. The committee can then consider approaches to correcting deficiencies and review factors that affect options available. The process of considering approaches and reviewing factors affecting options is described in the source documents as "environmental analysis."

Factors to be considered may include the financial resources available from either institutional sources or external bodies (government agencies, individual benefactors, foundations, corporations, user fees), support for change in both the university and library administrations, technology available within the university and in the field of librarianship, expertise of existing staff and availability of outside experts or consultants, receptiveness of staff to innovative approaches to service, and condition of physical facilities, to mention just a few.

In 1927 Works discussed the potential benefits of interlibrary cooperation. Forty years later the Booz, Allen and Hamilton report again called for greater use of interinstitutional cooperative efforts for addressing library management problems, for sharing the costs and personnel effort required to find solutions, and for developing and implementing pilot programs to test these solutions.

There are many ways of assessing the needs of a library. An institution could conduct a comprehensive formal survey of staff and users, it could conduct an informal survey, or library planners and administrators could merely review annual and internal reports and identify areas of concern. The comprehensiveness of the assessment of needs should be related to the scope of the planning effort to be undertaken. A major planning effort needs thorough documentation. A less ambitious effort can be effective with a smaller, though still perceptive, investment in needs assessment. As an absolute minimum, a library plan ought to include a review of the history and background of the library and the institution and an overall statement of mission, goals, and objectives in order to place planning efforts into an institutional and historical context.

Mechanisms for Establishing Priorities and Relating Them to Day-to-Day Activities

A third requirement of a library plan or planning system is the development of mechanisms for establishing priorities, for incorporating them into the library management system, and for relating them to day-to-day activities. Once a need for change has been realized and options for change have been reviewed, priorities must be established among desired goals, and selections made from available options. The library must then reorganize and reallocate resources to implement the courses of action selected.

Kemper describes this process as "organizing for change." Webster refers to it as the development of unit programs within the overall library plan and the assignment of responsibilities in developing and implementing them. Erickson's study was an attempt to determine the extent to which recommendations contained in library surveys were implemented by the institutions studied and to see whether "the general library survey . . . is an effective instrument in bringing about results conducive to the growth and development of college and university libraries" (Erickson, 1961, p. 7).

Although there are many basic differences between the library surveys by outside experts discussed earlier and the library plans as described by Kemper or Webster, in both cases the successes of the efforts can best be measured by the extent to which recommendations or decisions about priorities are actually implemented and the extent to which they are incorporated into the ongoing operations of the libraries.

Booz, Allen and Hamilton also discuss the importance of having mechanisms for establishing priorities and the importance of integrating planning priorities and objectives into a library's regular budget process as a key factor in addressing the library management problems they identified.

Management Information Systems

In addition to having administrative support, an apparatus for the assessment of needs, and mechanisms for establishing priorities, a library planning system needs an information network to gather, store, analyze, and interpret data documenting library operations and services provided. A library needs a record-keeping system that documents use or nonuse of materials, levels of satisfaction or dissatisfaction, efficiency of operations, and relative effectiveness of various approaches to providing services. Such an information gathering and processing network is described as a management information system by Kemper, Webster, and Booz, Allen and Hamilton.

Both the Works and the U.S. Office of Education reports cited inadequacy of documentation and inconsistency of terminology as major obstacles to objective analyses of the libraries they studied in the 1920s (with the exception of institutions that had library training programs). All of the source documents emphasize the importance of maintaining records of operations and of documenting transactions, processes, and procedures for both day-to-day management purposes and for later review and analysis.

With the introduction of new technologies such as electronic data processing, and an emphasis on quantitative analysis, documentation of activities is an even more important basic essential for studying use of library resources and services, for measuring effectiveness of services, and for analyzing user satisfaction or dissatisfaction. Although the term *management information system* may sound sophisticated and technical, it only means that a library should document its transactions, be consistent in compiling documentation of operations, and periodically review the data in an effort to come to some conclusions about the efficiency and effectiveness of its operations as compared with other institutions, or with desired levels of achievement.

Formal Planning Documents—Written Plans

A successful planning effort must have a tangible result, something physical that can be seen, shown, studied, and responded to. In 1947 Louis R. Wilson wrote that surveys result in the development of "a program of action." The findings and recommendations of a survey provide a written set of specific actions a library can take to correct specific problems or improve levels of service. Supported by the credibility of the surveyors and with a favorable predisposition of the university administration, such findings and recommendations have a higher likelihood of being implemented than the same proposals might have had if generated by the library staff itself.

The reports of surveys by outside experts resulted in the publication of documents that could be circulated to university administrators and librarians. Recommendations could be pulled from the reports and developed into specific proposals for action and incorporated into budget requests. Erickson's study showed that improvements packaged in this way were very successful, especially immediately after the surveys. Tauber discussed the importance of having a written document to serve as a guide in the development of specific projects to bring about improvements in services. Kemper said that the recommendations and proposals for improvement resulting from surveys and self-studies ought to be comprehensive. They should address specific problems as a part of the overall system, and their potential benefits should be viewed in a larger context than solving single problems. Booz, Allen and Hamilton also stressed the importance of comprehensiveness in developing recommendations and implementing change, and the importance of considering the system-wide ramifications of changes in any area.

Successful library plans are those that can be easily translated into specific goals and objectives to be addressed by each unit of the library and that can be related to existing or anticipated budgeting programs. Library strategic plans ought to stimulate unit strategic plans that are realistic and achievable. Once all participants in the plan see their individual contributions and the benefits to be derived from its success, implementation takes on greater meaning. "All participants" includes not only the library administration and staff; it also includes faculty, students, and university administrators.

Library plans and proposals for change must also be flexible; they must consider alternative approaches to specific problems and be open to periodic revisions based on changing circumstances, resources, personnel, successes or failures in meeting goals in many areas, or technology.

Programs of Implementation and Evaluation

The final, and perhaps most important, requirement of a "good" library plan is the provision for a program of implementation and evaluation. Once the need for change has been recognized and the administrative support for a planning effort has been obtained, and after priorities have been established and related to day-to-day operations with appropriate written documentation and information management systems, attention ought to move to mechanisms for implementation and evaluation of the plan.

It is at the stage of implementation and evaluation that many plans falter. An unrealistic ambitious plan is doomed before it can be begun. Those responsible for implementation must prioritize goals, set timetables, assign responsibility for each goal, and define criteria for evaluation. The comprehensiveness of the plan is important because progress or lack of progress in one area will affect the achievement of goals in other areas. Also, unexpected successes or failures in one area may require modifications or total revisions of goals in related areas. The flexibility built into the system must allow for intermediate revision of specific goals in order to increase the prospects of meeting the overall objectives of the planning effort.

Planning decisions must be tied to budgeting decisions, be revised based on availability of resources, personnel, technology, and be coordinated with activities in related areas of work. Planning decisions must also be responsive to possible changes in library or institutional goals and must accommodate the plan to the changes. The planning effort must include built-in monitoring systems that indicate how effectively goals are being met. Annual progress reviews and updates in the total plan are helpful.

REVIEW OF LIBRARY PLANNING COMPONENTS

The focus of this chapter has been on the library survey and library planning source documents summarized in the preceding chapters, and the basic library planning program components developed from the review. It is argued that each of these seven elements ought to be considered in a library planning document, be addressed in developing a library planning system, and be incorporated in a planning process being implemented by an organization. These elements are

1. statements of goals and objectives;
2. responsive, functional, organizational structures;
3. evaluations of resources and services, including: collections, reader and technical services, personnel, physical facilities, and general financial support;
4. use of contemporary technology and information management systems;
5. extent of interinstitutional cooperation;
6. examinations of the administrative relationship of the library to the university administration;
7. library planning systems that include administrative support, provisions for assessing needs and weighing options, mechanisms for establishing priorities and relating them to ongoing operations, use of management information systems, formal planning documents (written plans), and provisions for implementation and evaluation.

The next chapter is an analysis of planning documents and descriptions of planning efforts that were available in 1982–83 and in 1990–91. The objective is to determine the extent to which the elements described here and in the literature are considered in the plans and planning efforts as of those dates and to recommend ways in which changes in future library planning efforts might make them more effective in their implementation. Periodic updates would determine whether planning changed or improved in the period after the study.

Six

Surveys of Academic Library Planning Documents, 1982–83 and 1990–91

PURPOSE OF THE PLANNING STUDY

The primary objectives of the 1982–83 study were to (1) document the status of strategic long-range planning in academic libraries in the United States and Canada, (2) determine the extent to which planning efforts conformed to the criteria established by writers in management literature and library planning literature, and (3) develop an instrument for evaluating plans and for providing guidance to future academic library planning efforts. The purpose of the 1990–91 survey was to update the findings of the 1982–83 survey and to document the extent to which observations made were still valid.

This chapter reports on the survey of long-range strategic planning in Association of Research Libraries university libraries in 1982–83, and the analysis of the plans and planning efforts that were identified. It also reports on the 1990–91 update of the survey and on the differences observed. The ARL membership was chosen because it includes all of the largest academic libraries in the United States and Canada and those with the most comprehensive collections and programs of service.

SURVEYS OF ARL UNIVERSITY LIBRARY MEMBERS

The first survey began in the fall of 1982 with a review of the literature on academic library planning. Although there were many articles on academic library planning and a significant number on long-range planning in public libraries, there were relatively few references to the actual planning documents developed as a part of academic library planning efforts. Chapter 4 discussed those associated with the publication of the Booz, Allen and Hamilton report *Problems in University Library Management* (1970) at Columbia, Cornell, Stanford, the University of Chicago, and the University of Michigan.

Twenty-four Association of Research Libraries institutions had participated in the ARL's Management Review and Analysis Program (MRAP) by 1982, and others had participated in the Academic Library Program (ALP), Academic Library Development Program (ALDP), and the Planning Program for Small Academic Libraries (PPSAL), all assisted self-studies based on modifications of the MRAP model. The reports of these studies were at different stages of development and had different degrees of availability. Therefore, it was decided that the best approach to a study of long-range strategic planning in academic libraries would be to contact each ARL university library member institution directly about the status of its planning process. An initial letter was sent to each of the 101 university library directors in October 1982, with a first follow-up in November and a second follow-up in April 1983 with a progress report on responses.

The letters described the study as a research project on innovation and planning in academic libraries and requested the following documents or information:

1. each library's most recent annual report;
2. each library's 1980–81 annual report if it was not the most recent;
3. a current or recent organization chart with a note indicating the university administrator to whom the library director reports;
4. a current or recent long-range planning document (i.e., master plan, five-year plan, etc.), or formal statement of goals and objectives, or planning priorities; and
5. the name of a contact person who could provide additional information on library planning efforts or activities if needed.

The letters of inquiry brought responses from 83 of the 101 university library members of ARL. Forty-seven (56.6%) indicated that they had either developed a long-range plan (39) or were in the process of doing so (8). Seventeen of the 39 which had developed a plan (43.6%) indicated that planning was an ongoing process and that the plans were reviewed and updated annually. The dates of the plans submitted ranged from 1972

(Columbia University) to 1983 (Johns Hopkins University), in size from 5 to 210 pages, and in period covered from one to twenty years.

The 1990–91 survey update brought responses from 67 of the 101 ARL university library members canvassed in 1982–83. Of those responding, 58 (86.6%) reported either having developed a long-range plan (46) or being in the process of developing one at the time of the survey (12). Twenty-two of the 46 which had developed a plan (47.8%) indicated that planning was an ongoing process and that plans were reviewed and updated annually. The plans submitted were all developed between 1988 and 1991. They ranged in size from 3 to 124 pages and in period covered from 1 to 20 years, with the majority focusing on a five-year planning period.

Responses to Library Planning Letters, 1982–83 and 1990–91

	1982–83	1990–91
ARL University Library Members Contacted	101	101
Institutions Responding	83	67
Institutions Reporting Plans	39	46
% of Respondents Reporting Plans	47.0%	68.7%
Institutions Developing Plans	8	12
% of Respondents Developing Plans	9.6%	17.9%
Total Involved in Formal Planning Efforts	47	58
% Involved in Formal Planning Efforts	56.6%	86.6%
Copies of Plans Provided	34	44

The following section reports on the analyses of planning documents provided by 34 of the 39 libraries in 1982–83, the processes by which they were developed, and the extent to which they met the requirements set forth in Chapter 5. It was hoped that these analyses would demonstrate important differences between library-planning activities in the 1970s and 1980s, and those of earlier periods. If strategic long-range planning had become an integral part of library management, it would be demonstrated by the ways plans were developed and the ways in which they were to be implemented. The section also compares the results of the 1982–83 survey with a 1990–91 update.

OUTLINE FOR ANALYSES

The seven components of a university library program identified and discussed in the previous chapter as important factors to be considered in analyzing plans or planning systems were the following:

1. Statements of goals and objectives
2. Responsive, functional, organizational structures
3. Evaluations of resources and services
   a. Collections
   b. Reader and technical services
   c. Personnel
   d. Physical facilities—buildings and equipment
   e. General financial support
4. Use of contemporary technology and information management systems
5. Extent of interinstitutional cooperation
6. Examinations of the administrative relationships of the library to university administration
7. Library planning systems including
   a. Administrative support
   b. Provisions for assessing needs and weighing options—environmental analyses
   c. Mechanisms for establishing priorities and integrating them into ongoing operations
   d. Use of management information systems
   e. Formal planning documents—written plans
   f. Provisions for implementation and evaluation

In addition, the following factors were considered to the extent possible given the information provided in reviewing the plans and annual reports submitted: (1) by whom are plans initiated; (2) by whom are plans actually developed; and (3) purpose of planning efforts—improving service, controlling growth, maintaining services and resources, accommodating reductions in support, and so forth.

The following is an outline of the format used in completing the survey document form that was prepared for each of the plans analyzed, with brief explanations about each factor considered. The 1–4 rating system for some factors is explained at the end of the form. The ratings are subjective determinations of the extent to which each plan addressed the factor under consideration, based on the material received. The purpose of the ratings

was to demonstrate ranges of responses rather than characterize the
planning efforts of any individual institution.

ANALYSIS OF PLANNING DOCUMENTS   [Date]

1. NAME OF INSTITUTION: Name of library issuing plan.

2. PLANNING DOCUMENT: Bibliographic citation of plan.

3. RESPONSIBILITY FOR PLAN: What individual, office, agency, or
   committee was responsible for developing plan?

4. PURPOSE OF PLAN: For what purpose was plan developed?

5. FORMAL APPROVAL: To whom was plan submitted, or how did it
   attain formal approval?

6. STATEMENT OF MISSION, GOALS, AND OBJECTIVES: Does
   the plan include a full statement of mission, goals, and objectives for
   the library? [Rating 1–4, See rating schedule below.]

   Historical overview: Does the plan include a history of the institution
   and/or the library? [Rating 1–4]

   Organizational structure described: Does the library provide an organizational chart and a structure that shows how implementation of
   the plan might be achieved. [Rating 1–4]

   Administrative relationship to rest of university: What is the administrative relationship of the library to the rest of the university. To
   whom does the director of the library report?

7. ENVIRONMENTAL ANALYSIS: Does the plan address the environment in which it attempts to recommend change and review concerns,
   assets, liabilities, and constraints? [Rating 1–4]

8. KEY ISSUES: What are the key issues addressed in the plan, and what
   are the primary areas in which greater effort is required.

   Administration:
   Collections:

Services:

Personnel:

Facilities:

Financial support:

9. ALTERNATIVES: Does the plan consider alternatives in making its recommendations for action? [Rating 1–4]

   Contemporary technology and management systems: To what extent do alternatives involve the application of computer technology and/or new management systems? If so, describe applications.

   Interinstitutional cooperation: To what extent do alternatives rely on greater interinstitutional cooperation for achieving objectives? Give examples.

10. SPECIFIC RECOMMENDATIONS FOR ACTION: Does the plan make specific recommendations for action? Does it also include timetables and measurements for determining success? [Rating 1–4]

11. IMPLEMENTATION MECHANISMS: Does the plan make specific recommendations on how changes are to be effected? [Rating 1–4]

12. FORMAL PLANNING STRUCTURE: Does the library have a formal planning structure? [Rating 1–4]

13. DOCUMENTATION SUPPORTING RECOMMENDATIONS: Does the plan include documentation to support recommendations (growth projections, cost estimates, staffing requirements, etc.)? [Rating 1–4]

14. EVALUATION MECHANISMS: Does the plan include mechanisms for measuring progress toward achieving goals on a regular basis, and does it provide for formal periodic updating? [Rating 1–4]

15. GENERAL COMMENTS:

Rating System 1–4

The rating system measured the extent to which the plan addressed the areas of concern outlined in Chapter 5. Ratings were appropriate for questions 6, 7, 9, 10, 11, 12, 13, and 14.

1 None—no information provided on an area of concern.

2 Very little information provided.

3 Plan provided adequate consideration of a factor.

4 Plan provided extensive consideration of a factor.

ANALYSIS OF RESPONSES

The first items on the survey form (1 and 2) identified the institutions submitting the plans and provided bibliographic citations of the documents received. The second group of items (3–7) looked at responsibility for developing the plans, their purposes, sources of formal approval, whether they included mission statements or identifications of library goals and objectives (along with historical overviews, organizational structures, and university relationships), and whether they addressed the environmental factors that might influence choices available.

Item 8 listed the common key issues raised in most or many of the plans and the recommendations that were made for addressing them.

Items 9–14 looked at whether plans included the considerations of alternatives in making recommendations, whether they contained specific recommendations for action, whether they outlined mechanisms for implementing recommendations, whether the libraries had formal planning structures, whether the plans included documentation in support of their recommendations, and whether the plans identified mechanisms for measuring progress toward achieving desired ends. Item 15 was left for general comments.

The balance of this chapter is a summary of information the planning documents provided on each of the items included on the survey form. The raw results of the analysis are presented in the author's doctoral dissertation (Biddle, 1988, pp. A-52–63). The statements on the 1982–83 survey are followed by comments and observations drawn from the 1990–91 survey.

Strategic planning documents were received from thirty-four institutions in response to the 1982–83 survey and from forty-four in response to the 1990–91 survey. In light of the differences in the total responses (83 of 101 in 1982–83 and 67 from the same 101 in 1990–91), the fact that the second survey yielded ten more planning documents than the first illustrates the dramatic increase in involvement in formal planning that had occurred between the two surveys. In 1982–83, 56.6 percent of the respondents indicated that they were involved in such efforts. By 1990–91 that percentage had risen to 86.6 percent.

Of the thirty-four institutions providing planning documents in 1982–83, twenty-six were publicly supported universities and eight were privately supported. Twenty-nine were American institutions and five were Canadian. The largest group of plans came from university libraries in the South (10), with nine from institutions in the Midwest, seven in the Northeast, and three in the West.

Of the forty-four institutions providing plans in 1990–91, thirty-one were publicly supported and thirteen were private. Forty-one were American institutions and three were Canadian. Three of the four regions of the United States (South, Midwest, and Northeast) were represented by the same number of institutions each (11). Eight of the institutions were in the West.

Sources of University Library Plans	1982–83		1990–91	
Publicly supported	26	76.0%	31	70.0%
Private	8	24.0%	13	30.0%
Total	34	100.0%	44	100.0%
Northeast	7	20.0%	11	25.0%
South	10	29.4%	11	25.0%
Midwest	9	26.5%	11	25.0%
West	3	8.8%	8	18.2%
Subtotal U.S. Institutions	29	85.3%	41	93.2%
Canadian Institutions	5	14.7%	3	6.8%
Total	34	100.0%	44	100.0%

The third item on the survey form referred to direct responsibility for developing the planning document submitted.

Item 3: Responsibility for Plan: What individual, office, agency, or committee was responsible for developing plan?

Responsibility for Plan	1982–83		1990–91	
Library Administration	15	42.9%	19	43.2%
Library Staff Committee	9	25.7%	12	27.3%

Responsibility for Plan	1982–83		1990–91	
Library Director	4	11.4%	5	11.4%
Outside Consultant	3	8.6%	1	2.3%
University Administrative Committee	3	8.6%	2	4.5%
Developer not identified	1	2.9%	5	11.4%
Total	35*	100.1%	44	100.1%

Note: The total number of results recorded in Items 3, 4, and 5 is thirty-five rather than thirty-four because one institution submitted two documents prepared by different groups for different purposes.

The results showed that the largest group (15) of the thirty-five plans received in 1982–83 was developed by library administrations. Nine plans were developed by appointed library staff committees or task forces, four were developed by library directors themselves, three by outside consultants, three by committees established by university administrations, and one plan gave no indication of who had developed it. The overwhelming majority of the plans (31 or 91.2% of those of attributed responsibility) were developed by the librarians of the institutions themselves, either as administrators, library committees and task forces, or members of university committees or task forces. In only three cases were the plans developed by outside consultants. In two of them (Columbia and Cornell) librarians were actively involved, and both are landmark events in participative library planning.

The 1990–91 updated survey showed approximately the same percentages of plans being developed by library administrations, library staff committees or task forces, library directors, and university committees that included librarians in their membership as in 1982–83, with a reduction in the number of plans developed by outside consultants. If plans of unclear responsibility are excepted, local librarians were responsible for developing 92.3 percent of the plans submitted, nearly the same percentage as in 1982–83. Only one plan of the forty-four received in 1990–91 had been done by a consultant. However, several of the library planning efforts had employed consultants in various aspects of the process.

Item 4: Purpose of Plan: For what purpose was plan developed? The surveys addressed the reasons given for having each of the plans developed.

Purpose of Plan	1982–83		1990–91	
Required by parent institution for budget and/or planning purposes:	16	45.7%	24	54.5%

Purpose of Plan	1982–83		1990–91	
Self initiated (for budget and/or planning purposes, or to improve efficiency, effectiveness and/or management):	13	37.1%	16	36.4%
Externally funded project to improve management of the library:	2	5.7%	0	0.0%
Develop program for administering major donation:	2	5.7%	0	0.0%
Reason not indicated:	2	5.7%	4	9.0%
Total	35*	99.9%	44	99.9%

The largest group of plans in 1982–83 (16) was developed in response to institutional requirements for budgeting and/or planning purposes. The second largest group (13) was self-initiated by librarians in an effort to improve efficiency and effectiveness of operations or to develop better management systems. Two were externally funded projects to improve library management (presumably at the instigation of the library administration), two were associated with the receipt and administration of major donations, and two gave no indication of why the plans had been developed. It is important to note that fifteen plans (43%) were developed from initiatives of the librarians and that eighteen (51%) were stimulated by outside forces.

In the 1990–91 survey the majority of the plans (54.5%) were in response to requests by university administrations. Libraries initiated 36.4 percent of the planning efforts on there own, and four (9%) of the plans did not indicate why they had been developed.

Item 5: Formal Approval: To whom was plan submitted, or how did it attain formal approval? The plans followed several different routes to formal approval.

Formal Approval	1982–83		1990–91	
University Administration	21	60.0%	28	63.6%
Library Administration	9	25.7%	9	20.5%
Informational Document (no approval)	2	5.7%	1	2.3%
State legislative body	1	2.9%	0	0.0%
Route not indicated	2	5.7%	6	13.6%
Total	35*	100.0%	44	100.0%

Twenty-one of the 1982–83 plans were submitted to university administrations for formal approval, nine to library administrations, two were informational documents not requiring formal approval, one went directly to a state board of regents, and two provided no information on approval. Since one of the objectives of planning efforts is to gain institutional support for library initiatives by presenting a comprehensive and coordinated set of recommendations, the fact that nearly two-thirds (62.9%) of the plans were presented to the parent institution or funding body for formal approval demonstrates an appreciation of the importance of reconciling library planning with institutional planning. It also lays the groundwork for obtaining support for specific projects that develop out of the implementation process.

The 1990–91 plans were presented to university administrations in approximately the same proportions as planning documents in 1982–83, with 20.5 percent being approved by library administrations, and one plan serving as an informational vehicle rather than a directive for action.

Item 6: Statement of Mission, Goals, and Objectives. Under the category of "mission, goals, and objectives," four factors were considered: (1) Whether the plan included a clear statement of mission, goals, and objectives, (2) whether the plan included an historical overview placing the library and the university into a broader social, political, educational, economic, or technological context, (3) whether an organizational structure was described that could be used as a vehicle for implementing the provisions of the plan, and (4) whether the plan described the administrative relationship of the library to the rest of the university.

1. Statement of Mission, Goals, and Objectives: Does the plan include a full statement of mission, goals, and objectives for the library? [Rating 1–4]

Mission Statements	1982–83		1990–91	
1 No statements provided	1	2.9%	0	0.0%
2 Very little information provided	7	20.6%	4	9.1%
3 Document provides adequate coverage	3	8.8%	16	36.4%
4 Document provides extensive coverage	23	67.6%	24	54.5%
Total	34	100.0%	44	100.0%

The vast majority of the 1982–83 plans (26 or 76%) included either adequate or extensive statements of missions, goals, and objectives for the libraries. Seven provided very little information, and one provided none.

In light of the importance planning literature places on defining the mission of an organization, and on identifying and articulating specific goals and objectives necessary to fulfill a mission, it is reassuring to see that so many library plans include these elements. At the same time it is disturbing to see that several still provided very little information in the planning document itself on mission, goals or objectives. In some cases this may have been because the documents submitted were annual or periodic updates of existing plans prepared for internal distribution. It may not have seemed necessary to restate the library's mission or to recapitulate established goals and objectives in each update. However, when the update is separated from the base document as occurred with this survey, a recapitulation of mission, goals, and objectives becomes important again.

The 1990–91 plans showed an increase in the use of mission statements and defining of goals and objectives in the documents. More than 90 percent provided adequate or extensive statements of institutional and library missions and provided clear goals and objectives to be achieved through the implementation of planning efforts. It appears that the amount of effort and energy which went into developing a corps of library administrators equipped to articulate the position of the library in the university by the Association of Research Libraries, the Council on Library Resources, and the Association of College and Research Libraries has had a positive influence on the way librarians are able to present their cases to university administrations. Even plans that are a part of annual budget requests begin with a statement of the role of the library and an indication of how its operations support and augment the activities of other units of the university.

2. Historical overview: Does the plan include a history of the institution and/or the library? [Rating 1–4]

Historical Overview	1982–83		1990–91	
1 No historical information	15	44.1%	2	4.5%
2 Very little historical information	6	17.6%	16	36.4%
3 Adequate historical information	2	5.9%	10	22.7%
4 Extensive historical information	11	32.3%	16	36.4%
Total	34	100.0%	44	100.0%

Nearly two-thirds (21) of the 1982–83 planning documents provided little or no historical information on the library or the university. This is unfortunate because it may be assuming that everyone is familiar with the history of an institution and its library and is in agreement about the directions its development has taken over time. In reality, many librarians are not adequately familiar with the histories of their institutions and may not be aware of, or may have forgotten, many of the historical factors that explain why apparent idiosyncrasies may exist in facilities, resources, or services.

The other one-third (13) of the planning documents did provide adequate or extensive historical information on the libraries and institutions. These demonstrated an appreciation of the fact that good planning ought to be a part of a continuing process which builds upon the past and establishes directions and priorities for the future. It also showed that these libraries incorporated an awareness of changes in the educational needs of their users and the academic programs of their universities in their planning.

By the time of the 1990–91 survey the proportion of planning documents with little or no historical information on the library or the university had been reduced to just over 40 percent. The other 60 percent contained adequate or extensive information on the histories of the institutions and libraries and gave clearer illustrations of the bases upon which plans were to be developed. This increased emphasis on the continuing role the library has played in helping the university to achieve its current status in the academic community is another example of the increased sophistication of library administrators and their improved use of long-range planning strategies.

3.   Organizational structure described: Does the library provide an organizational chart and a structure that shows how implementation of the plan might be achieved? [Rating 1–4]

Organizational Structure	1982–83		1990–91	
1 No information on organizational structure	0	0.0%	2	4.5%
2 Little information on organization	2	5.9%	4	9.1%
3 Adequate description of organization	7	20.6%	9	20.5%
4 Document provides estensive coverage	25	73.5%	29	65.9%
Total	34	100.0%	44	100.0%

Every institution that submitted a planning document in 1982–83 provided information on the formal organizational structure of its library. Nearly all of the documents provided adequate or detailed information illustrating how duties and responsibilities were divided among units within the library. The libraries were almost universally organized along the traditional lines of public services, technical services, and administrative services, with some variation as to which specific functions fell in which areas. In nearly all cases formal planning is considered a part of central administration or administrative services.

However, in some cases the increasingly technological requirements of cataloging and acquisitions, and the advent of shared cataloging systems and computerization, seem to have stimulated the development of systems offices in technical services first. As the application of computers to circulation, budgeting and accounting, personnel records management, online data base services, and other electronic information handling systems has developed, the scope of systems offices has expanded, and their relationship to other library functions has been reexamined and revised. In several cases a library had both a planning office in administrative services and a systems office responsible for planning in technical services.

The 1990–91 survey documented a continuation of the trend toward greater use of planning functions, first in technical services, and later throughout the libraries. The advent of integrated library systems linking online catalogs with circulation, acquisitions, and serials systems required an expansion of the role of systems librarians and the development of new relationships among units being electronically linked. All of the planning documents received emphasized the importance of maximizing the use of computers and other electronic equipment to provide access to library resources and to extend the reach of library services.

Despite shifts in technologies used, the basic traditional structure still holds. Integrated computer systems are changing relationships among divisions, and the process will continue until it does alter the basic structure, but it has not done so yet.

4.   Administrative relationship to rest of University: What is the administrative relationship of the library to the rest of the university? To whom does the director of the library report?

Reporting Relationship	1982–83		1990–91	
Chief Academic Officer of the University	27	79.4%	34	77.3%
President of the University	3	8.8%	0	0.0%
University Vice President other than the Chief Academic Officer	2	5.9%	9	20.5%
University administrator not identified	2	5.9%	1	2.3%
Total	34	100.0%	44	100.1%

The administrative relationship of the library to the rest of the university was an important issue in the reports of the outside expert surveys reviewed by Erickson. It was also a major consideration discussed in the Booz, Allen and Hamilton report. It was considered important that the library hold a central position in the overall hierarchy of the university and that the library director report directly to the president or chief academic officer of the institution.

The 1982–83 review showed that thirty of the directors of university libraries (89%) reported to the chief academic officer (provost, vice president, or vice chancellor) or to the president of the university. Two reported to other university vice presidents, and two respondents did not identify the university administrators to whom the library directors reported.

The 1990–91 survey showed no basic change in the reporting structure for university librarians. However, there appears to be a movement toward centralizing information resource services (including media centers, administrative and academic computer centers, and libraries) under an umbrella at the vice presidential level. Nine of the libraries providing organization charts (20.5%) had their directors reporting to vice presidents other than for academic affairs.

The central role of the library in the priorities of the university and its importance to the educational process seems to be undisputed. This is reflected in the position of the library directors in university administrations. In fact, at several of the institutions the library directors also hold titles of dean, associate vice president, or associate provost.

Another question about the relationship between the library and the rest of the university that arose in many of the source documents was the issue of faculty status for librarians. The establishment of librarianship as a recognized and respected profession in higher education has been a recurring theme in library literature. The U.S. Office of Education report and the Works study recommended threshold educational requirements for librarians and a clear delineation between their functions and those of nonprofessional library workers. The outside expert surveys recommended that librarians' salaries and benefits be comparable to those of their classroom colleagues. Despite the fact that faculty status for librarians was being widely discussed in the late sixties, neither Kemper's report nor the Booz, Allen and Hamilton study gave much emphasis to the issue in their discussions of library management systems or strategic planning.

In reviewing the planning documents, it was impossible in most cases to determine which librarians had full faculty status, which had some of the requirements and benefits of faculty status, and which had other forms of academic status with different requirements and benefits. Therefore, it appears that faculty status is not viewed by library planners as a significant factor for strategic planning purposes. No attempt was made to determine the academic status of librarians in the 1990–91 survey.

Item 7: Environmental Analysis: Does the plan address the environment in which it attempts to recommend change and review concerns, assets, liabilities, and constraints? [Rating 1–4]

Environmental Analyses	1982–83		1990–91	
1 No discussion of environment	4	11.8%	1	2.3%
2 Little discussion of environment	7	20.6%	11	25.0%
3 Adequate discussion of environment	6	17.6%	9	20.5%
4 Extensive discussion of environment	17	50.0%	23	52.3%
Total	34	100.0%	44	100.1%

The next area covered in the survey was whether the plans addressed the environments in which they attempted to recommend change and whether they reviewed environmental concerns, assets, liabilities, and constraints. Environment is defined as the social, political, economic, educational, and technological context within which the plan is developed and in which it is intended to be implemented.

One-half (17) of the 1982–83 documents included extensive discussions of the environments in which the plans were being developed. Another six contained adequate discussion, seven very little, and four contained none. In the first two groups there were discussions of the economic factors the universities and higher education in general were facing, changes in demographics of students, greater social awareness of institutions and organizations, stronger support for cooperative endeavors among universities and their libraries, greater sense of social responsibility, and more emphasis on meeting the needs of the greater community beyond the walls of the university.

Many plans discussed the role computerization of library operations might have on organization, structure, goals, and objectives. Some also reviewed the changing nature of information resources themselves and addressed the need to move beyond primarily paper-based systems to incorporate access to electronic media through increased use of online bibliographic data-base vendors and nonbibliographic data in machine readable form.

The 1990–91 plans incorporated a great deal more attention to the impact of computer technology on libraries and on the nature and character of information resources themselves. Much of this attention could be attributed to the widespread implementation of integrated library systems linking a variety of functional operations through one machine. Telecommunications and computer technology make it possible, feasible, and, in the face of soaring prices and declining resources, economical to rely on interinstitutional arrangements to provide the depth and scope of access to information resources a first-rate university needs to have. The advent of CD-ROM and microcomputer technology and the ability to link these machines through local area networks with both local and remote access have revolutionized the profession. Library planners are examining their options and the long-range implications of these changes very closely.

Item 8: Key Issues: What are the key issues addressed in the plan, and what are the primary areas in which greater effort is required? Many common key issues were addressed in many or most of the plans and specific goals or objectives identified, regardless of the individual characteristics of the institutions. These were areas in which library planners in general felt the problems were most critical, or areas in which change was most acutely needed or desired. One beginning a new planning effort would benefit from reviewing the list of issues addressed in the plans reviewed here, and the goals and objectives defined, before developing a new list for a particular institution. Differences among plans tend to be in the solutions recommended rather than problems addressed.

On the survey review forms these issues were divided into six categories:

1. Administration
2. Collections
3. Services (technical services and reader/public services)
4. Personnel
5. Facilities (buildings and equipment)
6. Financial Support

The summary of all the issues raised, or goals and objectives identified and recommended in the 1982–83 planning documents, as well as the identifications of the libraries whose plans addressed each, appears in the author's doctoral dissertation (Biddle, 1988, pp. A-52–A-63).

Administration

Maintain better documentation of use of resources and services (regular periodic reports and improved management information systems):

1982/83   11   32.4%   1990/91   15   34.1%

Eleven of the 1982–83 planning documents identified a need for better documentation of resources and services. They recommended more statistical data collecting and reporting, more frequent reports of a broader range of information, and more sophisticated management information systems making greater use of statistical analysis and computer technology for interpretation. There was an assumption that if library managers had more information at their disposal, and if they could make more objective use of it, they would be able to make better decisions, would be more efficient in utilizing resources, and would be more effective in administering programs. There was no significant change in the 1990–91 survey, except for increased support for the use of cost/benefit analysis in evaluating options.

Develop and administer programs of library resources and services that support and are consistent with the mission, goals, and objectives of the university, efficiently and effectively:

1982/83   10   29.4%   1990/91   33   75.0%

Ten 1982–83 plans explicitly addressed the need to reconcile library plans, as well as efforts to develop resources and services, with the mission, goals, objectives, and plans of the parent institution. While maintaining an awareness of professional standards and criteria, library administrators were reminded that their first obligation was to satisfy the specific needs of their students, faculty, and administrations. A thorough knowledge of these needs and their relative priorities is essential to the development of appropriate library resources and the implementation of programs of service.

In 1990–91 there was a dramatic increase (from 29.4% to 75.0%) in the proportion of plans emphasizing the importance of linking library developmental efforts with overall university plans. A large number (54.5%) also referred to a need to improve communications with nonsystem libraries located on the campuses. It appeared that new technologies and higher costs of materials were forcing universities to reduce duplications of effort by linking previously autonomous and independent libraries with the university library systems.

Maintain quality of collections (rates of acquisitions) and services, and improve effectiveness, with static or declining total financial resources:

| 1982/83 | 7 | 20.6% | | 1990/91 | 37 | 84.1% |

Of the 1982–83 plans 20.6 percent specifically addressed the need to maintain qualities of collections and services with constant or declining financial resources. In these plans there were recommendations for greater selectiveness in acquisitions, for prioritization of new initiatives, with suggestions for reducing other services to release funds for the initiatives, and for careful examinations of the immediate and long-term ramifications of alternative possibilities for meeting fiscally mandated cut backs.

By the 1990–91 survey, the number of plans identifying maintenance of quality of collections as an area of serious concern had increased to more than 37 (84.1%). Inflation and escalating prices had taken their toll on even the most well-supported libraries.

The other two administrative goals identified in 1982–83 were (1) to foster a greater sense of unity and direction among library units and (2) to publicize the planning process (as well as progress toward achieving goals) and assess the extent to which it has been integrated into day-to-day operations and decision making. Both of these goals appeared again in 1990–91, with larger numbers of plans citing each.

Collections

Formulate comprehensive, objective, collection development policies (including gift policies) that take into account changes in academic programs and priorities, and resources available through cooperative arrangements with other libraries.

| 1982/83 | 22 | 64.7% | | 1990/91 | 30 | 68.2% |

Twenty-two (65%) of the 1982–83 plans recommended the formulation of comprehensive, objective, formal, collection development policies that would take into account changes in academic programs and priorities and would consider the additional resources that would become available through participation in cooperative arrangements with other research libraries. The Booz, Allen and Hamilton recommendation on inter-institutional cooperation in collection development, earlier advocated by George Works in 1927, seems to have finally been accepted as an integral part of an academic library's philosophy of service and a legitimate way of providing access to unique, rare, or infrequently used materials.

The 1990–91 plans showed a continuing emphasis on formalized collection development. Many recommended formal links between the library's collection development policy statement and the university's academic program plans (70.5%). Some (45.5%) recommended reallocations of existing funds based on changes and revisions in the policy statement over time. A few recommended approval plans, with strict monitoring of vendor performance. Several made a point of incorporating the need for more cultural diversity and a less Eurocentric focus in the library's collections.

The need for formal, written, collection development policy statements tailored to the specific needs of an institution seems to have been recognized by most library planners.

Provide greater access to electronic media (online bibliographic data-base searching, computer software, nonbibliographic machine readable data sets, compact disk technology).

| 1982/83 | 21 | 61.8% | 1990/91 | 44 | 100% |

The need to provide greater access to information resources in electronic media and machine readable form was cited by nearly the same number of plans in 1982–83 (21) as the need for formulating collection development policy statements. Online data-base searching had become, or ought to have become, an integral part of the reference service provided by all academic libraries. Many of the plans also addressed the need to expand the scope of their collections to include computer software, nonbibliographic machine readable data files on magnetic tape, and electronic media in other formats.

In 1990–91 every single plan (100%) cited the need for greater access to information resources in electronic media, reflecting the dramatic change the introduction of the CD-ROM and the microcomputer had brought about. Nearly all of the plans (95.5%) also called for the loading of external data bases on integrated library systems, linking systems with other institutions and providing remote access through mainframe systems and local-area networks. Nearly half also recommended the loading of graphic and full-text data bases as well.

As information technology continues to advance and develop, many libraries will find that many of their most basic reference sources will become available only online or in machine readable form. Forward looking library administrators are preparing themselves, their staffs, and their clientele for that eventuality.

Improve stack maintenance and place greater emphasis on physical preservation of collections (periodic weeding of holdings, regular schedule for binding materials, restricted access to mutilation-prone periodicals, microfilm rather than bind periodicals).

1982/83   17   50.0%   1990/91   40   90.9%

The problem of the physical preservation of library materials was addressed in seventeen (50%) of the 1982–83 plans and in forty (90.9%) of the 1990–91 plans. Recommendations in both surveys called for increased emphasis on stack maintenance (i.e., reshelving returned materials and shifting stacks as sections of the collections grow at different rates, weeding stacks to identify out-of-date and damaged books, establishing regular schedules for binding materials, restricting access to periodicals that are subject to mutilation, and purchasing microfilm copies where practical rather than binding some periodicals).

The decade of the 1980s saw a tremendous increase in awareness of the fragile nature of paper and the printed word, perhaps this society's primary medium for storing and transmitting information. Planning documents conjured up images of millions of volumes literally disintegrating on the shelves in the stacks of the libraries. Dramatic measures were called for to preserve the nation's heritage.

The concern for preservation was demonstrated again in the area of facilities, where many of these same plans recommended the construction of off-site storage facilities, installation of high density and compact shelving units, and the development of document preservation programs.

Conduct a comprehensive analysis of collections (weeding and retrospective purchasing where appropriate, monitoring continuing relevance of serial titles).

1982/83   13   38.2%   1990/91   24   54.5%

Many of the 1982–83 plans (38.2%) recommended that a comprehensive analysis of the collections be undertaken with the intent of weeding titles that were no longer relevant to the library's current emphasis and instituting retrospective purchasing programs to correct deficiencies in collections. There was a special concern about reviewing periodical and serial titles for continuing relevance and eliminating titles that were no longer appropriate to current and projected scholarly and academic needs.

More than half of the 1990–91 plans (54.5%) recommended comprehensive analyses of collections. A new dimension was added with the proliferation of electronic media and computer systems capable of providing access to a far broader range of information resources. The emphasis on interinstitutional cooperation carried with it a responsibility to have more accurate records of an institution's own holdings and a responsibility to consider resource sharing agreements when deciding to reduce levels of collecting in a discipline or to drop an area of concentration entirely. Pressures on acquisitions budgets and lack of space seem to have invalidated the attitude that a periodical or serial title should be continued once begun because of the completeness of a run. The trend seems to be to build in areas of strength and to rely on cooperative agreements to support resource needs in lower priority areas.

Another factor introduced by the electronic indexing systems and remote access to bibliographic data bases has been an increase in the demand for heretofore obscure items. Sophisticated indexes employed in electronic systems are able to identify, locate, and direct library patrons to relevant resources that would never have been found through manual systems. Therefore it is vitally important that librarians be able to verify their holdings and be able to refer patrons and requests to appropriate alternative sources when items are not held locally.

Greater emphasis on acquiring and providing bibliographic and physical access to microform and audiovisual resources.

| 1982/83 | 12 | 35.3% | 1990/91 | 40 | 90.9% |

Many of the 1982–83 plans (35.3%) also called for expanding collection development by placing greater emphasis on acquiring periodical and research materials in microform (both on microfilm and microfiche) and by including material in audiovisual formats (motion picture film, audiotapes, videotapes, computer software). Where this process has already begun, plans also call for better bibliographic access by placing a higher priority on including these resources in catalogs and in local bibliographic data bases.

The overwhelming majority of the 1990–91 plans (90.9%) recommended placing a higher priority on acquiring and providing bibliographic access to microform and audiovisual resources. As just noted, electronic indexing systems have provided library patrons with powerful tools for finding relevant resources. Many libraries have purchased large collections in microform that are virtually inaccessible unless cataloged and incorporated into the institution's data base.

Other 1982–83 recommendations on collections included (1) increasing the rate of growth of collections, (2) building on strengths of special collections (primarily rare books, archives, and instructional materials centers), (3) encouraging more classroom faculty participation in collection development, (4) increasing the number of relevant foreign publications, and (5) more careful monitoring and evaluating of the performance of library material vendors.

In 1990–91 other issues were added in the area of collection development. Twenty-four plans (54.5%) recommended comprehensive analyses of media collections as well as of monograph and periodical holdings. Nineteen recommended the initiation of retrospective collection development efforts in the wake of the collection analysis projects. Several expressed a concern about the ratio of expenditures for electronic versus paper media, and for serials versus monographs. There were suggestions that librarians seek to establish indexing formulas tied to rates of inflation in presenting their arguments to university administrators in order not to have the libraries appear as bottomless pits when soliciting increased funding. One proposal advanced was to make greater use of government depository programs to increase acquisitions at reasonable costs. Another area likely to receive increased attention in the future was a recommendation in three plans that the university libraries assume a responsibility for university records management.

Services

Three major service recommendations were common to nearly two-thirds of the 1982–83 plans. These recommendations appeared again, with even greater support, in the 1990–91 plans.

Improve bibliographic access to all library materials through computerization of bibliographic records (retrospective conversion and development of online public access catalog).

| 1982/83 | 29 | 85.3% | 1990/91 | 43 | 97.7% |

Twenty-nine of the 1982–83 plans (85%) recommended improving bibliographic access to all library materials through the computerization of bibliographic records and the development of online public access catalogs. By 1990–91 the number had increased to 43 (97.7%). Most of the plans urged a high priority for retrospective conversion efforts required to generate the data base for online catalogs and recommended that the scope of the data base be expanded to include resources not included in many card catalogs (information on microform holdings, newspapers and periodicals, archival record groups, manuscript collections, audiovisual media, computer software, nonbibliographic data on magnetic tape, availability of access to commercial online systems, etc.).

A large number of the plans (77.3%) recognized the need to standardize all cataloging going into the university bibliographic data base, including the records of previously unaffiliated campus libraries and other information resource centers. Recognizing the critical role computers and electronics play in information technology, nearly half of the plans called for the establishment of university policies on machine readable data to help clarify the relative roles of computer centers and libraries.

Develop or acquire and install a computer-based integrated library system providing online access to acquisitions, processing, cataloging, binding, circulation, interlibrary loan, and periodicals records.

1982/83	27	79.4%	1990/91	42	95.5%

Twenty-seven 1982–83 plans (79%) and forty-two 1990–91 plans (95.5%) recommended that the library develop or install a computer-based integrated library system which would provide access not only to the bibliographic data base but also to acquisitions, processing, binding, circulation, reserve, interlibrary loan, and periodicals records. Many also stipulated that the integrated library system also be linked with other campus computer systems and be capable of communicating with regional and national computer networks.

The 1990–91 plans went even further than earlier proposals by emphasizing the importance of remote access to library bibliographic data bases through university mainframes and via modem-equipped microcomputers located in faculty members' and students' homes and offices. A surprising 86 percent of the plans urged libraries to become active participants in the development and refinement of university telecommunications systems in order to guarantee the level of computer and communications support library operations are going to need.

Many of the plans, from both surveys, discussed the improved management information capabilities of integrated library systems and argued that improved efficiency and effectiveness would help offset the considerable costs of implementation and operation.

Place greater emphasis on bibliographic instruction.

1982/83	21	61.8%	1990/91	37	84.1%

The third major recommendation common to most plans (21 or nearly 62% of the 1982–83 plans and 37 or more than 84% of the 1990–91 plans) was to place greater emphasis on bibliographic instruction and the development of library-use skills. Many of the plans noted that libraries were meeting student and faculty needs but that users were frequently frustrated because they did not know what resources were available or where or how to ask for them. Technological advances provide users with access to a greater variety of information resources, and the tools tend to change more rapidly than users can adapt to them. Therefore the librarian is under even greater pressure to keep his or her self current in the use of new information resources and capable of teaching patrons how those resources can be most effectively utilized.

Many of the plans focused on the need for greater proficiency on the part of the reader service librarians in negotiating among electronic resources and providing library users with the levels of assistance they would need to master new tools. They suggested seminars, minicourses, and frequent workshops as vehicles for delivering these services. Many also suggested closer working relationships between librarians and computer center staffs. As new technologies are introduced and updated, staff and users must be kept informed of new developments and be prepared to take advantage of them as they become operational.

Initiate or improve public relations programs (communications with faculty, students, administrators, and staff through greater use of exhibits, library newsletters, formal library policy statements, etc.).

1982/83   13   38.2%   1990/91   24   54.5%

Along with greater emphasis on bibliographic instruction, several 1982–83 plans recommended initiating or improving upon existing public relations programs by increasing communications with faculty, students, staff, and administrators. By 1990–91 the number of plans calling for more vigorous public relations efforts had increased to a majority (24 or 54.5%). Methods suggested included formulating and distributing formal library policy statements, publishing library newsletters, and making more effective use of exhibits to publicize resources, services, and key personnel. More than two-thirds also recommended series of seminars and workshops, supported by pamphlets, brochures, flyers, and other handouts, introducing and explaining new resources and services made possible by the integrated library systems and by the CD-ROM and microcomputer-based systems being installed.

Place greater emphasis on user satisfaction in reader services (improve hit rates in catalog searches, more specialized user services, longer hours, open stacks, etc.).

1982/83   12   35.3%   1990/91   21   47.7%

Both surveys showed plans recommending improving public services by giving more weight to user satisfaction as a criterion for success (12 or 35.3% in 1982–83 and 21 or 47.7% in 1990–91). Specific measures included improving hit rates in catalog searches (a comprehensive collection inventory would remove lost, stolen, and missing items from the data base, and retrospective collection development would fill in gaps), tailoring specialized services to meet expressed needs of users (facilities for users with visual, hearing, or mobility disabilities), adjusting hours to meet unusual scheduling of some groups of users, initiating journal article photocopying and document delivery systems for faculty, open stacks for all students, and restricted access to high casualty journals.

A significant number in 1990–91 (14 or nearly 32%) specifically mentioned placing greater emphasis on meeting the needs of undergraduate students more effectively. This would seem to address a general concern in society about higher education's commitment to general education as opposed to research and professional education.

Provide for more user involvement in evaluating and prioritizing services.

1982/83	2	5.9%		1990/91	17	38.6%

In 1982–83 two plans recommended formal user involvement in evaluating and prioritizing services. By 1990–91 the number of plans recommending formal user involvement had increased to 17, 38.6 percent of the total.

Increase emphasis on resource sharing through duplication, interlibrary loan, and document delivery services.

1982/83	9	26.5%		1990/91	42	95.5%

Approximately one-quarter of the 1982–83 plans called for placing more emphasis on the use of resource sharing arrangements with other libraries through publicizing interlibrary loan and document delivery systems. In 1990–91 virtually every plan not only recommended more interinstitutional cooperation, but gave this recommendation a high priority. Technological advances such as the implementation of integrated library systems capable of being accessed from the outside, advances in facsimile transmission (fax), and the acknowledgement of limitations on every institution's ability to purchase and house material have all contributed to this dramatic change in emphasis. Many of the institutions also recommended more active use of the Center for Research Libraries. A few even recommended loading the center's records into their local data base as a way of maximizing use of the service.

Planners at several libraries felt that a few basic recommendations needed to be formalized in their planning documents nevertheless: (1) maintaining levels of service despite reductions in funding, (2) formulating and publicizing formal public service priorities, (3) promoting high ethical standards (freedom of access to information, privacy of user records), and (4) improving library services to off-campus university facilities. There seems to be a continuing debate about the ethics of fee-based access to some services and no universally acceptable solution to photocopying services.

Personnel

There was less unanimity about problems, or solutions, in the area of library personnel. Only one recommendation was shared by a majority of the plans in either survey. This may have been because some institutions had already implemented the measures recommended for others, or it may be that the differences among libraries is so great that there actually are no commonly shared problems. It may also be that many plans did not give personnel administration as much attention as others, and therefore recommendations which would have been appropriate were not made.

A review of the recommendations that were made shows there are few an enlightened administrator would not support.

Provide more support for professional development of librarians (including travel funds and financial support for research efforts).

1982/83	21	61.8%	1990/91	37	84.1%

Twenty-one (62%) of the 1982–83 plans and 37 (84.1%) of the 1990–91 plans recommended more support for the professional development of librarians. Specific forms included funds for travel and attendance at seminars, workshops, and professional meetings, and financial support for research and publishing efforts. One institution stated that its professional development goal was to provide institutional leadership in the profession through research, publications, and participation in professional organizations.

The other personnel recommendations fell into five groups dealing with (1) recruitment, (2) training and evaluation, (3) personnel policy, position descriptions, and staffing patterns, (4) benefits, and (5) interaction with classroom faculty.

In the area of recruitment, plans called for the library administrations to:

Recruit the best qualified library faculty and staff.

1982/83	5	14.7%	1990/91	20	45.5%

Intensify commitment to Affirmative Action.

1982/83	4	11.8%	1990/91	15	34.1%

Recruit specialists in computer science and telecommunications.

1982/83	1	2.9%	1990/91	12	27.3%

It is noteworthy that in each area there was a dramatic increase in the number and percentage of plans making recommendations between the 1982–83 and the 1990–91 surveys. It is also noteworthy that in the 1990–91 plans 34.1 percent (15 plans) the need to pursue greater cultural and ethnic diversity in staffing was cited. The plans recommend the recruitment, hiring, and promotion of larger numbers of individuals from under-represented minority groups, reflecting the changing composition of student bodies, work forces, and the general population in many areas of the country.

Under training and evaluation, the plans recommended that library administrations:

Provide for cross-training and in-service training (especially in areas being heavily computerized) of staff.

1982/83	13	38.2%	1990/91	25	56.8%

Thirteen of the 1982–83 plans (38%) and 25 of the 1990–91 plans (56.8%) specifically recommended cross-training and in-service training for staff. This was especially important in view of the great emphasis on computerization in all areas of library work and the need to be able to shift staff and functions as computer-driven reorganization changes structural patterns within the organization. This recommendation also recognizes the need to keep staff continuously current on changes in computer systems and fully prepared to adjust to upgrades and enhancements as they are implemented.

Other plans recommend that library administrations undertake training and evaluation efforts that would:

Provide better orientation and training programs for new employees.

1982/83	8	23.5%	1990/91	9	20.5%

Develop (or refine) criteria for evaluating the performance of librarians.

| 1982/83 | 8 | 23.5% | 1990/91 | 12 | 27.3% |

Develop (or refine) criteria for evaluating nonlibrarian professional staff.

| 1982/83 | 3 | 8.8% | 1990/91 | 11 | 25.0% |

Establish (or expand existing) formal staff development program.

| 1982/83 | 4 | 11.8% | 1990/91 | 32 | 72.7% |

Provide training to develop career paths and upward mobility for support staff.

| 1982/83 | 10 | 29.4% | 1990/91 | 19 | 43.2% |

Two recommendations appeared in roughly one-third of the 1990–91 plans that had not appeared in the 1982–83 group. These were (1) to improve management skills and (2) to increase productivity. Both reflect a higher level of professionalism among planners and a wider use of a mainstream management approach to library operations.

Personnel policies, position descriptions, staffing patterns, and numbers of staff were discussed in several of the plans. Recommendations included:

Develop (or update) a handbook of library policies, procedures, and practices.

| 1982/83 | 5 | 14.7% | 1990/91 | 3 | 6.8% |

Update, expand, and refine job descriptions, and review classifications of personnel (analyze skills requirements and workloads).

| 1982/83 | 7 | 20.6% | 1990/91 | 17 | 38.6% |

Review staffing patterns library-wide and make appropriate adjustments.

| 1982/83 | 1 | 2.9% | 1990/91 | 20 | 45.5% |

Increase/restore number of professional staff.

| 1982/83 | 9 | 26.5% | 1990/91 | 18 | 40.9% |

Increase or restore number of support positions.

| 1982/83 | 9 | 26.5% | 1990/91 | 20 | 45.5% |

Increase or restore student assistant support (also cover increases in minimum wages).

| 1982/83 | 5 | 14.7% | 1990/91 | 12 | 27.3% |

Only eight 1982–83 plans addressed professional salaries and benefits, and just one plan explicitly called for greater interaction between librarians and classroom faculty.

A significant development was expected, but it did not occur. There was no groundswell of support for participative management, democratization of library administration, or radical changes in administrative or organizational structures except in response to computerization of operations. There was little discussion of new management systems, except to call for the hiring or training of professionals in various fields of computer technology.

The final general areas of recommendations in the 1990–91 plans included recommendations to improve communications among library staff and library administrators and recommendations to encourage more interaction between librarians and classroom faculty.

Physical Facilities

There was more agreement among plans about facility needs (buildings and equipment) than about personnel. A majority of the plans made recommendations for new construction or major renovations of existing buildings. A large minority of the plans made specific recommendations about security, storage, preservation, equipment, and overall space allocation and utilization.

Renovate and/or expand existing facilities or plan for construction of new facilities (equipped to support heavy computerization of operations).

| 1982/83 | 19 | 55.9% | 1990/91 | 42 | 95.5% |

Nineteen of the 1982–83 plans (56%) and forty-two of the 1990–91 plans (95.5%) recommended major renovations or expansions of existing facilities or supported efforts to begin planning for construction of new facilities. There is a serious concern that these renovated and/or newly constructed facilities be equipped to handle the extensive computerization of library operations anticipated.

Improve security for resources and personnel (book detection systems, temperature and humidity environmental controls, building guards, closed stacks, etc.).

| 1982/83 | 17 | 50.0% | 1990/91 | 26 | 59.1% |

One-half of the 1982–83 plans (17) and nearly 60 percent of the 1990–91 plans recommended improvements in security for both personnel and resources. Specific measures included book detection systems, building guards, and closed stacks for high-theft items, as well as environmental controls to monitor and regulate temperature, humidity, and levels of air pollution.

Develop (or expand) off-site storage facilities (also consider use of compact shelving) and review policy regarding use.

1982/83   16   47.1%   1990/91   25   56.8%

Sixteen of the 1982–83 plans (47%) and twenty-five of the 1990–91 plans (56.8%) recommended the development or expansion of off-site storage facilities (sometimes as a part of a regional resource sharing arrangement), or a review of policy regarding use where such facilities already exist. Compact shelving was recommended by many plans as a way of increasing the storage capacity where there are large numbers of low-use volumes.

Plan and develop facilities for preservation activities (document restoration, in-house binding, microfilming, etc.).

1982/83   16   47.1%   1990/91   37   84.1%

A large number of the 1982–83 plans and the overwhelming majority of the 1990–91 plans recommended the development or expansion of preservation facilities for the restoration of documents, in-house binding of library materials, and microfilming of documents. Again, these recommendations often were advanced in support of regional resource sharing efforts that could be planned and undertaken with other institutions.

General upgrading of equipment (computers, printers, OCLC terminals, photo-copying machines, A/V equipment, microform readers and reader/printers, etc.).

1982/83   15   44.1%   1990/91   39   88.6%

With the proliferation of information resources into a wide range of media, there was a widespread concern about the availability of adequate equipment to provide access to the materials. Fifteen 1982–83 plans (44%) and thirty-nine of the 1990–91 plans called for a general upgrading of such equipment as terminals, computers, printers, photocopying machines, audiovisual equipment, and microfilm and microfiche readers and reader/printers. As the movement of information resources to machine-readable form gains momentum, equipment and support staff with technical skills have become an increasingly important area of concern for library administrators. Several 1990–91 plans even recommended that equipment amortization schedules be set up in order to monitor and project future equipment needs.

Conduct a comprehensive review of total utilization of library space.

1982/83   12   35.3%   1990/91   38   86.4%

Twelve of the 1982–83 plans (35%) and thirty-eight of the 1990–91 plans (86.4%) recommended a comprehensive review of total space utilization by libraries. There was an assumption that such comprehensive reviews would identify more efficient ways of using existing space and that recommendations for renovation and new construction would more likely be supported by governing bodies if they were well documented and demonstrated that alternatives had been considered and adopted where feasible.

The other facilities' recommendations dealt with the need for (1) disaster preparedness plans, (2) improved signage, and (3) facilities for persons with disabilities.

Financial Support

The final category of key issues addressed, or goals and objectives identified in the plans, dealt with financial support.

Seek alternative sources of funds (philanthropists, corporations, government grants [NEH, Title II-C, etc.], special service user charges and library fees, Friends of the Library groups).

1982/83   21   61.8%   1990/91   38   86.4%

Twenty-one of the 1982–83 plans (62%) and thirty-eight of the 1990–91 plans (86.4%) recommended that library administrators and university officials seek alternative sources of funds. Specific examples were philanthropists, corporations, federal government programs such as the National Endowment for the Humanities, National Endowment for the Arts, National Science Foundation, and HEA Title II–C. Some plans recommended imposing user fees for special services or services to special nonuniversity clientele, and others advocated the creation or revitalization of friends of the library groups to take the initiative in external fund-raising. Several plans noted the close working relationship between library administrators and university development offices and urged its continuation.

Improve documentation of need for increases in general funding (also tie expansions in academic programs to increases in library funding).

1982/83   20   58.8%   1990/91   38   86.3%

For improving financial support, the other major recommendation in twenty 1982–83 plans (59%) and thirty-eight 1990–91 plans (86.3%) was to improve documentation of the need for increases in general funding from the university administration. Examples included references to expansions in academic programs already being supported, increased costs of resources in specialized disciplines, benefits of participation in resource sharing arrangements, aged or deteriorating physical plants, obsolete equipment, violations of current building and/or health codes, and new initiatives in support of high priority university goals and objectives.

The other recommendations dealt with (1) making effective use of major gifts and grants already received or pending, (2) identifying existing library funds that could be channeled to new initiatives, and (3) pressing for an appropriate share of overhead funds generated by university research grants.

Items 9–14 of the survey review form dealt with the consideration of alternative courses of action, the implementation of recommendations included in the planning documents, and the formal planning systems of libraries. They examined whether the documents demonstrated a consideration of alternatives, whether they contained recommendations for specific actions to be taken, whether they recommended specific mechanisms for implementing changes, whether they provided documentation in support of recommendations, and whether they provided mechanisms for measuring progress toward achieving desired ends. Item 12 examined existing and proposed formal planning systems within libraries based on the plans and organizational information provided.

Item 9: Alternatives: Does the plan consider alternatives in making its recommendations for action? [Rating 1–4]

Alternatives	1982–83		1990–91	
1 No discussion of alternatives	1	2.9%	2	4.5%
2 Very little discussion	11	32.3%	11	25.0%
3 Adequate discussion	10	29.4%	10	22.7%
4 Extensive discussion	12	35.3%	21	47.7%
Total	34	99.9%	44	99.9%

Planning theorists emphasized the importance of weighing alternative courses of action in their writings and the importance of projecting the long-term consequences of using different approaches to solving a problem. Item 9 examined whether the library planning documents collected demonstrated considerations of alternative choices in making recommendations on how to address key issues and the extent to which these alternatives involved the application of computer technology, new management systems, or interinstitutional cooperation.

Twenty-two (65%) of the 1982–83 plans and twenty-one (47.7%) of the 1990–91 plans demonstrated adequate or extensive consideration of alternatives in developing recommendations. Eleven of each (32% and 25% respectively) included very little discussion of alternatives. One 1982–83 plan contained no discussion of alternatives. It should be noted that the one plan was specifically charged with developing a building program for new construction once a decision had been made to fund it, and the charge did not include a discussion of alternative choices or elements which might be included. In the 1990–91 survey there were two plans with no discussions of alternative possibilities.

It should also be kept in mind that many of the plans were updates of previously prepared planning documents. Therefore it cannot be assumed that the small amount of discussion of alternative courses in many of the plans means that alternatives were not considered when goals and objectives were originally identified. In many of the plans that discuss alternatives, there are reaffirmations of choices made earlier, or revisions of decisions based on new resources, new problems, or technological advances which change the feasibility of some options.

Contemporary Technology and Management Systems: To what extent do alternatives involve the application of computer technology and/or new management systems? If so, describe applications.

Nearly all of the planning documents called for greater use of computer technology in addressing the problems of library management and improving library operations. Thirty of the 1982–83 plans (88%) and thirty-nine of the 1990–91 plans (88.6%) urged more research on computer applications to library operations and the development of specific applications to problems identified at the individual institutions. Twenty-nine 1982–83 plans and nearly all of the 1990–91 plans recommended the development or acquisition of computer-based integrated library systems, either independently or as a part of a cooperative effort on the part of several institutions.

The increased emphasis on electronic media and information resources in machine-readable form was noted by nearly all plans. Many of them recommended an expansion of collection development policy statements to include these new formats and a reorientation of reader services policy to make more effective use of emerging information technology.

There was almost no support for the implementation of new management systems in either survey. This may have been because so many of the plans were developed by library directors, other library administrators charged by library directors, committees appointed by library directors, or committees appointed by university administrators.

Only two of the 1982–83 plans, Columbia University and the University of Texas at Austin, recommended basic changes in management systems. The Columbia report, developed by Booz, Allen and Hamilton in cooperation with the Association of Research Libraries and the American Council on Education, was described earlier. The University of Texas report made very general statements about organizational innovation and participatory management, but made no specific recommendations on how these goals might be achieved. A third plan at Cornell University suggested major changes, but left it to future committees and task forces to recommend specific measures to be taken.

Other plans recommended centralizing or decentralizing functions, reorganizing along geographic or functional lines, reassigning personnel and functions in response to changes brought about by computerization of operations, and bringing in new staff with specialized expertise in a variety of areas reflecting the current priorities of the libraries and/or the universities.

Interinstitutional Cooperation: To what extent do alternatives rely on greater interinstitutional cooperation for achieving objectives? Give examples.

Making greater use of interinstitutional cooperative arrangements to distribute and share the burden of supporting scholarship and research was one of the strongest recommendations of the Booz, Allen and Hamilton report on problems in university library management.

Twenty-five of the 1982–83 plans (74%) and forty-two of the 1990–91 plans (95.5%) recommended increased participation in regional, state, national, and international cooperative library service programs. Many specifically referred to cooperative collection development and reciprocal resource sharing programs. Some recommended cooperative development of computer software programs, and others recommended special cooperative arrangements among institutions with related special collections.

The success of the Online Computerized Library Center (OCLC), the Research Libraries Information Network (RLIN), the University of Toronto Library Automation Systems (UTLAS), and the Washington Library Network (WLN) probably had a great deal to do with changing many libraries' attitudes about cooperative efforts and resource sharing. Advances in computer technology make it possible to identify and locate specific items more easily through regional or national data bases than in the large and increasingly complex local card catalogs maintained by individual libraries. It is only a matter of time before formal agreements become commonplace in taking advantage of this resource sharing potential.

Further evidence of the change in attitude about interinstitutional cooperation is demonstrated by the extent to which major research libraries have reviewed their collection development policies under programs such as ARL's Collection Analysis Project (CAP) and the Research Libraries Group's (RLG's) resource sharing projects. Participating libraries assume a primary responsibility for collecting in agreed-upon areas of specialization, with the understanding that they will be able to provide their users with relatively easy access to the holdings of other institutions in those areas in which they have agreed not to specialize.

Another important factor was the availability for a period of time of external funding for cooperative programs through state agencies, the federal government, and several important foundations. The roles played by several of these funding sources in addressing problems of academic libraries were discussed earlier in Chapter 4.

Item 10: Specific Recommendations for Action: Does the plan make specific recommendations for action? Does it also include timetables and measurements for determining success? [Rating 1–4]

Specific Recommendations	1982–83		1990–91	
1 No recommendations for action	1	2.9%	0	0.0%
2 Very few recommendations for action	8	23.5%	4	9.1%
3 Many recommendations for action	6	17.6%	11	25.0%
4 Extensive recommendations for action	19	55.9%	29	65.9%
Total	34	100.0%	44	100.0%

Writers on planning emphasize the importance of an action orientation for a planning effort. Item 10 examined the extent to which the planning documents received made recommendations of specific actions to be taken to achieve the goals and objectives identified.

Twenty-five (74%) of the 1982–83 planning documents made many or extensive recommendations for specific actions to be taken upon approval of the plan. Eight made very few, and one made none. The one with no specific recommendations is interesting because it demonstrated a good understanding of the problems facing academic libraries, it identified areas in which significant progress might be made, and it described the kinds of changes that would be beneficial. However, it did not charge anyone with doing anything to advance its recommendations. By contrast, in the 1990–91 survey forty of the planning documents (90.9%) made many or extensive recommendations for specific actions to be taken. Only four plans made a few, and not a single one made none.

Some of the plans directed that specific individuals or offices take clearly defined steps toward achieving goals. These steps included conducting space utilization studies, investigating the feasibility of adapting specific computer hardware or software for handling particular types of transactions or records, investigating the benefits of participating in particular resource sharing programs, preparing or revising job descriptions and initiating searches for individuals with special skills, and preparing cost-benefit analyses of various approaches to handling operations.

Several of the plans called upon division heads to respond to the recommendations affecting their areas of responsibility and to develop implementation schedules. Others incorporated the planning recommendations into the budgeting system and required annual progress reports to the library administration as a part of funding requests. Two 1982–83 plans called for the development of loose-leaf planning notebooks in which each objective would be represented. Sections of the notebook would be updated as progress was made. Another plan proposed the establishment of a formal procedure within the library administration for getting planning initiatives approved and implemented.

In general the documents demonstrated an appreciation for the importance of making the plans an active component in library administration and of assigning responsibilities for initiating actions that could lead to implementation. Although actions taken to implement plans ultimately depend on the amount of support library and university administrators give them, most of the plans included in this survey do not appear to be in danger of being set aside and forgotten.

Item 11: Implementation Mechanisms: Does the plan make specific recommendations on how changes are to be effected? [Rating 1–4]

Implementation Mechanisms	1982–83		1990–91	
1 No implementation mechanisms	2	5.9%	1	2.3%
2 Very few implementation mechanisms	11	32.4%	12	27.3%
3 Adequate mechanisms	3	8.8%	11	25.0%
4 Extensive mechanisms	18	52.9%	20	45.5%
Total	34	100.0%	44	100.1%

Effective plans need to contain mechanisms to stimulate the implementation of goals and objectives identified and recommended. Item 11 examined the extent to which planning documents recommended mechanisms for implementing the proposed changes.

Many of the plans called for annual reviews of progress toward meeting goals and objectives and annual updates based on new developments. The loose-leaf planning notebook previously mentioned was one method described for handling this process. Plans also incorporated the implementation of planning recommendations into the annual budget cycle and required progress reports of all administrators. At some libraries planning was incorporated into the job descriptions of administrators; at others monitoring strategic planning initiatives was made the primary responsibility of one senior administrator.

A few plans recommended the establishment of a formal research and planning office or the appointment of an implementation task force to coordinate and monitor progress toward meeting planning objectives and to organize new planning initiatives on an ongoing basis.

Implementation of recommendations at three institutions in the 1982–83 survey was to be funded by major grants they had received to improve the quality of library resources and/or services.

The message from planning literature that implementation can be the most important element in a planning effort seems to have been received. The majority of the planning documents examined include specific recommendations on how planning goals and objectives should be incorporated into the administrative priorities of the libraries, and on how monitoring progress toward achieving them could be made a part of every administrator's responsibilities.

Item 12: Formal Planning Structure: Does the library have a formal planning structure? [Rating 1–4]

Formal Planning Structure	1982–83		1990–91	
1 No formal planning structure	6	17.6%	1	2.3%
2 Little provision for formal planning	7	20.6%	19	43.2%
3 Adequate provision for formal planning	5	14.7%	8	18.2%
4 Extensive provisions for formal planning	16	47.1%	16	36.4%
Total	34	100.0%	44	100.1%

Examining the formal planning structures of the libraries included in the surveys proved more difficult than anticipated. Although every institution provided information on its formal organizational structure, including several elaborate charts, it was not always apparent how strategic planning related to the structure or administrative processes, or how decision making was handled. Most of the libraries do not have a separate organizational body for planning, but have made it an integral part of every administrator's responsibilities. Approximately one-half of the libraries in both surveys indicated that they conduct a formal review of their plan each year and that goals and objectives are adjusted as circumstances warrant.

Some libraries identified senior administrators whose primary responsibilities were planning, coordinating, and monitoring the implementation of plan recommendations, and collecting, organizing, and analyzing data for future planning activities. These individuals held different titles at different institutions, and their actual responsibilities varied considerably. Several were assistant university librarians for planning or planning and development. Others were identified as assistant university librarians for administrative services. Their responsibilities often included budgeting, accounting, physical facilities, fund-raising, and administrative computerization as well as planning. Still other institutions identified the heads of their systems offices as their primary planning officers. In several of these cases automation of technical services seems to have been the initial focus of planning efforts that later expanded into other areas of library operation.

A few institutions recommended or established formal planning committees or planning task forces with the specific charge of coordinating and monitoring the implementation of plan recommendations. One planning document recommended the establishment of a "Planning Sequence Organization," which would provide a formal structure for the development, approval, implementation, and evaluation of planning initiatives.

The majority of the libraries that have developed strategic plans have incorporated long-term planning into their administrative structure either by making it a part of the ongoing responsibilities of each administrator, by incorporating it into their budgeting systems, or by identifying a particular group or individual as being primarily responsible for coordinating and monitoring the implementation of plans.

Item 13: Documentation Supporting Recommendations: Does the plan include documentation to support recommendations (growth projections, cost estimates, staffing requirements, etc.)? [Rating 1–4]

Documentation Supporting Recommendations	1982–83		1990–91	
1 No documentation	3	8.8%	0	0.0%
2 Very little documentation	8	23.5%	16	36.4%

Documentation Supporting Recommendations	1982–83		1990–91	
3 Adequate documentation	8	17.6%	12	27.3%
4 Extensive documentation	17	50.0%	16	36.4%
Total	34	100.0%	44	100.0%

Comprehensive documentation of trends, problems, and alternative solutions is another important element of effective planning described in the writings. Item 13 examined the kinds and amounts of supporting documentation contained in the planning documents received in an effort to determine the extent to which library planners used objective data in conducting their analyses and recommending solutions. Types of documentation sought included growth projections for collections and clientele, effects of inflation on purchasing power, costs of continuing current levels of service, costs of implementing changes in service patterns, costs of expanding use of computers, service benefits of resource sharing arrangements, projected staffing requirements of continuing existing patterns and of implementing recommendations, and so on.

The planning documents fell into several groups, some with subgroups. In the 1982–83 survey eleven (32%) had little or no documentation, and twenty-three (68%) had adequate or extensive documentation. In the 1990–91 survey none had no documentation and sixteen (36.4%) had very little. Twenty-eight (63.6%) had adequate or extensive documentation.

It should be pointed out once again that many of the planning documents were annual updates of existing long-term plans. The absence of documentation in the update received does not necessarily mean that the institution did not conduct a careful analysis of the problems and weigh options in selecting courses of action to recommend when planning goals and objectives were originally established. At the University of Michigan, for example, extensive documentation is required when a planning initiative is first recommended. Once it has been formally adopted, only progress reports are required unless priorities or goals are changed significantly.

Many of the planning documents included general essays on the problems of higher education and of academic libraries drawing data from the literature and from institutional projections. They discussed the changing demographics of the college-age population, institutional projections of student body growth patterns, institutional priorities for development of academic programs, the effects of inflation on purchasing power, the increasing costs of maintaining current levels of staffing, changes in the volume and nature of scholarly publishing, the need for increased computerization to handle larger volumes of transactions, an increased awareness of the problems of preserving library materials in paper form, the need to hire or train specialists in areas that had not previously been considered librarianship (systems analysts and computer programmers, preservation experts, staff development officers, fund-raisers, etc.), and the ever-present problems of providing enough space to adequately house and provide user access to library materials.

Several of the plans used data from their local situations to document the issues drawn from the literature and weighed the costs and benefits of solutions being tried or suggested at other institutions. Some of the plans included the general essay, but only provided local documentation in those areas in which they made their own recommendations. A few used the ARL annual statistics to document their status relative to peer institutions and to support recommendations for increased funding. One institution used an outside consultant to conduct a formal needs assessment survey and self-study committees to document staff perceptions of areas of concern.

In general the planning documents were well documented and provided both quantitative and qualitative evidence of the scope of the problems being addressed. The data presented demonstrated that the recommendations selected were based on a realistic review of the alternatives available and the assets, liabilities, and constraints on the individual institutions.

Item 14: Evaluation Mechanisms: Does the plan include mechanisms for measuring progress toward achieving goals on a regular basis and does it provide for formal periodic updating? [Rating 1–4]

Evaluation Mechanisms	1982–83		1990–91	
1 No evaluation mechanisms	7	20.6%	3	6.8%
2 Very few evaluation mechanisms	6	17.6%	15	34.1%
3 Adequate evaluation mechanisms	3	8.8%	12	27.3%
4 Extensive evaluation mechanisms	18	52.9%	14	31.8%
Total	34	100.0%	44	100.0%

The final area covered on the survey analysis form was the question of mechanisms for continuously evaluating progress toward achieving the goals and objectives identified and provisions for formal updating of plans.

Many people are cynical about planning efforts, and planning in general, because they have seen too many efforts fail to produce desired results. Sometimes planning has been used as a delay to postpone taking action, or as a tactic to avoid confronting an issue until it becomes a crisis. Sometimes planning has even been used as a mechanism for legitimizing courses of action already decided upon.

One way of avoiding or undermining this inherent cynicism is for a planning effort to incorporate a sound system of monitoring implementation and evaluating progress. The literature discusses the importance of evaluation systems to planning and the danger to the success of an effort if evaluation is not given enough emphasis and support.

Item 14 examined the evaluation mechanisms included in the library planning documents studied and sought to determine whether they met the standards recommended in the literature.

Thirteen of the 1982–83 plans (38%) provided very few or no mechanisms to evaluate progress toward meeting the goals and objectives identified in the reports, or for evaluating progress toward implementing the recommendations made. Only three of the 1990–91 plans lacked specific evaluation mechanisms. Fifteen (34%) included a few, and twenty-six (59%) included adequate or extensive provisions for evaluations of implementation efforts. On the other hand, twenty-one of the 1982–83 plans (62%) and forty-one of the 1990–91 plans (93.29%) provided adequate or extensive information on how progress should be measured and implementation evaluated.

Many of the plans either proposed formal annual reviews of progress toward meeting planning program goals and objectives or indicated that such a procedure had already been implemented. These annual reviews are conducted by library directors, library planning officers, and by the individual unit administrators themselves. Several of the institutions indicated that these annual reviews include a reexamination of goals and objectives, the establishment and revision of timetables for accomplishing specific tasks, and the coordination of efforts among units to meet overall library or institutional priorities. Two institutions indicated that their planning systems require monthly reports of all administrators involved in major planning project implementations.

Where planning has been incorporated into the individual unit head job descriptions, the evaluation of planning success becomes a part of the overall administrative review of the individual and the unit he or she is responsible for administering. Some institutions do not have a formal review of planning; however, they do review specific planning projects that have been approved and initiated.

CONCLUSIONS AND COMMENTS

Most of the planning documents received were prepared by librarians themselves, either as directors, administrators, members of library committees or task forces, or members of university committees or task forces.

Where outside consultants were used, they worked closely with librarians or provided technical support and advice to the planning effort.

The reasons given for undertaking the planning efforts were divided between those that were self-initiated by librarians for budgeting or planning purposes or to improve efficiency, effectiveness, and/or overall management, and those that were required by parent institutions for budget and/or planning purposes. The only other reason given for developing a long-term plan was for the administration of major donations for library projects. In both surveys, more than 60 percent of the plans were submitted to university administrations or governing bodies for formal approval. The balance were either approved by library administrations or were informational documents for working purposes.

More than three-fourths of the plans in the first survey and more than 90 percent of the plans in the second survey provided adequate or comprehensive mission statements and delineations of general library goals and objectives. However, nearly two-thirds of the planning documents in the first survey provided little or no historical information about the libraries or the universities. Although some of the documents were annual updates of ongoing plans being implemented, the absence of historical information in so many reports indicates a need for a greater appreciation of the significance of planning and the importance of having it become a part of the library's continuous growth as an organization. Planning needs to build upon the past and incorporate the individual characteristics of an institution and its historical approach to resources, facilities, and patterns of service. Fortunately, in the second survey the percentage providing little or no historical information had dropped to about 40 percent. The majority of the documents provided a historical context for the planning effort.

All of the libraries provided information on their formal organizational structures. However, these personnel lists and organization charts did not reveal how libraries actually operated or how decision-making processes differed. Although most revealed the traditional organizational structure along functional lines of technical services, public services, and administrative services, the role of planning in administration was not defined. Usually it was an administrative function with more involvement of technical service and systems people at those institutions who were more involved in computer technology.

All of the directors who identified their university administrators reported to chief academic officers, presidents, or other university vice presidents. This reaffirms the importance all of the university administrators place on their libraries' roles as critical functions in their institutions' educational missions. The question of faculty status for librarians did not emerge as an important issue for strategic planning purposes in any of the documents.

Most of the plans demonstrated an appreciation for the importance of incorporating an environmental analysis in their considerations and discussed such issues as the changing role of higher education, changes in the economy, advances in technology, and the need for more cooperation among libraries.

The issues addressed by the individual plans and the goals and objectives recommended covered the whole range of library operations, resources, services, and facilities. Computerization emerged as the most important factor, with nearly all plans recommending major investments in efforts to increase the application of computer technology to their operations and use of information resources in machine-readable form. Interlibrary cooperation emerged as another high priority for most plans, as did staff development.

The development or application of dramatic new management systems had almost no support in the recommendations. The heavy involvement of current administrations in initiating and supporting the planning efforts may have influenced the extent to which they would be critical of the systems that produced them.

Most of the plans produced specific recommendations for immediate action and identified individuals or groups who should take them. Most of the plans also included provisions for implementation. In many cases implementation involved annual reviews of progress on recommendations made, with timetables and deadlines for specific projects.

Few of the libraries had separate formal planning structures; in most cases planning was a part of all administrators' job descriptions. However, in many cases libraries had identified planning officers and had charged them with coordinating, monitoring, and evaluating planning efforts.

The amounts of supporting documentation provided in the plans describing issues addressed or recommendations made varied. Some plans focused on general issues in academic library administration and higher education, and only provided specific local documentation in those areas where specific recommendations for action were made. Most of the plans provided for regular evaluation of planning activities either in an annual planning review, a general administrative review for budget purposes, or an individual project review. Although many of the plans failed to meet some of the requirements discussed by writers, the majority of the plans demonstrated a sophisticated awareness of the value of effective planning and had developed planning programs that generally conform to the criteria outlined by planning writers.

The contrast between the planning documents received in the first survey and the second was dramatic. The number of libraries actively involved in strategic long-range planning efforts increased from 56.6 percent of the total responding in 1982–83 to 86.6 percent of those responding in 1990–91. The general quality and comprehensiveness of the documents received also improved, with the second group more closely meeting the requirements outlined in the literature. When comparing the products of library planning efforts received in these surveys with the conditions described by the Booz, Allen and Hamilton report in 1970, one can appreciate the progress library administration has made in the intervening years. Many libraries now have comprehensive, well-documented, long-term plans that incorporate the elements of effective planning described in the literature. More important perhaps, they have also planned the implementation and evaluation of these planning efforts to maximize the long-term benefits of the endeavors and integrated them into the ongoing administrative programs of their organizations.

Seven

Conclusions and Recommendations for Further Research

OVERVIEW OF LIBRARY PLANNING DOCUMENT SURVEY

Strategic long-range planning has become widely accepted as a legitimate tool for improving the management of academic libraries, and as a mechanism for implementing the changes necessary for their survival and the achievement of identified goals and objectives. Of the eighty-three ARL libraries that responded to the 1982–83 survey of library planning efforts, 57 percent (47) had either developed a long-range planning document or were in the process of doing so. Of the sixty-seven that responded to the 1990–91 update, 87 percent (58) had either developed a document or were in the process of doing so. Even among those libraries that had not developed a comprehensive plan, many had undertaken targeted planning efforts in defined areas such as collection development, automation of library operations, space utilization, and future directions for bibliographic control.

The scope of the plans varied considerably, with some focusing on library resources and services for a particular number of years (five, ten, or the year 2000), others concentrating on automation and the introduction and utilization of new technologies, and still others struggling with the problems of maintaining basic levels of service through the next funding cycle. Many were annual updates of ongoing planning programs conducted by their parent institutions, and several were installments on three- or five-year plans.

The sophistication of the plans also varied considerably. Some were brief outlines of objectives to be achieved during a particular period of time; others demonstrated that a comprehensive planning effort had been undertaken using committees and task forces and utilizing formal planning methods and techniques described in the literature. The responses to the 1990–91 survey tended to be more comprehensive than those to the 1982–83 survey, demonstrating an increased level of sophistication on the part of library planners.

CONCLUSIONS ABOUT PLANNING EFFORTS DRAWN FROM ANALYSIS

Most of the planning documents were developed by librarians themselves. Where outside help was provided, it was usually for a specific part of the overall effort or in the form of technical advice and support such as that provided by the Association of Research Libraries through the Office of Management Studies programs. None of the plans was the result of outside expert intervention characteristic of the library surveys described in Chapter 3.

More than half of the library plans were developed in response to requests from university administrations. This shows that, whatever the individual library director's attitude, the real pressure to engage in strategic planning comes from the university administration or the university governing body. Most of the other plans were self-initiated by librarians to improve efficiency, effectiveness, and/or overall management. In both surveys more than 60 percent of the plans were submitted to university administrations for formal approval. Another quarter were formally approved by library administrations, and the balance were informational documents not requiring formal approval.

The vast majority of library directors reported to the chief academic officers of their institutions, with three reporting directly to presidents, and two reporting to other university vice presidents. Several library directors held the title of dean, vice president, or associate provost. The administrative relationships of the university librarians to the university administrations at these institutions reaffirms the important role the libraries play in the overall missions of most universities. This relationship appears to address the point made in some of the source documents that library directors should become more actively involved in university administration and that they should participate in planning and decision making at the highest levels.

In analyzing the planning documents themselves, it was encouraging to see the proportion that provided either adequate or comprehensive mission statements and articulated clear library goals and objectives. In the first survey it was discouraging to see that nearly two-thirds provided little or no historical information on the development of the libraries or the universities. In strategic planning it is important to determine where an organization stands in its historical development and to understand the influences which brought it to that position, before one can effectively develop a program for moving it to another level. The 1990–91 planning documents corrected the earlier situation, with nearly 60 percent providing adequate or extensive historical information. Libraries initiating strategic planning efforts should place greater emphasis on reviewing the histories of their institutions before defining goals and objectives and charting courses for the future.

It was also encouraging to see that so many of the planning documents incorporated comprehensive environmental analyses in identifying problems and recommending solutions. This demonstrated a good understanding of the forces that control the real options available to an organization and showed that planners adjusted their expectations to realistic, achievable goals and objectives. Unrealistic expectations lead to frustration and failure. A plan based on false assumptions of what is possible performs a disservice to those involved in the effort and reinforces the general cynicism about planning.

Formal organization charts were not especially helpful, except in those cases where there was a clearly defined planning officer or designated office for research, planning, or development. The presence of systems offices was sometimes misleading because many dealt only with automation or technical services and did not serve a library-wide planning function.

Item 8 on the survey form displayed the range of issues addressed in the recommendations set forth in the planning documents. It demonstrated the great interest in computerization of library operations, the integration of electronic media into the information resources libraries provide access to, an increased appreciation of the importance of bibliographic instruction in teaching library patrons to maximize effective use of resources and services, a concern for preservation of materials, a desire to emphasize staff development and professional growth in an increasingly technological environment, and a heightened appreciation for the potential benefits of resource sharing and interlibrary cooperation.

The recommendations show the directions in which library planners feel academic libraries should move, and the implementation schedules demonstrated ways of initiating or continuing the process.

A substantial number of the planning documents met the criteria for effective planning outlined in the source documents. They identified missions, goals, and objectives; they documented important key issues of concern; and they made specific recommendations about what should be done, by whom, and when. They considered alternative approaches to problems in many areas and projected long-term consequences of options. One plan even included a projection of the consequences of taking no action and letting the problem develop into a major crisis.

The most widely used mechanism for implementation was the incorporation of plan recommendations into the annual budget cycle. Many library unit administrators would be required to provide progress reports on plan implementation in their areas of responsibility, either when they presented their annual budget requests or as a separate periodic update on implementation of plan recommendations. Two institutions proposed the maintenance of a loose-leaf planning notebook in which individual projects would be documented and monitored.

The amount of documentation contained in the planning documents also varied. The standard approach was to describe trends in higher education and academic libraries in general terms and to provide local data in areas of particular local concern. Thus most of the plans only provided data where a problem was perceived or recommendations made. Enrollment was not discussed unless it was increasing or decreasing dramatically; institutional funding was not discussed unless it was scheduled to increase or was considered inadequate; staffing patterns were not discussed unless there was a need to move personnel to support new priorities, develop new programs or services, or launch new initiatives.

Although every plan supported increased computerization of library operations and the introduction or expansion of new technologies, not a single one presented a detailed cost-benefit analysis of specific automation applications or contrasted them with the costs of continuing existing manual systems.

The final and perhaps most critical element in a library planning program is the evaluation component. Sixty-two percent of the 1982–83 planning documents (21) and 60 percent of the 1990–91 documents (22) included either adequate or extensive recommendations or provisions for the evaluation of the implementation of the plans. The evaluation element is also the planning component in greatest need of further research. Some plans incorporated evaluation of plan implementation into the annual report requirements of individual library unit administrators, others incorporated it into the budget request for the coming funding cycle, and still others set up a separate annual review and evaluation of planning activities.

However, none of the responding libraries provided documentary evidence of how they actually evaluate the implementation of their plans, or of how the plans are changed in response to unsuccessful implementation. The evaluation of planning program implementation is a topic that warrants its own research. This issue is discussed in more detail under recommendations for further research at the end of this chapter.

The analysis showed that a formal, separate planning structure is not required in order for a library to undertake a comprehensive planning effort or to implement the results of one. If a planning effort has the appropriate administrative support, and it is seen as a high priority by all major participants, it does not need a separate staff or mandate. In fact, there is a danger that if planning becomes the primary responsibility of one office or group of staff, it may be seen as a secondary responsibility for other unit administrators. Participation in the planning effort and in the implementation of plan recommendations must become an integral part of every unit administrator's job. Implementing plan recommendations cannot be seen as taking away from meeting one's day-to-day obligations but must be perceived as an investment in improving the long-term quality of service.

The staff assigned to a planning office or appointed to planning committees and task forces must be seen as coordinators of a library-wide effort, not as individuals on a separate special project or as a group with their own goals and objectives to achieve. Where conflicts arise between immediate operational requirements and long-term planning goals, administrators must modify priorities in order to accomplish both. It must be understood that short-term reductions in productivity are expected when effort is diverted to planning and implementing changes. This must also be taken into account when the evaluation of the effort is done.

The Booz, Allen and Hamilton report recommended the establishment of planning offices with the appropriate staffing and skills to develop, implement, and evaluate strategic planning endeavors. Although several university libraries did establish planning offices, the trend has been to expand the scope of an existing administrative staff office to include planning as a major responsibility. Associate or assistant directors for administrative services have been given the responsibility for coordinating planning activities and developing and maintaining management information systems in addition to budgeting, accounting, facilities and equipment, supervising library mail distribution, administering grants, writing proposals, and other related activities. The separate planning offices recommended by some experts have not appeared; however, the planning function has become accepted as an integral part of the overall library administration.

It seems to be generally accepted that the planning process does not end with the publication of "The Plan," but that library planning continues through the implementation of recommendations and to the evaluation of results. The planning documents received in response to the 1982–83 survey demonstrate the extent to which library planning has developed since the Booz, Allen and Hamilton study in 1969. They also demonstrate how much more sophisticated library staffs and administrations have become since the era of the outside expert surveys. During the intervening period, programs such as those offered by the ARL Office of Management Studies and the Council on Library Resources, which are supported by several major foundations, have helped develop a corps of librarians and library administrators who are better trained and better equipped to apply the results of research in management theory and organization theory to the operations of libraries. Strategic planning is one of the management tools that has become recognized as effective in improving the administration of libraries.

GUIDELINES FOR FUTURE LIBRARY PLANNING EFFORTS

One of the objectives of this study was to develop a model or guide for library planners that would enable them to capitalize on the successes of others in conducting comprehensive strategic planning efforts and in developing and implementing long-term planning programs.

The form that was developed for the analysis of planning documents in Chapter 6 incorporated the basic program components for study drawn from the nine library survey and library planning source documents discussed in Chapter 5. The analysis of the thirty-four planning documents received from the 1982–83 survey demonstrated how the elements identified could serve as measures for examining library planning documents and for providing guidance to those developing or initiating new library planning efforts. The analysis of the forty-four documents received from the 1990–91 survey confirmed the usefulness of the outline of elements incorporated into the form. The seven program components a library survey or planning effort should contain or examine were the following:

1. statements of goals and objectives
2. responsive, functional, organizational structures
3. evaluations of resources and services, including collections, services (technical and reader), personnel, physical facilities, and general financial support
4. use of contemporary technology and information management systems
5. extent of interinstitutional cooperation
6. the administrative relationships of the library to the university administration
7. library planning systems that include administrative support, capabilities for assessing needs and weighing options, mechanisms for establishing priorities and relating them to day-to-day activities, management information systems, formal planning documents—written plans, and programs for implementation and evaluation

Since the application of contemporary technology was found to be appropriate for nearly all areas of activity in the plans reviewed, it can be deleted as a separate category.

The introduction of new management systems, beyond the application of what are now considered good personnel practices and procedures emphasizing individual development and appropriate participation in decision making, did not emerge as a significant element in the plans reviewed.

The administrative relationship of the library to the rest of the university also seems to be less of an issue now than it was when many of the source documents were written. The informational requirements of contemporary instructional programs, research, and scholarship, and the tremendous costs of satisfying them, seem to have answered any questions about the role of the library in the life of the university. All of the library directors whose institutions were included in the survey serve as officers of the university administrations. The extent of their involvement and the weight of their advice depends more on personal interactions and local circumstances than on the formal relationship between the university librarian and the vice president, provost, or president of the university.

The analysis of the thirty-four planning documents received in response to the 1982–83 survey showed that university library management had changed considerably since the Booz, Allen and Hamilton report. The responses to the request to update the survey in 1990–91 added another decade to the record of growth and development. University libraries individually and as a group have moved to address the problems identified in the report. The planning documents reflect this in the ways the institutions approached their planning efforts, the problems they identified, and the solutions they recommended. Library management was much more sophisticated in 1982–83 than when the Booz, Allan and Hamilton report was written, and its approach to planning demonstrated a greater understanding of the issues involved. In 1991, the documents demonstrated that the process of development was continuing.

Therefore, based on the analysis of the 1982–83 and 1990–91 plans, the seven library program components identified in Chapter 5 can be revised to five basic areas that need to be emphasized in the analysis of a library planning program, or in developing a framework for initiating one today: (1) statements of goals and objectives; (2) organizational structure; (3) resources and services; (4) interlibrary cooperation; and (5) library planning programs.

Statements of Goals and Objectives

A library plan should begin with a clear statement of the ultimate mission of the university and of the library system. The university mission statement should incorporate an understanding of the historical development of the university and of the role it has defined for itself in the field of higher education. The library mission statement can then define the role the library will play in fulfilling the university mission, taking into consideration the extent to which library resources, programs, and services have been developed to date.

The goals and objectives that are then defined are specific achievements which will enable the library to redirect its energies and reallocate its resources toward developing the programs, services, and information resources needed to fulfill both the library's and the university's missions.

The goals and objectives need to be both long range to achieve strategic ends and short range to give participants a sense of progress and direction as they move toward implementation. They also need to be concise and quantifiable so that progress can be easily monitored and evaluated. Failures in meeting some short-range goals are to be expected. They are a part of the process and provide feedback so that corrections can be made early enough to minimize their effect on achieving long-term goals.

The source documents and the publications of the ARL Office of Management Studies provide detailed guidelines for identifying and defining appropriate library planning goals and objectives. The ARL SPEC Kits also provide examples of existing statements of goals and objectives that can be adapted to meet individual library situations.

Organizational Structure

Organizational structure addresses the issue of how a library is organized, how duties and responsibilities are distributed, how decision making is conducted, how administrative priorities are communicated through the organization, and how they are enforced. The dramatic growth of academic libraries in the past several decades is reflected in the organizational structures they have developed. All of the libraries in the planning survey had well-developed, central administrative offices with delineations of authority and responsibility among functional units of the library. Most were responsible for nearly all university-wide library services (financial administration, acquisitions, cataloging, personnel, facilities, public services, etc.) with the exceptions of law and medicine, which were discussed earlier in this book.

Library directors are now generally members of the university administration and are actively involved in university decision making. They are therefore in a position to link library planning to university planning and to reconcile the differences between the two. Since many of the library plans include major investments in computerization, it is especially important that university administrations fully understand the rationale behind these recommendations and integrate them into their university-wide plans for computerization.

As the administrative structures of university libraries have grown and matured, they have also had to develop written policies and procedures to guide their day-to-day activities. For planning purposes it is important that the library administration and the university administration demonstrate their support of the planning effort and that they communicate this support through the appropriate channels. The fact that more than 94 percent of the plans included in the analysis were initiated by either university administrations or library administrations underscores the importance administrative support has been in developing those plans that were available at the time of the survey.

In addition to voicing support for the planning effort, library administrators must provide the staff and technical support to enable the planning group to complete its assignment. This means releasing some staff temporarily, relaxing some deadlines or modifying priorities on other projects or activities, and sometimes diverting funds needed for the effort.

The whole organization should be involved in developing the recommendations that result from a planning effort. Once the recommendations have been approved by the appropriate authorities, the whole organization should be involved in implementing them through existing administrative channels and in evaluating the results.

Resources and Services

The library planning program should include a review and analysis of all library programs, resources, and services. The form used in this study outlines the major areas, illustrates the kinds of problems that were identified, the kinds of solutions that were recommended, and the kinds of alternatives that were selected by other institutions. In examining its resources and services, a library planning group must apply its own institution's mission, goals, and objectives in selecting appropriate recommendations. There are no right or wrong ways of achieving goals, only those that are appropriate for a particular library given its history, resources, and stage of development.

Interlibrary Cooperation

Interlibrary cooperation is an issue that was discussed in all of the source documents and supported as a way of maximizing the utilization of resources. With the advent of computer technology, resource sharing has finally become a feasible and acceptable vehicle for providing access to certain services and classes of material for all institutions. OCLC demonstrated what could be done first with its shared cataloging system and later a whole range of cooperative resource ventures. The Council on Library Resources, many foundations, and several federal and state government agencies have supported extensive research and funded many cooperative library programs that have been widely replicated.

Any library planning program must demonstrate an awareness of the potential for cooperative ventures and resource-sharing agreements in developing its recommendations, both as effective ways of achieving goals and potential sources of funding for implementation.

Library Planning Programs

The planning process a library adopts, and the planning program it eventually implements, can be many things. As academic libraries have become more sophisticated over the years, more and more of the components described as essential for strategic planning efforts in the source documents have begun to appear in the ongoing administrative programs of libraries. Technological advances, economic pressures, and demands for greater accountability from university administrations have stimulated the development of many of the capabilities library planners had been advocating in the source documents. It is useful to review some of the library planning program components discussed in those documents.

Attitude About Planning

Perhaps the first element is the institution's attitude about planning. Today planning must be seen as an integral part of library administration. Planning is not a special project to be undertaken to deal with an emergency or to solve a particular problem, but is an organizational function that is a part of the ongoing responsibility of every member of the organization.

Formal Documentation

Effective library planning is based on formal documentation that includes a statement of the basic mission of the university and the library, an understanding of its historical development, and a set of accepted long-range and short-range goals and objectives which will enable the organization to fulfill its mission. The goals and objectives should be specific, have timetables, and provide quantitative or qualitative data for evaluation.

Needs Assessment and Prioritization of Objectives

The library plan should include mechanisms for assessing needs at the beginning of the process and for monitoring them as they are modified by the implementation of various aspects of the plan. The priorities of different objectives must be flexible enough to respond to changes in perceptions of needs and to successes and failures in implementing elements of the plan. Some goals may be deleted entirely as implementation proceeds, and new objectives may be added as staff and users become more familiar with the changes being introduced.

Management Information Systems

Effective library planning requires the continuous documentation of library operations and the interpretation of the information generated by operations to monitor efficiency and effectiveness. Computerized systems can provide a great deal of the information needed, but the interpretation of data and the initiation of changes in programs based on the results must remain a high priority for the administrator.

Personnel

The personnel needs for planning depend on the sophistication of the library administration and the level of support it provides in general. In a highly developed system, the basic components for implementing a planning program probably already exist and may in fact already be functioning informally. In a more traditional structure planning may have to be explicitly defined and specific individuals charged with coordinating initial planning efforts. In the latter case, planning must not be allowed to develop as a separate function but must be merged with existing administrative functions as soon as possible. In some cases this might require a complete review of job descriptions and the incorporation of planning into the evaluation system for all personnel.

Implementation and Evaluation

After a planning program has been developed, accepted, and formally approved, implementation and evaluation become crucial to its success. Most of the planning documents included in the analysis recommended implementation through incorporation into the annual programs of library units, with periodic evaluations and updates. Since so many of the plans were developed in response to university administration requests, it is fair to assume that progress is monitored by those administrations, and successes and failures to meet objectives noted.

Most of the plans showed an appreciation of the importance of continuing planning as an ongoing process. In fact, many of the institutions have been operating with formalized planning programs for many years. These programs are monitored by library and university administrators and are tied to the budgeting programs in most instances.

Planning has established itself as a powerful management tool in government, business, and industry. As social institutions, libraries are not isolated from the pressures, demands, or influences of their environments. In order to survive and prosper, they must develop mechanisms for controlling their environments and minimizing harmful effects. Significant efforts have been and still are being undertaken to make planning an integral part of library management in specific institutions. It is hoped that the analyses in this study can be used as criteria for evaluating library planning efforts and provide guidance in making planning a more effective instrument for improving library management.

RECOMMENDATIONS FOR FURTHER RESEARCH

The focus of this investigation has been on the application of strategic planning to academic libraries, an analysis of planning documents available in 1982–83, and an analysis of documents available in 1991. The findings suggest further research that might be undertaken to provide a better understanding of the role strategic planning plays, or can play, in the administration of academic libraries.

Recommendation 1

A study ought to be made of the extent to which recommendations of long-range planning documents have been implemented in a selected group of libraries five or ten years after the drafting of a formal plan. This would be an updating of E. Walfred Erickson's 1961 study of the implementation of library survey recommendations. It would provide valuable information on the implementation of library plans and the kinds of problems libraries encounter, and provide additional guidance to those involved in new planning efforts.

Recommendation 2

Research is needed on the important role the Association of Research Libraries' Office of Management Studies has played in developing library management personnel and in helping to create an environment in which the application of contemporary management theory to libraries has been fostered and encouraged through its various programs and projects. This research should also examine the extent to which the support of the Council on Library Resources, library-oriented foundations, and government agencies have encouraged cooperative approaches to solving academic and research library problems and stimulated resource sharing among institutions.

Recommendation 3

Despite the amount of time, money, and energy that has been invested in strategic planning by university libraries over the years, and despite the general impression that formal long-range planning increases a library's efficiency and effectiveness, there have been no statistical analyses of groups of libraries to validate this impression. Therefore it would be appropriate to conduct a statistical analysis of two groups of libraries, one consisting of libraries that have implemented formal planning programs and one that have not, to determine whether there are statistically significant differences in efficiency or effectiveness as demonstrated by preselected characteristics (i.e., per unit costs of technical service processing, user satisfaction, ratio of professional to nonprofessional staff, ratio of library staff to patrons served, bibliographic data-base hit rates, overall costs of computerized operations, etc.). The model for such an investigation could be based on the effects of formal planning in selected industries as described by Charles W. Hofer in Chapter 2 (Hofer, 1976).

Recommendation 4

There is also a need to have more research published in the literature on the implementation of formal planning programs and on the evaluation of planning and implementation. The fact that the planning is being done and that implementation is being evaluated is evidenced by the responses to the surveys and by the number of planning documents provided. However, scant documentation of evaluations of planning implementation appears in library literature. To many administrators the evaluations, especially the regular planning updates, are considered internal reports. These need to be shared more generally and to be analyzed, discussed, and studied for their general implications for library planning.

Appendix A

Responses to the 1982–83 Planning Survey of ARL University Libraries

Below is a partial list of the responses to the fall 1982 and spring 1983 letters inquiring about the status of long-range planning of the 101 ARL University Library members (total responses 83). It includes those institutions that either reported having a long-range plan (39) or being in the process of developing one at the time of the survey (9). Thirty-four of those reporting long-range plans provided copies. A complete listing of respondents is included in the author's dissertation (Biddle, 1988).

ARL University Library Members Contacted		101
Responding Institutions		83
Institutions Reporting Plans		39
Institutions Developing Plans		9
	Total	48
Copies of Plans Provided		34

RESPONSES

Institution	Have Plan	Time Frame of Plan	Plan Date	Copy Rec'd
University of Arizona	No	Developing	----	---
Arizona State University	No	Developing	----	---
Boston University	No	Developing	----	---
Brown University	No	Developing	----	---

Appendix A

Institution	Have Plan	Time Frame of Plan	Plan Date	Copy Rec'd
Univ. of California, Berkeley	No	Developing	_____	___
Univ. of California, Davis	Yes	On Going*	1982	Yes
Univ. of California, Los Angeles	Yes	???	197?	No
Univ. of California, Riverside	Yes	10 Years*	1981	Yes
Univ. of California, Santa Barbara	No	Developing	----	---
University of Cincinnati	Yes	On Going*	1981	Yes
Columbia University	Yes	___	1981	Yes
University of Connecticut	Yes	On Going*	1982	Yes
Cornell University	Yes	On Going*	1973	Yes
Duke University	Yes		1978	Yes
Emory University	Yes	On Going*	1981	Yes
Florida State University	Yes	On Going*	1977	Yes
University of Guelph	Yes	5 Years*	Annual	Yes
University of Hawaii	No	Developing	----	---
Howard University	Yes	---	1976	Yes
Indiana University	Yes	2 Years*	1980	Yes
University of Iowa	Yes	5 Years	1982	Yes
Johns Hopkins University	Yes	20 Years	1983	Yes
University of Kentucky	Yes	5 Years	1978	Yes
Louisiana State University	Yes	5 Years	1982	Yes
McMaster University	Yes	10 Years	1980	Yes
University of Manitoba	Yes	4 Years*	1979	Yes
University of Maryland	Yes	5 Years*	1981	Yes
University of Massachusetts	Yes	On Going*	1982	Yes
University of Miami	No	Developing	----	---
University of Michigan	Yes	On Going*	1980	Yes
University of Minnesota	Yes	3 Years	1979	Yes
University of Nebraska	Yes	5 Years*	1981	Yes

Institution	Have Plan	Time Frame of Plan	Plan Date	Copy Rec'd
State Univ. of New York, Albany	Yes	5 Years*	1981	Yes
University of North Carolina	Yes	20 Years	1974	No
University of Notre Dame	Yes	5 Years	1982	Yes
University of Oklahoma	Yes	5 Years	1979	No
Oklahoma State University	Yes	5 Years	1980	No
University of Pennsylvania	No	Developing	----	---
University of Pittsburgh	Yes	5 Years	1979	Yes
Southern Illinois University	Yes	On Going*	Annual	No
Temple University	Yes	10 Years	1979	Yes
University of Tennessee	Yes	1 Year*	1981	Yes
University of Texas (Austin)	Yes	___	1982	Yes
Washington State University	Yes	6 Years	1979	Yes
Washington Univ. (St. Louis)	Yes	On Going*	1980	Yes
Wayne State University	Yes	3 Years	1982	Yes
Western Ontario University	Yes	3 Years*	Annual	Yes
York University	Yes	5 Years*	1981	Yes

*Plans are updated annually.

Appendix B

Responses to the 1990–91 Planning Survey of ARL University Libraries

Below is a partial list of the responses to the fall 1990 and spring 1991 letters inquiring about the status of long-range planning of the 101 ARL University Library members (total responses 67). It includes the fifty-eight institutions that reported either having developed a long-range plan (46) or being in the process of developing one at the time of the survey (12). Forty-four of those reporting plans provided copies. Time frames of plans submitted ranged from one to twenty years.

ARL University Library Members Contacted		101
Responding Institutions		67
Institutions Reporting Plans		46
Institutions Developing Plans		12
	Total	58
Copies of Plans Provided		44

RESPONSES

Institution	Have Plan	Time Frame of Plan	Plan Date	Copy Rec'd
University of Alabama	Yes	Annual*	1990	Yes
University of Alberta	Yes	5 years	1990	Yes
University of Arizona	Yes	20 years	1990	Yes
Arizona State University	Yes	Annual*	1990	Yes

Institution	Have Plan	Time Frame of Plan	Plan Date	Copy Rec'd
Brigham Young University	Yes		1989	Yes
University of British Columbia	No	Developing		No
Univ. of California, Berkeley	No	Dispersed		No
Univ. of California, Los Angeles	No	Developing		No
Univ. of California, San Diego	Yes		1989	Yes
University of Chicago	Yes	10 years*	1990	Yes
University of Cincinnati	Yes	5 years*	1989	Yes
Colorado State University	Yes	5 years*	1989	Yes
Duke University	Yes	5 years	1988	Yes
University of Florida	No	5 years		No
Florida State University	Yes	3 years*	1990	Yes
Georgetown University	No	Developing		No
University of Georgia	Yes	5 years*	1989	Yes
Harvard University	No	Developing		No
Indiana University	Yes	Annual*	1988	Yes
University of Iowa	Yes	5 years*	1989	Yes
Johns Hopkins University	No	Developing		No
Kent State University	Yes	5 years	1990	Yes
McGill University	No	Developing		No
Mass. Institute of Technology	Yes	5 years*	1989	Yes
University of Miami	Yes	5 years*	1990	Yes
University of Michigan	Yes		1989	Yes
Michigan State University	Yes	10 Years*	1990	Yes
University of Minnesota	No	Developing		No
University of Missouri	Yes	5 years*	----	Yes
University of Nebraska	Yes	10 years	1990	Yes
University of New Mexico	Yes	5 years	1989	Yes

Institution	Have Plan	Time Frame of Plan	Plan Date	Copy Rec'd
State Univ. of New York, Albany	Yes	5 years	1990	Yes
State Univ. of New York, Buffalo	Yes	10 years	1986	Yes
New York University	Yes	5 years	1986	Yes
University of North Carolina	No	Developing		No
Northwestern University	Yes	10 years	1990	Yes
University of Notre Dame	Yes	5 years	1989	Yes
Ohio State University	Yes	*	1988	Yes
University of Pennsylvania	Yes	5 years	1990	Yes
Pennsylvania State University	Yes	5 years*	1991	Yes
Princeton University	No	Acquisitions		No
Rutgers University	Yes	Annual*	1988	Yes
University of South Carolina	Yes	5 years	1990	Yes
Southern Illinois University	Yes	5 years*	1990	Yes
Stanford University	Yes	3 years	1991	Yes
Syracuse University	Yes		1988	Yes
University of Texas (Austin)	Yes	5 years*	19--	Yes
Texas A & M University	Yes	5 years*	199-	Yes
Tulane University	Yes	5 years	1989	Yes
Vanderbilt University	Yes		19--	Yes
University of Virginia	No	Dispersed		No
Virginia Polytechnic Institute	Yes	10 years*	1986	Yes
Washington State University	Yes	5 years	1990	Yes
Washington Univ. (St. Louis)	No	Developing		No
Wayne State University	Yes	5 years	1989	Yes
University of Western Ontario	Yes	3 years*	1990	Yes
Yale University	No	Developing		No
York University	Yes	3 years*	1988	Yes

*   Plans are reviewed and updated annually.

Bibliography

Ackoff, Russell L. 1970. *A Concept of Corporate Planning.* New York: Wiley Interscience, 158pp.

Administration and Change: Continuing Education in Library Administration. 1969. New Brunswick, N.J.: Rutgers University Press, 60pp.

Anthony, Robert N. *Planning and Control Systems: A Framework for Analysis.* 1965. Boston: Division of Research, Graduate School of Business Administration, Harvard University.

ARL/OMS. Association of Research Libraries, Office of University Library Management Studies. 1978. "Collection Analysis in Research Libraries: An Interim Report on a Self-Study Process." Washington, D.C.: Association of Research Libraries, 29pp.

_____ . 1977. *Library Management in the 1970's: Summary of Issues and Selected Bibliography.* Washington, D.C.: Association of Research Libraries, 16pp.

_____ . 1974. "Review of the Formulation and Use of Objectives in Academic and Research Libraries." *ARL Management Supplement* 2, no. 1 (January): 4pp.

_____ . "Review of Budgeting Techniques in Academic and Research Libraries." 1973a. *ARL Management Supplement* 1, no. 2 (April): 4pp.

_____ . 1973b. "Review of Management Training Activities in Academic and Research Libraries." *ARL Management Supplement* 1, no. 4 (September): 4pp.

_____ . 1972. "Review of Planning Activities in Academic and Research Libraries." *ARL Management Supplement* 1, no. 1 (December): 4pp.

_____ , and McGill University Libraries. 1976. *Staff Performance Evaluation Program at McGill University Libraries: A Program Description of a*

Goals-Based Evaluation Process with Accompanying Supervisor's Manual. Washington, D.C.

ARL/OMS/SPEC Association of Research Libraries, Office of University Library Management Studies, Systems and Procedures Exchange Center. 1979. "Cost Studies and Fiscal Planning." *SPEC Flyer*, no. 52 (March): 2pp.

——— . 1976. "The Systems Function in ARL Libraries." *SPEC Flyer*, no. 29 (September): 2pp.

——— . 1975. "Managerial and Technical Specialists in ARL Libraries." *SPEC Flyer*, no. 20 (September): 2pp.

——— . 1974. "Planning Systems." *SPEC Flyer*, no. 13 (November): 2pp.

——— . [Promotional Brochure]. N.d. "SPEC Systems and Procedures Exchange Center—devoted to the acquisition, organization, analysis, and dissemination of information related to academic and research library management," 4pp.

Atherson, P. A. 1973. "Applications of Ideas of Management, Instruction and Technology in Staff Practices in the Academic Library." *LACUNY Journal* 2 (Spring): 26–28.

Axford, H. William. 1975. "Interrelations of Structure, Governance and Effective Resource Utilization in Academic Libraries." *Library Trends* 23 (April): 551–71.

Bailey, Martha J., Michael K. Buckland, and Joseph M. Dagnese. 1975. "Influencing Change: The Role of the Professional." *Special Libraries* 66 (April): 183–87.

Baker, N. R. 1969. "Organizational Analysis and the Simulation Studies of University Libraries." In *Automation Problems of 1968: Papers Presented at the Meeting, October 4–5, 1968.* Purdue University Libraries, pp. 45–69.

Beckman, Margaret, and Nancy Ann Brown. 1975. "Role of the Librarian in Management." *Special Libraries* 66 (January): 19–26.

Bellomy, Fred J. 1969. "Management Planning for Library Systems Development." *Journal of Library Automation* 2, no. 4 (December): 187–217.

Bennis, Warren J., et al. 1976. *The Planning of Change.* 3d ed. New York: Holt, Rinehart and Winston.

Biddle, Stanton F. 1988. "The Planning Function in the Management of University Libraries: Survey, Analysis, Conclusions, and Recommendations." Ph.D. diss., University of California, Berkeley, December 20, 1988, 346pp.

Bolton, Earl C. 1972. "Response of University Library Management to Changing Modes of University Governance and Control." *College and Research Libraries* 33 (July): 302–11.

Bommer, Michael. 1975. "Operations Research in Libraries: A Critical Assessment." *Journal of the American Society for Information Sciences* 26 (May): 137–39.

_____. 1972. "The Development of a Management System for Effective Decision Making and Planning in a University Library." Ph.D. diss., University of Pennsylvania, December 1972, 307pp., 2vols.

Booz, Allen and Hamilton, Inc. 1973. *Organization and Staffing of the Libraries of Columbia University: A Case Study.* Prepared by Booz, Allen and Hamilton, Inc. Sponsored by the Association of Research Libraries in cooperation with the American Council on Education, under a grant from the Council on Library Resources. Westport, Conn.: Redgrave Information Resources, 210pp.

_____. 1970. *Problems in University Library Management, A Study Conducted by Booz, Allen and Hamilton, Inc., for the Association of Research Libraries and the American Council on Education.* Washington, D.C.: Association of Research Libraries, 63pp.

Boston University. 1974. "Management Review and Analysis Report: Boston University Libraries." Karl Bynoe, Study Team Chair, 167pp.

Bracker, Jeffrey. 1980. "The Historical Development of the Strategic Management Concept." *Academy of Management Review* 5, no. 2 (April): 219–24.

British Columbia, University of. 1978. "Objectives of the University of British Columbia Library, April 1978," 10pp.

Brough, Kenneth J. 1953. *Scholar's Workshop: Evolving Conception of Library Service.* Urbana: University of Illinois Press.

Brown, Charles Harvey. 1932. "Is the Librarian a Victim or a Beneficiary of the Land-Grant Survey?" *ALA Bulletin* 26 (July): 431–35.

Bryant, Douglas W. 1975. "Changing Research Libraries." *Library Scene* 4 (September): 2–4.

Buckland, Michael K., ed. 1976. "The Management Review and Analysis Program: A Symposium." *Journal of Academic Librarianship* 1 (January): 4–14.

_____. 1970. "Systems Analysis of a University Library. Final Report of a Research Project." Edited by Michael K. Buckland, Anthony Hindle, A. Graham MacKenzie, and I. Woodburn. *Library Occasional Papers*, no. 4. University of Lancaster Library, 100pp.

Bundy, Mary Lee. 1968. "Automation as Innovation." *Drexel Library Quarterly* 4 (January): 100.

Burns, Robert W. 1971. "A Generalized Methodology for Library Systems Analysis." *College and Research Libraries* 32 (July): 295–303. [Reprinted in *Library Systems Analysis*, pp. 53–62.]

California, University of. 1977. *The University of California Libraries: A Plan for Development, 1978–1988.* Prepared by the Office of the Executive Director of Universitywide Library Planning. Systemwide Administration. Berkeley, Calif.: University of California, July 1977, 210pp.

_____. 1974. "Report of the Library Policy Task Force, Library Policy to 1980–81."

_____ (Irvine). 1982. "Goals and Objectives, UC Irvine Library, September 30, 1982," 9pp.

_____ (Los Angeles). 1977. University Library. *MRAP: Management Review and Analysis Program/UCLA Library, 1974–77*. Final Report on UCLA MRAP Study. Judy Corin, chair of design team. Los Angeles: UCLA Library, February 1977, 138pp.

Carlton, W. N. C., and N. Chattin. 1907. "College Libraries in the Mid-Nineteenth Century." *Library Journal* 32: 479–86.

Chapman, Edward A., Paul J. Pierre, and John Lubans, Jr. 1970. *Library Systems Analysis Guidelines*. New York: Wiley, 226pp.

Chicago, University of. 1976. "Statement of Long Range Planning Guidelines." Approved by the Board of the Library in 1973 and reaffirmed in 1976, 1p.

_____ . Graduate Library School. 1973. *Management Education: Implications for Librarians and Library Schools*. 36th Annual Conference, April 9–10, 1973. Edited by H. H. Fussler et al. Chicago: University of Chicago Press, 115pp.

_____ . Graduate Library School. 1972. *Operations Research: Implications for Libraries: 35th Annual Conference, August 2–4, 1971*. Edited by D. R. Swanson and A. Bookstein. Chicago: University of Chicago Press, 160pp.

Cohn, William L. 1976. "Overview of ARL Directors, 1933–1973." *College and Research Libraries* 37 (March): 137–44.

Colorado, University of (Boulder). 1982. "Administrative Document I. *Mission Statement*." Adopted February 3, 1982, 1p.

_____ . 1978. "Administrative Document II. *Goals of the University Libraries*." Adopted by the Library Staff and Director, June 1978, 3pp.

Colorado State University. 1975. "The Libraries at Colorado State University: A Statement of Mission, Goals, Objectives and Requirements." May 1975, 14pp.

Commager, Henry Steele. 1969. "Crisis of the Academic Library." *Wilson Library Bulletin* 43 (February): 518–25.

Current Issues in Library Administration: Papers Presented Before the Library Institute at the University of Chicago, August 1–12, 1938. 1939. Edited with an introduction by Carleton B. Joechel. Chicago: University of Chicago Press, 392pp.

DeProspro, Ernest R. 1971. "Management by Objectives: An Approach to Staff Development." In *New Directions in Staff Development*. Edited by Elizabeth W. Stone. Chicago: Library Administration Division, American Library Association, pp. 38–47.

Dill, William R. 1958. "Environment as an Influence on Managerial Autonomy." *Administrative Science Quarterly* (March): 104–28.

Dix, William S. 1972. "Two Decisive Decades: Cause and Effect on University Libraries." *American Libraries* 3 (July): 725–31.

Dougherty, Richard M., and Fred J. Heinritz. 1974. "Problems Confronting Academic Managers of Academic Libraries." *Idaho Librarian* 26 (October): 135–40.

———. 1966. *Scientific Management of Library Operations*. New York: Scarecrow Press, 285pp.

Downs, Robert B. 1976. "Role of the Academic Librarian, 1876–1976." *College and Research Libraries* 37 (November): 491–502.

Drake, M. A. 1976. "Forecasting Academic Library Growth." *College and Research Libraries* 37 (January): 53–59.

Drucker, Peter F. 1974. *Management: Tasks, Responsibilities, Practices*. New York: Harper & Row.

Dunlop, Connie R. 1976. "Organizational Patterns in Academic Libraries, 1876–1976." *College and Research Libraries* 37 (September): 395–407.

Edelman, Hendrik. 1976. "Redefining the Academic Library." *Library Journal* 101 (January 1): 53–56.

"Effecting Change in the Management of Libraries: The Management Review and Analysis Program." 1973. In *Association of Research Libraries, Minutes of the 82nd Meeting, New Orleans, LA*. Washington, D.C.: Association of Research Libraries, pp. 41–80.

Ellsworth, Ralph. 1944. "Trends in University Expenditures for Library Resources and Total Educational Purposes, 1921–1941." *Library Quarterly* 14: 1–8.

Erickson, E. Walfred. 1961. *College and University Library Surveys, 1938–1952*. ACRL Monograph No. 25. Chicago: American Library Association, 115pp.

Evans, G. Edward. 1976. *Management Techniques for Librarians*. New York: Academic Press, 276pp.

Ewing, David W., ed. 1972. *Long-Range Planning for Management*. 3d ed. New York: Harper & Row, 464pp.

"First Full Year of Activity for the Office of University Library Management Studies." 1972. *College and Research Libraries News* (March): 63–64.

Flener, Jane G. 1975. "New Approaches to Personnel Management: Personalizing Management." *Journal of Academic Librarianship* 1 (March): 17–20.

———. 1973. "Staff Participation in Management in Large University Libraries." *College and Research Libraries* 34 (July): 275–79.

Fussler, Herman H. 1973. *Research Libraries and Technology: A Report to the Sloan Foundation*. Chicago: University of Chicago Press, 91pp.

Galvin, Thomas J. 1976. "Beyond Survival: Library Management for the Future." *Library Journal* 101 (September 15): 1833–35.

Gardner, Jeffrey J., and Duane E. Webster. 1979. *Resource Notebook on Planning*. Office of Management Studies, Association of Research Libraries. Washington, D.C.: Association of Research Libraries, February 1979, 155pp.

_____. 1974. "The Formulation and Use of Goals and Objectives Statements in Academic and Research Libraries." *Occasional Papers*, no. 3. Office of Management Studies, Association of Research Libraries, Washington, D.C., August 1974.

Gelfand, Morris A. 1958. "Technique of Library Evaluations in the Middle States Association." *College and Research Libraries* 19 (July): 305–20.

Goldberg, Robert L. 1976. *A Systems Approach to Library Program Development*. Metuchen, N.J.: Scarecrow Press, 172pp.

_____. 1975. "The Pies Model: A Systems Approach to Library Program Development." Ph.D. diss., Rutgers University, 201pp.

Goldhor, Herbert. 1950. "Critique of the Library Survey." *Illinois Libraries* 32 (November): 609–12.

Goyal, S. K. 1973. "Allocation of Library Funds to Different Departments of a University: An Operational Research Approach." *College and Research Libraries* 34 (May): 219–22.

Greenwood, James W., Jr. 1962. "Organizing and Planning; and, Conduct of the System Analysis." *EDP: The Feasibility Study; Analysis and Improvement of Data Processing*. Systems Education Monograph No. 4. Washington, D.C.: Systems and Procedures Association. [Reprinted in *Reader in Library Systems Analysis*, pp. 315–27.]

Gull, C. D. 1968. "Logical Flow Charts and Other New Techniques for the Administration of Libraries and Information Centers." *Library Resources and Technical Services* 12 (Winter): 47–66. [Reprinted in *Reader in Library Systems Analysis*, pp. 269–89.]

Haak, John R. 1971. "Goal Determination." *Library Journal* 96 (May 1): 1573–78.

Haas, Warren J. 1974. "Management in Research Libraries: Implications for Library Education." *Management Education: Library Implications for Libraries and Library Schools*. The 36th Annual Conference of the Graduate Library School, April 9–10, 1973. Chicago: University of Chicago Press, pp. 83–104.

_____. 1968. "Research Library Management." In *Minutes of the 72nd Meeting of the Association of Research Libraries, June 22, 1968, Kansas City, Missouri*. Washington, D.C.: Association of Research Libraries, pp. 19–29.

Hamburg, Morris, Leonard Ramist, and Michael Bommer. 1972. "Library Objectives and Performance Measures and Their Use in Decision Making." *Library Quarterly* (January): 107–28.

_____, Richard C. Clelland, Michael R. W. Bommer, Leonard E. Ramist, and Ronald W. Whitefield, eds. 1974. *Library Planning and Decision-Making Systems*. Cambridge, Mass.: MIT Press, 274pp.

Hamlin, Arthur T. 1981. *The University Library in the United States: Its Origins and Development*. Philadelphia: University of Pennsylvania Press, 271pp.

Hammer, Donald P. 1969. "Casting for Automation: New Roles for Administrators, Librarians, Systems Analyst, Programmer." *Library Journal* 94 (December 15): 4492–95.

Haro, Robert P. 1972. "Change in Academic Libraries." *College and Research Libraries* 33 (March): 97–103.

Heiliger, Edward M., and Paul B. Henderson, Jr. 1971. *Library Automation: Experience, Methodology, and Technology of the Library as an Information System.* New York: McGraw-Hill, 333pp.

Heinritz, Fred J. 1975. "Modern Scientific Management in the Academic Library." *Journal of Academic Librarianship* 1 (July): 19–22.

_____ . 1970. "Quantitative Management in Libraries." *College and Research Libraries* 31 (July): 232–38.

Hofer, Charles W. 1976. "Research on Strategic Planning: A Summary of Past Studies and Suggestions for Future Efforts." *Journal of Economics and Business* 28 (Spring–Summer): 261–86.

Holbrook, A. 1976. "Librarian as Manager." *New Library World* 77 (May): 95–97.

Holley, Edward. 1975. *Emerging University Libraries: Lessons from the Sixties.* State University of New York at Stony Brook, 17pp.

_____ . 1973. "Who Runs Libraries? The Emergence of Library Governance in Higher Education." *Wilson Library Bulletin* 48 (September): 42–50.

_____ . 1972a. "Academic Library Finance in the 70's: The Picture Blurs." *Texas Library Journal* 48 (March): 25.

_____ . 1972b. "Organization and Administration of Urban University Libraries." *College and Research Libraries* 33 (May): 175–89.

_____ . 1971. *American University Libraries: Organization and Administration.* Texas A & M University Libraries, 15pp.

Holtz, V. H., and P. E. Olson. 1976. "Planning a Meaningful Change in Libraries and Library Networks: A First Step." *Medical Library Association Bulletin* 64 (October): 376–81.

Horn, Roger G. 1975. "Idea of Academic Library Management." *College and Research Libraries* 36 (November): 464–72.

_____ . 1972. "Think Big: The Evolution of Bureaucracy." *College and Research Libraries* 33 (January): 13–17.

Howard, Helen. 1977. "The Relationship Between Certain Organizational Variables and the Rate of Innovation in Selected University Libraries." Ph.D. diss., Rutgers University, 281pp.

Indiana State University. Library Science Institute. 1972. *Library Management: Quantifying Goals.* Edited by Choong H. Kim, in collaboration with Robert D. Little and William H. Kurth. Terre Haute: Department of Library Science, Indiana State University, April 27–29, 1972, 81pp.

Jackson, Ivan F. 1967. "Approach to Library Automation Problems." *College and Research Libraries* 28 (March): 133–37.

Johnson, Edward R. 1981. "Academic Library Planning, Self-Study, and Management Review." *Journal of Library Administration* 2, nos. 2, 3, and 4 (Summer–Fall–Winter): 67–79.

———. 1973. "Applying 'Management By Objectives' to the University Library." *College and Research Libraries* 34 (November): 436–39.

———, and Stuart H. Mann. 1980. *Organization Development for Academic Libraries: An Evaluation of the Management Review and Analysis Program.* Westport, Conn.: Greenwood Press, 199pp.

———, Stuart H. Mann, and Carol Whiting. 1979. "Evaluating the Impact of MRAP on Several Research Libraries: Some Thoughts on Assessment." In *Library Research Round Table 1977 Research Forums, Proceedings.* Meetings held at the 96th Annual Conference of the American Library Association, Detroit, Michigan, July 17–23, 1977. Edited by Charles C. Curran, published for ALA Library Research Round Table by University Microfilms International, pp. 69–86.

Kaser, David E. 1977. "The Effect of the Revolution of 1969–70 on University Library Administration." In *Academic Libraries by the Year 2000: Essays Honoring Jerrald Orne.* Edited by Herbert Poole. New York: R. R. Bowker, pp. 64–75.

———. 1974. "Dialectic for Planning in Academic Libraries." In *Academic Library: Essays in Honor of Guy R. Lyle.* Edited by Evan Ira Farber and Ruth Walling. New York: Scarecrow Press, pp. 96–104.

———. 1973. *Report from the Director of University Libraries, 1972–73.* Ithaca, N.Y.: Cornell University Libraries.

———. 1971. "Planning in University Libraries: Context and Process." *Southeastern Librarian* 21 (Winter): 207–13.

———. 1970. "Modernizing the University Library Structure." *College and Research Libraries* 31 (July): 227–31.

Keller, George. 1983. *Academic Strategy: The Management Revolution in American Higher Education.* Baltimore: Johns Hopkins University Press, 211pp.

Keller, John E. 1969. "Program Budgeting and Cost Benefit Analysis in Libraries." *College and Research Libraries* 30 (March): 156–60.

Kells, H. R. 1983. *Self-Study Process: A Guide for Postsecondary Institutions.* Washington, D.C.: American Council on Education, 156pp.

Kemper, Robert E. 1970. "Library Planning: The Challenge of Change." In *Advances in Librarianship.* Vol. 1. Edited by Melvin J. Voight. New York: Academic Press, 1970, pp. 207–38.

———. 1967. "Strategic Planning for Library Systems." D.B.A. diss., University of Washington, 295pp.

Kent, Allan. 1965. *Library Planning for Automation: Based on the Proceedings of a Conference Held at the University of Pittsburgh, June 2–3, 1964.* New York: Spartan Books.

Kessler, M. M. 1973. "Application of Ideas of Management, Instruction, and Technology in the Administration of the Academic Library." *LACUNY Journal* 2 (September): 23–25.

Kilpela, Raymond E. O. 1968. "Administrative Structure of the University Library." *College and Research Libraries* 29 (November): 511–16.

Kingery, Robert E. 1954. "What Happens When the Management Engineers Leave?" *College and Research Libraries* 15 (April): 202–04.

Kittle, Arthur T. 1961. "Management Theories in Public Library Administration in the United States, 1925–55." D.L.S. diss., Columbia University, 289pp.

Kountz, John. "Library Cost Analysis: A Recipe." 1972. *Library Journal* (February): 459–64.

Kraus, J. W. 1973. "Book Collections of Early American College Libraries." *Library Quarterly* 43: 142–59.

Kunz, A. H. 1976. "Use of Data Gathering Instruments in Library Planning." *Library Trends* 24 (January): 459–72.

Lancaster, F. W. 1977. *The Measurement and Evaluation of Library Services*. With the assistance of M. J. Joncich. Washington, D.C.: Information Resources Press, 395pp.

_____. 1973. "Systems Design and Analysis for Libraries." *Library Trends* 21, no. 4 (April): 461–612.

LeBreton, Preston P., and Dale A. Henning. 1961. *Planning Theory*. Englewood Cliffs, N.J.: Prentice-Hall, 357pp.

Lee, Sul H., ed. 1973. *Planning-Programming-Budgeting System (PPBS): Implications of Library Management*. Ann Arbor, Michigan: Pierian Press, 112pp.

"The Library and the Graduate School." 1913. *Journal of Proceedings and Addresses of the Fifteenth Annual Conference of the Association of American Universities, 1913*.

Litterer, Joseph A. *The Analysis of Organizations*. 1965. New York: Wiley, 471pp.

Lyman, Richard W. 1972. "New Trends in Higher Education: The Impact on the University Library." *College and Research Libraries* 33 (July): 298–304.

Lynch, Beverly P. 1982. "Options for the 80's: Directions in Academic and Research Library Development." *College and Research Libraries* 43 (March): 124–29.

_____. 1976. "The Role of Middle Managers in Libraries." In *Advances in Librarianship* 6: 253–77.

_____. 1974a. "Academic Library and Its Environment." *College and Research Libraries* 35 (March): 126–32.

_____. 1974b. "Organizational Structure and the Academic Library." *Illinois Librarian* 56 (March): 201–06.

_____. 1972. "Library Technology: A Comparison of the Work of Functional Departments in Academic Libraries." Ph.D. diss., University of Wisconsin, Madison, 207pp.

McAllister, Caryl, and John M. Bell. 1971. "Human Factors in the Design of an Interactive Library System." *Journal of the American Society for Information Science* (March–April): 96–104.

McAnally, Arthur M., and Robert B. Downs. 1973. "Changing Role of Directors of University Libraries." *College and Research Libraries* 34, no. 2 (March): 103–25.

McCarthy, Stephen A. 1967. "Administrative Organization and Management." In *Library Surveys*, by Stephen A. McCarthy and M. F. Tauber. New York: Columbia University Press, pp. 142–56.

McClure, Charles R. 1982. *Strategies for Library Administration: Concepts and Approaches*. Littleton, Colo.: Libraries Unlimited, 451pp.

———. 1981. "Planning Strategy for Library Services: Lessons and Opportunities." *Journal of Library Administration* 2, nos. 2, 3, and 4 (Summer–Fall–Winter): 7–28.

———. 1978. "The Planning Process: Strategies for Action." *College and Research Libraries* 39 (November): 456–66.

McDiarmid, Errett. 1954. "Scientific Method and Library Administration." *Library Trends* 2 (January): 89–96.

———. 1940. *The Library Survey: Problems and Methods*. Chicago: American Library Association, 243pp.

McGrath, William E. 1973. *Development of a Long-Range Strategic Plan for a University Library: The Cornell Experience—Chronicle and Evaluation of the First Year's Effort*. Ithaca, N.Y.: Cornell University Libraries, 185pp.

Mackenzie, A. Graham. 1976. "Whither Our Academic Libraries: A Partial View of Management Research." *Journal of Documentation* 32 (June): 126–33.

———. 1968. "Systems Analysis of a University Library." *Program* 2 (April): 7–14. [Reprinted in *Reader in Library Systems Analysis*, pp. 97–108.]

McMullen, Charles H. 1950. "The Administration of the University of Chicago Libraries, 1892–1928." Ph.D. diss., University of Chicago, 181pp.

McNeal, A. L. 1969. "Changing Personnel Patterns in College and University Libraries." *MLA Quarterly* 30 (June): 159.

Maag, A. F. 1975. "Some Correlates of Program Change in Large Academic Libraries." Ph.D. diss., Ohio State University, 218pp.

"Management Review and Analysis Program: The University of Tennessee Experience." 1974. *Southeastern Librarian* 24 (Fall): 22–40.

March, James G., ed. 1965. *Handbook of Organizations*. Chicago: Rand McNally, 1247pp.

———, and Herbert A. Simon. 1958. *Organizations*. With the collaboration of Harold Guetzkow, Graduate School of Industrial Administration, Carnegie Institute of Technology. New York: Wiley. [9th printing, April 1967, 262p.]

Marchant, Maurice P. 1976. *Participative Management in Academic Libraries*. Westport, Conn.: Greenwood Press.

_____ . 1972. "Participative Management as Related to Personnel Development." *Library Trends* 20 (July): 48–59. [Comment and rejoiner by Beverly Lynch. 1972. *College and Research Libraries* 33 (September): 382–97.]

_____ . 1971. "Participative Management in Libraries." In *New Directions in Staff Development*. Chicago: American Library Association, pp. 28–38.

_____ . 1970. *The Effects of the Decision Making Process and Related Organizational Factors on Alternative Measures of Performance in University Libraries*. Ann Arbor: University of Michigan, 305pp.

Martell, Charles R. 1972. "Administration: Which Way—Traditional Practice or Modern Theory." *College and Research Libraries* 33 (March): 104–12.

Mason, Ellsworth. 1971. "The Great Gas Bubble Prick't; or, Computers Revealed—by a Gentleman of Quality." *College and Research Libraries* 32 (May): 183–96. [Reprinted in *Reader in Library Systems Analysis*, pp. 179–93.]

Mason, Thomas R. 1969. "Program Planning for Research Libraries in a University Setting." In *Minutes of the 73rd Meeting of the Association of Research Libraries, January 26, 1969, Washington, D.C.* Paper Presented by Thomas R. Mason, director of Institutional Research, University of Colorado. Washington, D.C.: Association of Research Libraries, pp. 10–25.

Massachusetts Institute of Technology. 1979. "Review and Analysis of Environmental Factors." Massachusetts Institute of Technology. [1977]. In *ARL Resource Notebook on Planning*. Washington, D.C.: Association of Research Libraries, pp. 20–46.

Meier, Richard L. 1961. "Efficiency Criteria for the Operation of Large Libraries." *Library Quarterly* 31 (July): 215–43.

Miami, University of [Florida]. 1982. "The University of Miami Libraries: Outlook for the 1980's." February 1982, 12pp.

Michalko, J. 1975. "Management by Objectives and the Academic Librarian: A Critical Overview." *Library Quarterly* 45 (July): 235–52.

Michigan, University of. 1974. "Organization and the Individual: Planning and Change in the University of Michigan Library. Report Submitted to the Director by the University Library Planning Committee," December 6, 1974.

Middle States Association of Colleges and Secondary Schools. Commission on Institutions of Higher Education. 1957. *Evaluating the Library: Suggestions for the Use of Faculties and Evaluation Teams*. Document No. 4.81, October 1957.

Minder, Thomas. 1966. "Library Systems Analyst: A Job Description." *College and Research Libraries* 27: 271–76. [Reprinted in *Reader in Library Systems Analysis*, pp. 63–69.]

Mitchell, Elizabeth P. 1976. "Don Diener, Systems Librarian: Hard Nosed at Harvard." *American Libraries* 7 (June): 363–65.

Mohrhardt, Foster E. 1967. "Office of the Librarian." *Wilson Library Bulletin* 42 (December): 391–96.

Moore, John A. 1978. "A Study of an Academic Library. Part 1." University of California, Riverside, August 1978, 148pp.

Moran, Barbara B. 1984. *The Changing Knowledge Centers of Colleges and Universities.* ASHE-ERIC Higher Education Research Report No. 8, 1984. Washington, D.C.: Association for the Study of Higher Education, 97pp.

Morein, P. Grady, et al. 1977. "The Academic Library Development Program." *College and Research Libraries* 38 (January): 34–45.

Morelock, Molete, and F. F. Leimkuhler. 1964. "Library Operations Research and Systems Engineering Studies." *College and Research Libraries* 25 (November): 501–3.

Moriarty, J. H. 1970. "Academic Library Management: Traditional." In *Papers Delivered at the Library Dedication.* Indiana University Library, Bloomington, October 9–10, 1970, pp. 50–59.

Morris, T. D. 1954. "The Management Consultant in the Library." *College and Research Libraries* 15 (April): 196–201.

Morse, Philip M. 1968. *Library Effectiveness: A Systems Approach.* Cambridge, Mass.: MIT Press, 207pp.

Morton, Donald J. 1975. "Applying Theory Y to Library Management." *College and Research Libraries* 36 (July): 302–7.

Munn, Robert F. 1968. "The Bottomless Pit, or the Academic Library as Viewed from the Administration Building." *College and Research Libraries* 29 (January): 51.

Mussmann, Klaus. 1978. "Socio-Technical Theory and Job Design in Libraries." *College and Research Libraries* 39 (January): 20–28.

Myrick, William J. 1974. *CUNY Dean for Libraries: A Brief History of the Office.* New York: Library Association of the City University of New York, 35pp. [Also excerpted in *LACUNY Journal.*]

New Directions in Staff Development: Moving from Ideas to Action. 1971. Edited by Elizabeth W. Stone. Chicago: American Library Association, 65pp.

New York, State University of (Stony Brook). 1982. "1983/84 Budget Proposal—Libraries," October 18, 1982, 19pp.

North Carolina, University of (Chapel Hill). 1979. "A Plan for Library Services at the University of North Carolina at Chapel Hill Through 1995." "Forward," in *ARL Resource Notebook on Planning, 1979,* pp. 93–99.

————— (Charlotte). 1976. *Academic Library Development Program: A Self Study.* J. Murray Atkins Library, University of North Carolina at Charlotte, December 1976, 176pp.

Oklahoma, University of (Norman). 1979. "The Challenge of Academic Excellence: A Progress Report, July, 1979." 4pp.

————— . N.d. "The University of Oklahoma Libraries: Progress Report, 1979–81." Sul H. Lee, dean, University Libraries, 16pp.

Orne, J. 1974. "Future Academic Library Administration—Whither or Whether?" In *Academic Library: Essays in Honor of Guy R. Lyle.* New York: Scarecrow Press, pp. 82–95.

Parsons, Jerry L. 1976. "Characteristics of Research Library Directors, 1958 and 1973." *Wilson Library Bulletin* 50 (April): 613–17.

Pennsylvania State University (University Park). 1982a. "University Libraries: Planning and Budget Review Questions, 1982," 2pp.

———. 1982b. "University Libraries Budget Proposal, 1982–83." Stuart Forth, dean of University Libraries, January 12, 1982, 17pp.

———. 1981. "The Quality of the Collections in Support of Instruction and Research at Penn State, December 17, 1981," 6pp.

———. 1975. "Management Review and Analysis Program at the Pennsylvania State University Libraries, 1974–75." Edward R. Johnson, chair, September 19, 1975, 123pp., appendices.

Peterson, Fred McCraw. 1975. "The Use of Committees in the Governance, Management, and Operations of Three Major University Libraries." Ph.D. diss., Indiana University, 415pp.

Plate, Kenneth H. 1970. *Management Personnel in Libraries: A Theoretical Model for Analysis.* Rockaway, N.J.: American Faculty Press, 100pp.

———. 1969. "Middle Management in University Libraries: The Development of a Theoretical Model for Analysis." Ph.D. diss., Rutgers University, 109pp.

Presthus, Robert B. 1970. *Technological Change and Occupational Response: A Study of Librarians.* Part of a Program of Research into the Identification of Manpower Requirements, the Educational Preparation and the Utilization of Manpower in the Library and Information Profession. Bureau of Research, Office of Education, U.S. Department of Health, Education and Welfare, Washington, D.C., June 1970, 110pp.

Princeton University. 1976. "Princeton University Library Ongoing Program Goals." Appendix to Annual Report, 1975–76, 2pp.

Quinn, James Brian, Henry Mintzberg, and Robert M. James. 1988. *The Strategy Process: Concepts, Contexts, and Cases.* Englewood Cliffs, N.J.: Prentice-Hall, 998pp.

Raffel, Jeffrey A., and S. Shisko. 1969. *Systematic Analysis of University Libraries: An Application of Cost Benefit Analysis to the M.I.T. Libraries.* Massachusetts Institute of Technology, 107pp.

Reader in Library Administration. 1968. Edited by Paul Wasserman and Mary Lee Bundy. Reader Series in Library and Information Science. Washington, D.C.: NCR Microcard Editions. [4th printing, 1972, 403pp.]

Reader in Library Systems Analysis. 1975. Edited by John Lubans, Jr., and Edward A. Chapman. Reader Series in Library and Information Science. Englewood, Colo.: Microcard Editions, 471pp.

Reader in Operations Research for Libraries. 1976. Edited by Peter Brophy, Michael K. Buckland, and Anthony Hindle. Reader Series in Library and Information Science. Englewood, Colo.: Information Handling Services, 392pp.

Reader in Research Methods for Librarianship. 1970. Edited by Mary Lee Bundy and Paul Wasserman, with Gayle Araghi. Reader Series in Library and Information Science. Washington, D.C.: Microcard Editions, 363pp.

Reader in the Academic Library. 1970. Edited by Michael M. Reynolds. Reader Series in Library and Information Science. Englewood, Colo.: Microcard Editions, 378pp.

"Report of ARL-ACRL Joint Committee on University Library Standards (Revised)." 1975. Robert B. Downs, chair, March 1975, 28pp.

Rider, Fremont. 1936. "Library Cost Accounting." *Library Quarterly* 6 (October): 331–81. [Reprinted in *Reader in Library Systems Analysis*, pp. 9–26.]

Riggs, Donald E. 1986. "Strategic Planning: What Library Managers Need to Know." *LAMA Newsletter* 12, no. 1 (January): 1–4.

———. 1984. *Strategic Planning for Library Managers.* Phoenix: Oryx Press, 137pp.

Rizzo, John R. 1980. *Management for Librarians: Fundamentals and Issues.* Contributions in Librarianship and Information Science, No. 33. Westport, Conn.: Greenwood Press, 339pp.

Robinson, F. 1971. "Systems Analysis in Libraries: The Role of Management." From *Interface; Library Automation with Special Reference to Computing Activity.* Edited by C. E. Balmforth and N.S.M. Cox. Cambridge, Mass.: MIT Press, pp. 101–11. [Reprinted in *Reader in Library Systems Analysis*, pp. 71–82.]

Rochester, University of. 1974. "Management Review and Analysis of the University of Rochester: Final Report of the MRAP Study Team in Two Volumes." Sul H. Lee, chair, June 28, 1974, 325pp.

Rogers, Rutherford D., and David C. Weber. 1971. *University Library Administration.* New York: H. W. Wilson, 454pp.

Rosenlof, G. W. 1929. *Library Facilities of Teacher-Training Institutions.*

Ross, Johanna C. 1972. "Scientific Management in Libraries." *California Librarian* 33 (April): 83–87.

Rutgers University. 1980. "Rutgers Libraries: Growing Greater."

———. 1974. "Final Report of the Management Review and Analysis Study Team." Don Luck, team leader, Virginia Whitney, library director, 190pp.

Schendel, Dan E., and Charles W. Hofer, eds. 1979. *Strategic Management: A New View of Business Policy and Planning.* Boston: Little, Brown, 538pp.

Schmidt, C. James. 1975. "Resource Allocation in University Libraries in the 1970's and Beyond." *Library Trends* 23 (April): 643–48.

Shaw, Ralph R. 1954. "Scientific Management in Libraries." *Library Trends* 2 (January): 359.

_____ . 1947. "Scientific Management in the Library." *Wilson Library Bulletin* 21 (January): 349–57.

Shores, Louis. 1934. *Origins of the American College Library, 1638–1800.* New York: Barnes and Noble.

_____ . 1957. *Administrative Behavior.* 2d ed. New York: Macmillan, 259pp.

_____ . 1965. "Administrative Decision Making." *Public Administration Review* 25 (March): 31–37.

Slocum, Grace P. 1971. "Participation by Committee." In *New Directions in Staff Development.* Chicago: Library Administration Division, American Library Association, pp. 51–57.

Smith, J. C. 1971. "Planning Library Facilities and Services within Budgetary Constraints." *Southeastern Librarian* 21 (Summer): 118–22.

South Carolina, University of (Columbia). 1981. "Self-Study, 1980—The University of South Carolina, Columbia, February, 1981." (Sections of Study Dealing With Planning in the University Libraries), 5pp.

Southern Illinois University at Carbondale. 1979. "MRAP Report." April, 93pp.

Sparks, Rita. 1976. "Library Management: Considerations and Structures." *Journal of Academic Librarianship* 2 (May): 66–71.

Speller, Benjamin F., Jr. 1973. "Perceptions of Academic Personnel Concerning Who Should be Involved in Formulating Objectives for Academic Libraries: Three Case Studies." Ph.D. diss., Indiana University, 140pp.

Spence, Paul H. 1969. "A Comparative Study of University Library Organizational Structures." Ph.D. diss., University of Illinois at Urbana, Champaign, 149pp.

Stanford University. 1981. "Stanford University Libraries—Statement of Mission and Library Objectives for 1981–84." November 1981, 13pp.

Steiner, George A. 1979. *Strategic Planning: What Every Manager Must Know.* New York: Free Press, 383pp.

Stevens, Norman D. 1975. "The Management and Review and Analysis Program at the University of Connecticut." *Journal of Academic Librarianship* 1 (July): 4–10.

Stueart, Robert D., and John Taylor Eastlick. 1977. *Library Management.* Littleton, Colo.: Libraries Unlimited, 180pp.

Swihart, Stanley J., and Beryl F. Hefley. 1973. *Computer Systems in the Library: A Handbook for Managers and Designers.* Los Angeles: Melville Publishing, 338pp.

Syracuse University. 1976. "Report on Library Objectives, November, 1976," 16pp.

Tauber, Maurice. 1954. "Management Improvements in Libraries: Surveys by Librarians." *College and Research Libraries* 15, no. 2 (April): 188–96.

_____ . 1964. "Survey Method in Approaching Library Problems." *Library Trends* 13 (July): 22.

_____ , and Irlene Roemer Stephens, eds. 1967. *Library Surveys.* Conference on Library Surveys, Columbia University, 1965. New York: Columbia University Press, 286pp.

Taylor, R. S. 1972. *Making of a Library: The Academic Library in Transition.* New York: Wiley, 250pp.

Texas A & M University (College Station). 1982. "Nominal Group Technique Priorities of the Library Faculty." June 17, 1982.

―――― . 1981. "Five Year Staffing Plan," November 16, 1981, 2pp.

Thune, Stanley S., and Robert J. House. 1970. "Where Long-Range Planning Pays Off: Findings of a Survey of Formal, Informal Planners." *Business Horizons* 13 (August): 81–87.

Three Thousand Futures: The Next Twenty Years for Higher Education. 1980. Final Report of the Carnegie Council on Policy Studies in Higher Education. San Francisco: Jossey-Bass, 155pp.

Toronto, University of. 1976. "MRAP Report." June 1976, 384pp.

Toward a Theory of Librarianship: Papers in Honor of Jesse H. Shera. 1973. Edited by Conrad H. Rawski. Metuchen, N.J.: Scarecrow Press, 564pp.

Trueswell, Richard W. 1976. "Growing Libraries: Who Needs Them?" In *Farewell to Alexandria: Solutions to Space, Growth and Performance Problems of Libraries.* Westport, Conn.: Greenwood Press, pp. 74–104.

U.S. Office of Education. 1930. "Survey of Land Grant Colleges and Universities: The Library." Section of *Bulletin, 1930.* Vol. 1, no. 9, pt. 8. Washington, D.C.: Government Printing Office, pp. 609–714.

"University Library Management Study."1970. In *Minutes of the 75th Meeting of the Association of Research Libraries*, January 17–18, 1970. Chicago, Ill., pp. 52–58. Washington, D.C.: Association of Research Libraries.

Utah, University of (Salt Lake City). 1975. "MRAP Report," November 1975, 207pp.

―――― . 1980. "Marriott Library—Future Library Catalog Committee—Final Report, March 20, 1980."

Vanderbilt University. 1982. "Vanderbilt University Libraries, Overview, October 22, 1982." Keith M. Cottam, acting director, 4pp.

―――― . 1974. "Comprehensive Organizational/Operational Planning." *ARL SPEC Kit*, no. 13 (November): 15pp.

Vasi, John. 1983. "Budget Allocation Systems for Research Libraries." *Occasional Papers*, no. 7. Office of Management Studies, Association of Research Libraries. Washington, D.C.: Association of Research Libraries, 39pp.

Veaner, Allen B. 1970. "Major Decision Points in Library Automation." *College and Research Libraries* 31 (September): 299–312.

Volkersz, C. J. 1975. "Library Organization in Academia: Changes From Hierarchial to Collegial Relationship." In *New Dimensions for Academic Library Service.* Metuchen, N.J.: Scarecrow Press.

Washington, University of. 1974a. "The Libraries Planning Guide, Adapted from the University of Washington Planning Guide for Fiscal Years 1974–81," November 1973, 28p. *ARL SPEC Kit*, no. 13 (November).

———. 1974b. "University of Washington Libraries. Unit Plan, 1975–81 (Revised)," 25pp. In *ARL SPEC Kit*, no. 13 (November).

———. 1973a. "Report of the Management Study of the University of Washington Libraries, April–November, 1973." Millicent Abell, study team chair, 162pp.

Wasserman, Paul. 1965. *Librarian and the Machine: Observations on the Applications of the Machines in Administration of College and University Libraries.* Detroit: Gale Research, 170pp.

Way, H. E. 1972. "Management Techniques." *RQ* 11 (Spring): 215–21.

Webb, William H. 1972. " 'Will the Resources Head Wag the Imperative Tail?' Carnegie Commission on Higher Education Report Entitled—The More Effective Use of Resources: An Imperative for Higher Education: Implications for Libraries." *College and Research Libraries* 33 (July): 269–70.

Weber, David C. 1971. "Personnel Aspects of Library Automation." *Journal of Library Automation* 4 (March): 27–37.

Webster, Duane E. 1980. "Description of the Management Review and Analysis Program." In *Organization Development for Academic Libraries: An Evaluation of the Management Review and Analysis Program.* Edited by Edward R. Johnson and Stuart H. Mann. Westport, Conn.: Greenwood Press, pp. 52–64.

———. 1974. "The Management Review and Analysis Program: An Assisted Self-Study to Secure Constructive Change in Management of Research Libraries." *College and Research Libraries* 35 (March): 114–25.

———. 1973. *Library Management Review and Analysis Program: A Handbook for Guiding Change and Improvement in Research Library Management.* Washington, D.C.: Association of Research Libraries.

———. 1971. "Planning Aids for the University Library Director." *Occasional Papers*, no. 1. Office of University Library Management Studies, Association of Research Libraries, Washington, D.C., December, 27pp.

———, and Jeffery Gardner. 1975a. *A Structure for Implementation of Study Recommendations.* Washington, D.C.: Association of Research Libraries, August 18, 1975, 39pp.

———, and Jeffery Gardner. 1975b. "Strategies for Improving the Performance of Academic Libraries." *Journal of Academic Librarianship* 1 (May): 13–18.

———, and John G. Lorenz. 1980. "Effective Use of Library Consultants." *Library Trends* 28 (Winter): 345–62.

———, and Maxine K. Sitts. 1981. "A Planning Program for the Small Academic Library: The PPSAL." *Journal of Library Administration* 2, nos. 2, 3, and 4 (Summer–Fall–Winter): 129–44.

Weiss, Carole. 1978. "Closing the Catalog: Automated Alternatives to the Card Catalog—Impact on Users." Paper presented by Carole Weiss, Reference Department, University of Toronto Library, February 6, University of California, Berkeley.

Williams, Harry. 1966. *Planning for Effective Resource Allocation in Universi-ties.* Prepared for the Commission on Administrative Affairs of the ACE. Washington, D.C.: American Council on Education, 78pp.

Wilson, Louis R. 1947. "The University Library Survey: Its Results." *College and Research Libraries* 8, no. 3, pt. 2 (July): 368–75.

———. 1931. "Emergence of the College Library." *ALA Bulletin* 25, no. 9 (September): 439–46.

———, and Maurice F. Tauber. 1956. *The University Library: The Organiza-tion, Administration, and Functions of Academic Libraries.* 2d ed. New York: Columbia University Press, 641pp.

———, and Maurice F. Tauber. 1945. *The University Library: Its Organiza-tion, Administration, and Functions.* Chicago: University of Chicago Press, 570pp.

Wilson, T. D. 1977. "Organization Development in Library Management." In *Studies in Library Management.* Vol. 4. Edited by Gelson Holroyd. Hamlin, Conn.: Linnet Books, 178pp.

Works, George A. 1927. *College and University Library Problems: A Study of a Selected Group of Institutions Prepared for the Association of American Universities.* Chicago: American Library Association, 142pp.

Yarvarkovski, Jerome. 1975. "Management Planning to Achieve Academic Library Goals." In *New Dimensions for Academic Library Service.* Metuchen, N.J.: Scarecrow Press.

Young, Harold Chester. 1976. *Planning, Programming, Budgeting Systems in Academic Libraries: An Exploratory Study of PPBS in University Li-braries Having Membership in the Association of Research Libraries.* Detroit: Gale Research Company, 227pp.

Index

About the Author

STANTON F. BIDDLE is Professor and Administrative Services Librarian at Baruch College, The City University of New York. He is the author of numerous professional articles and has contributed chapters to professional books.